The Duke of Rutland's Hounds
THE BELVOIR

Michael Clayton

By the same author:

A Hunting We Will Go
Foxhunting Companion
The Hunter
The Golden Thread
The Chase
Foxhunting in Paradise
Endangered Species
Peterborough Royal Foxhound Show – A History

The Duke of Rutland's Hounds
THE BELVOIR

Merlin Unwin Books

First published in Great Britain by Merlin Unwin Books, 2011

Text © Michael Clayton, 2011

All rights reserved, including the right to reproduce this book or portions thereof in any form or by any means, electronic or mechanical, including photocopying, recording, or by an information storage and retrieval system, without permission from the publisher. All enquiries should be addressed to:

Merlin Unwin Books Ltd
Palmers House
7 Corve Street
Ludlow, Shropshire SY8 1DB
U.K.

www.merlinunwin.co.uk

The author asserts his moral right to be identified as the author of this work.
A CIP catalogue record for this book is available from the British Library.

ISBN 978-1-906122-31-7

Designed and set in Bembo by Merlin Unwin
Printed and bound by 1010 Printing International Ltd.

Contents

Foreword by His Grace the Duke of Rutland		7
Acknowledgements		9
Introduction		11
Chapter 1	Casting Off	13
Chapter 2	Early Glory	21
Chapter 3	Turning Point	33
Chapter 4	Surviving the Great War	35
Chapter 5	Between the Wars	53
Chapter 6	Second War Challenge	73
Chapter 7	Post War Triumph	79
Chapter 8	The Webster Way	85
Chapter 9	20th Century Sport	97
Chapter 10	Recollections of a Master	113
Chapter 11	Fateful 1990s – and into the 21st century	123
Chapter 12	Hounds of the Belvoir	149
Chapter 13	Supporters All	163
Chapter 14	Point-to-point	177
Chapter 15	Belvoir Pony Club	185
Chapter 16	Memories, memories	191
Appendix I	Masters and Huntsmen	211
Appendix II	Chairmen and Secretaries	213
Appendix III	Supporters' Club Officers	215
Appendix IV	Point-to-Point Members' Race Winners	217
Index		219

To Marilyn
– without whose support this book,
and much else, would not have been possible.

Foreword by His Grace the Duke of Rutland

As owner of the hounds, and President of the Hunt, I am delighted that Michael Clayton has written a new account of our pack of fox hounds at Belvoir, founded by the 3rd Duke of Rutland in the mid-18th century.

My family is proud that the Belvoir Hunt has entertained so many generations of sporting people, and continues to attract significant support, despite the restrictions of the iniquitous Hunting Act since 2005.

There was hunting on the Belvoir estates long before the Normans arrived to impose new order and discipline on the sport. Belvoir Castle's first owner was a Norman baron who was William the Conqueror's Standard Bearer at Hastings in 1066.

Deer remained the traditional quarry of most packs of hounds throughout England until the mid-18th century when the clearance of forests changed the terrain. The 3rd Duke was one of the first Masters of Hounds to make the historic move from deer to foxhunting after 1730.

I am pleased the Belvoir hounds have remained in the possession of my family. The pack had an illustrious record in the 19th and 20th centuries, with staunch local support, and attracting many visitors. Our hounds have been hunted by some of the finest huntsmen in the history of the sport.

Successive Dukes of Rutland have maintained a policy of breeding only the Old English type of Foxhound, in their traditional 'livery' of black, tan and white. They saw that all Masters and huntsmen adhered to this policy, and I am equally firm in ensuring it continues.

The Belvoir hounds have had a crucial influence on Foxhound breeding, and the lines we have in the kennels are of great value.

The resilience and fortitude of its members and supporters have ensured the Hunt's survival under the Hunting Act. The Belvoir Hunt's great history is well worth telling anew. I am sure there will be many more achievements to be recorded in the future.

Rutland

His Grace the Duke of Rutland

Acknowledgements

I have received help from many who support the Belvoir Hunt. Warmest thanks are due to the Duke and Duchess of Rutland who allowed reproduction of historic Belvoir hunting pictures by Ferneley and others, which hang in Belvoir Castle. We are indebted to the Duke of Rutland, President of the Hunt and owner of the hounds, for kindly providing the Foreword to this book.

As well as Michael Saunby, whose key contribution I describe in the Introduction, I would like to thank especially the following: Tor Owen for reading and correcting where necessary the manuscript; Foster Edwards for distributing 'memory questionnaires', relaying contributions from supporters, checking the text of the Belvoir Hunt Supporters' Club chapter, and providing past copies of 'Belvoir Tan'.

For a superb array of postwar Belvoir pictures I am principally indebted to Jim Meads, the doyen of hunting photographers, to Trevor Meeks for his remarkable colour work, including the crucial meet the day before the 'ban', and for more recent excellent pictures Matt Barnard of Belvoir Photography; all these fine professionals have been most generous and supportive in making their work available; Tony Fenwick kindly allowed me access to the historic pictures he has assembled in the Duke's Room at the Hunt Kennels which he has restored magnificently as a valuable archive of Belvoir history; access to family albums and lovely prints has been generously made by Lord (Peter) Daresbury; the Hon. Vicky Westropp, who accessed the remarkable pre-war albums of her godmother, the late Monica Sherriffe; Mrs Carol Taylor, for the album of her mother, the late Hon. Ursula (Urky) Newton; similarly Mrs Fiona Gibson for pictures and prints of her parents, Mrs Jean Parry and her husband, the late John Parry; Mrs Sally Skelton and Mrs Susan Bealby provided Pony Club pictures. Mr Tim Hall-Wilson, grandson of Major Charles Tonge, made available family pictures.

Mrs Ann Clark allowed usage of Belvoir photographs by her grandfather, the sporting photographer Howard Barrett. Nico Morgan, sporting photographer of Uppingham has provided the excellent pictures from the 2010–11 season.

Mr John Bryant kindly gave access to Belvoir sporting prints by Munnings and Lionel Edwards. Others have sent individual or groups of pictures and documentary information, for which many thanks, including Mr and Mrs Johnny Fountain and Mr William Moore, son of Supporters' Club Hon. Treasurer Mr John Moore, and Mrs Margaret Shipman for Croxton Park history. Mr Hugh Condry, retired deputy editor of Horse and Hound, gave advice and information on Belvoir point-to-point history, including the list of Members' Race winners; local point-to-point information came from Mr Ian Manchester.

Special thanks are due to Mr Rupert Inglesant, Master and huntsman 2006–10, who wrote the important chapter on past and present breeding of the Belvoir hounds; Mr Robert Henson, former Joint Master (1978–87) for his engaging chapter of memories;

and Mrs Sally Skelton for the informative and interesting chapter on the Pony Club. Those who filled Waltham village hall for a 'History Evening' when I talked about the Belvoir's past were most enthusiastic and encouraged me to continue this project.

Appreciation is due to everyone who has contacted me, including those who responded by sending in their 'Memory questionnaires'.

Introduction

As every ardent foxhunter knows, there are moments in the hunting field which remain unforgettably in the mind's eye, and continue to refresh one's hunting memories for the rest of a life-time.

Such images are especially abundant in my memories of riding frequently in pursuit of the Belvoir hounds, as a subscriber and as a visitor, during the last 30 years of the 20th century. I can so easily conjure up the thrilling spectacle of the Belvoir hounds running hard over the brow of a hill, hunting together in a group 'you could throw a blanket over', in the phrase coined by Surtees.

In their traditional handsome livery of black and tan and white, the Belvoir pack, as it surges across the countryside, remains remarkably similar to its ancestors, celebrated so often in words and pictures. They are a superb example of a living tradition which still enhances our way of life.

Riding down the hill above Long Clawson, after hounds had found in Clawson Thorns, then arriving in the delights of the Belvoir Vale below the village, and tackling the hedges as hounds run on over the grass, remain among my favourite hunting memories.

As a hunting correspondent for over 40 years, I was fortunate to ride in the mounted fields of nearly 250 packs at home and abroad, but the Belvoir has a special place in my memory. The wonderful variety of its country, upland and vale, and huge swathes of land down to the Fens, have always been essential ingredients in the success of the Hunt in attracting visitors from all over the world.

All of us who have relished sport with these hounds are indebted to their owners, the Dukes of Rutland. The ducal family has maintained through the tumult of history its 1,000-year-old inheritance of Belvoir Castle and its contribution to rural life, in which hunting has always played a major part. The Dukes' insistence that Old English type breeding is strictly adhered to in the Belvoir Foxhounds has ensured they are today one of only three British packs which can claim this breeding without acknowledged outcrosses.

Those huntsmen who came to Belvoir having previously hunted only 'modern' Foxhounds soon appreciated warmly the performance virtues of the Old English type; its drive and ability to work together closely in the hunting field. All these assets remain in today's Belvoir kennel, however 'unfashionable' the Old English type remains in the hound show ring, although Peterborough Royal Foxhound Show, part of the annual Festival of Hunting, now includes special classes for Old English hounds.

Generations of followers of the Belvoir are indebted to the farmers and landowners throughout the country who have for so long made hounds welcome on their land, creating such a marvellous tradition of foxhunting at the highest levels, since the Hunt changed from its ancient quarry of deer to fox in the mid-18th century.

For all these reasons, perhaps unwisely, I was unable to resist accepting an invitation from former Hunt Chairman, Mrs Tor Owen, and Mr Foster Edwards, Chairman of the Belvoir Hunt Supporters Club, to undertake the daunting task of writing a new history of the Belvoir, updating the Hunt history by T.F. Dale, published in 1899.

There has been a splendid opportunity to find a new, valuable source of the earlier history of the Manners family, through the publication in 2009 of the excellent book Belvoir Castle –1000 Years of Family, Art and Architecture, by the Duchess of Rutland.

There is now an opportunity to tell for the first time the history of the Hunt throughout the turbulent 20th century, and into the 21st. Most crucial is the Hunt's survival and the support it has received within the country, since the imposition of the iniquitous anti-hunting legislation introduced by the Labour government in 2005.

This illustrious Hunt, still kennelled in traditional style in the beautiful park of Belvoir Castle, has such a long and varied history, that I could not possibly guarantee justice has been done to everyone who has made that history possible. The Belvoir Hunt button has changed in design four, and perhaps five times, but it has always borne the ducal crest, and it has always been worn with pride by those fortunate enough to ride after these wonderful hounds.

I have been increasingly aware that my labours are inadequate in covering the full extent of the Hunt's past achievements. I hope, however, that what has been produced will revive happy memories for everyone fortunate to have enjoyed sport with the Belvoir, whether on horseback, on foot or on wheels. I hope it will inform new generations of foxhunters about a truly great Hunt whose contribution to our way of life in the countryside is immeasurable. A Hunt history is to some degree rural social history. It is wonderful to see new young recruits responding to the challenge of following the Belvoir hounds in the hunting field each season.

I pay special tribute to Mr Michael Saunby of Grantham, who has for many years collated and maintained his own meticulous and detailed records of the Hunt's history in every aspect. Without his help this history would have lacked a great deal of detailed information he has been able to provide.

His collection of Belvoir records has been the self-imposed task of a true enthusiast, and how fortunate the Belvoir has been in having such a supporter. A retired Metropolitan Police Officer, Michael has long nurtured a keen enthusiasm for foxhunting, and a great interest in Hunt staff and Masterships who make it possible.

Michael's adherence to the Belvoir as a follower, and as an excellent reporter of its hunting days in the sporting press under the pseudonym 'Old Bill', a reference of course to his Metropolitan Police background, have been tremendous assets to the Hunt.

The history of the Belvoir, and foxhunting generally, is far from over in the British Isles, no matter what is produced through prejudice and ignorance in opposition. The Hunt is indispensable in maintaining the best of English country life. I am sure there will be ample reason to update this history again by some equally enthusiastic foxhunter later in the 21st century.

There is every reason for confidence at the start of a second decade in the 21st century in wishing all Belvoir followers – Good Hunting!

MICHAEL CLAYTON
Morcott, Rutland
January 2011

CHAPTER ONE

Casting Off

What glory awaits when riding after hounds into the Vale...

How fortunate the Belvoir Hunt has been since its inception in hunting two widely varying terrains, Leicestershire and Lincolnshire – both ideal for the sport in different ways.

It was the grassland and fences of Leicestershire which attracted most visitors, but the staunch support of the resident sporting community in Lincolnshire has always been a major asset.

On both sides of the country the continuing generous welcome of farmers and landowners has made the history of the Belvoir Hunt possible.

To achieve a vision of the attractions of Leicestershire to the mounted foxhunter, pause at the top of Broughton Hill on the A606 road from Melton Mowbray to Nottingham. The huge sweep of the Vale of Belvoir lies below.

The Quorn country is mainly to your left; the Belvoir to your right. The boundary lies to the right of the road; it is the river Smite, a famous name in Shires foxhunting, since so many foxes were found on its banks, and many famous runs crossed the narrow river in both directions. There have been countless duckings for intrepid souls crossing the Smite in a hurry.

The range of hills eastwards from Broughton Hill is broken in your vision by woodland coverts which have been vital to foxhunting in the Belvoir country.

Holwell Mouth is a dense, sprawling covert clothing the hillside; the Smite runs down from it into the Vale. Foxes abound in this covert, and it needs persistent work by hounds to get a fox away for a good hunt in the open, but it can be done. And what glory has faced generations of foxhunters when hounds race from the hillside covert into the expanse of old turf and hedges guarded by ditches in the famous Vale.

Further east along the hillside is one of the Belvoir's most renowned coverts, Clawson Thorns, overlooking the village of Long Clawson, the village true to its name, stretching one and a quarter miles, with 14 right-angle bends. Stilton cheese is made in Long Clawson, originally relying entirely on milk supplied by the small dairy farms which covered the floor of the Vale, keeping it mainly down to grass. During the late 20th century farming economics encouraged a steady swing from pastoral to arable farming in the East Midlands, and much of the former grassland in the Vale is now ploughed up, but there remain headlands, fences and coverts –

'Going Away from Clawson Thorns' by Cecil Aldin.

and the greatest prize of all, the goodwill and welcome of Vale farmers and landowners.

The old windmill stands above Long Clawson, but below the covert. Long Clawson is the Belvoir's traditional fixture for its first Vale Saturday meet, and traditionally this meet was supported by a great gathering of mounted and foot followers from far and wide.

Villagers in the Vale of Belvoir have been staunch supporters of the Duke of Rutland's hounds for nearly three centuries. They have been brought up with foxhunting as a central part of their lives; they love it, and many are among the most knowledgeable of the Belvoir hounds' regular followers.

A good hunt from Clawson Thorns, soaring down past the village to right or left, involving the clearance of daunting drop fences, and going down to the pastures below, has been a treat for Belvoir mounted followers which they recall with a warm glow for the rest of their lives.

Further east from Clawson is Brock Hill, and the range of the Harby Hills overlooking the village of Harby, the largest in the Vale, and another centre of Stilton cheese production. Foxes live in the coverts all along the hillside, and have been hunted for generations down to the Vale.

Above the hill between the Vale and Melton Mowbray is Old Hills, the covert just south of the village of Holwell, surrounded by pastures and strange little hollows, a reminder of old ironstone mining projects, marked by warnings of possible subsidence, although this has never curtailed riding to hounds over a delightful stretch of grass country.

Other famous coverts in this upland area are Scalford Ashes, and Melton. Just on the south side of the old Grantham Canal Lane in the Vale is Hose Thorns, a marvellous covert affording hunts throughout the Leicestershire side.

The Belvoir country is a remarkable example of foxhunting surviving huge changes in the countryside. Pessimists said the arrival of the canals would kill the sport, and they feared the same when railway lines were put in, originally to convey iron ore from the new mines in the 19th century.

None of these proved to be obstacles to the sport, and since both canals and railway lines in the Vale area were closed down, the spinneys clothing the disused railway embankments have been used by foxes as sanctuary for many years, and therefore proved to be useful coverts for hounds to draw.

Belvoir Castle, the Gothic-style home of the Dukes of Rutland, creators of the Hunt, and proud owners of the pack, offers breath-taking views of hunting country from its romantic turrets, towers and battlements. The Dukes could take their hounds in any direction from the Castle Kennels, sure they would be able to enjoy hunting without ever leaving their great estate, which latterly encompassed some 18,000 acres.

Leicestershire opening meets of the Belvoir traditionally take place at Croxton Park on the estate, where the Manners family built their own hunting lodge. The parkland and surrounding areas form one of the most beautiful, unspoilt settings for sport and recreation you could find.

Across the Great North Road, nowadays the A1, the Belvoir rejoices in an entirely different setting which has seen some of the best hunting by hounds since the environment of spacious acres, leading eastwards to the Fens, has long offered remarkable opportunities for long, arduous hunts in pursuit of strong foxes.

We are now in Lincolnshire, and no-one could be more sporting than the farmers and landowners of that great county. Generations of them have been devoted Belvoir followers, attending meets at such venues as Leadenham where the Lincolnshire opening meet was held until the early 1970s,

Pre-war 'sea of grass': the Belvoir hounds moving to Barrowby Thorns, on October 8, 1938.

The Belvoir

since when the Hoare family at Rauceby Hall have welcomed the Hunt.

Before one talks of hounds, of huntsman and Field Masters, it is the hunting country itself which is the crucial factor in ensuring that a Hunt can touch greatness. The Belvoir from its inception has been fortunate in enjoying one of the most remarkably varied and challenging environments for our great national countrysport of foxhunting. It has ensured the regular pilgrimage of hunting devotees from far and wide throughout its history, and most importantly, it has maintained the core loyalty of those who live and work within the hunt boundaries.

This is the Belvoir country. Let us see how one of the world's great Hunts was created in such a superb setting for our finest rural sport.

'The Belvoir at Newman's' by Lionel Edwards 1935. George Tongue is hunting hounds.

IN THE BEGINNING...

The history of the Duke of Rutland's hounds started, similarly to all the major Foxhound packs, with deer hunting.

Like other aristocratic hunting families, the Manners, who were to become Dukes of Rutland, originally enjoyed hunting red and fallow deer in England's large forests which abounded in the East Midlands.

Their occupancy of the Belvoir estate, and much other land in the Midlands, including Derbyshire, began just after the Conquest. Robert de Todeni from Tosni on the Seine in Normandy, was Standard Bearer for William the Conqueror at the Battle of Hastings.

His reward was lands and estates in 11 counties; the original Belvoir estate was created by the adoption of 35 manors in Lincolnshsire and 16 in Leicestershire, all wrested from Anglo Saxons.

The first Earl of Rutland, Sir Thomas Manners, began rebuilding Belvoir Castle on its hilltop site west of Grantham in 1528,

Coming up Lings Hill in the 1930s.

two years after he was created an Earl. It had been badly damaged in battle in the previous century.

During England's Civil War the Castle, as a royalist garrison, was demolished again in 1649, by consent of the 8th Earl who was a Parliamentarian. He retired to the family's other great home, Haddon House in Derbyshire, and later rebuilt Belvoir as a mansion, but the family did not regard it as their premier home until the early 18th century, although kennels continued to operate at Belvoir.

No-one in the family was more keen on hunting than the 9th Earl who was created the first Duke of Rutland in the second year of Queen Anne's reign, 1666. He loved buck hunting in the Belvoir Vale and the wooded hill country above, but the gradual clearance of forests to cope with the growing demands of agriculture led to a decline in deer hunting in England in the late 17th and early 18th centuries.

The Belvoir

FOUNDATION OF THE FOX HUNT

T.F. Dale in his History of the Belvoir Hunt credits the 3rd Duke of Rutland (1696–1779) with making the historic move from deer to foxhunting from 1730, although some sources say he did not form his own pack until 1750, and it did not become entirely a Foxhound pack until somewhat after that; it may not have been entirely a foxhunting pack until 1762.

John, the 3rd Duke, succeeded to the title in 1721. He moved the main family home back from Haddon Hall in Derbyshire to Belvoir, and built the hunting lodge in the deer park at Croxton, to which the family retired for relaxation at times.

The 3rd Duke loved his hunting, but he had many other interests and public duties, which may explain why he soon entered into a curious joint hunting arrangement, long before 'hunt amalgamations' existed. The 3rd Duke arranged with the Earl of Cardigan, the Earl of Gainsborough, Lord Gower and Lord Howe, that each should pay £150 annually to cover the cost of a pack of foxhounds: the keep of hounds, horses and staff.

These hounds were kept from 15 October to 30 November at Croxton Park on the Rutland estate; from 1 December to 31 January at Cottesmore; from 1 February to 1 March at Thawson, near Towcester; and from 1 April to 14 October 'at such places as shall be determined by the parties'.

The Hunt establishment comprised one huntsman, six whippers-in, a steward and two cooks; clearly refreshment after hunting was an important part of the entertainment. This joint venture hunted a large area up and down the East Midlands until the end of the 18th century.

John Manners, 3rd Duke of Rutland (1721-79) founder of the Belvoir Foxhounds. Painting by Charles Jervas, 1725.

Costs increased and there was inevitably some dissatisfaction among the sporting fraternity that hounds kept moving on out of the district, and some angst among the noble Masters that their costs were increasing. In 1732 the Earl of Gainsborough separated from the arrangement and took 25 couple of hounds to hunt from Cottesmore as an independent pack.

At Belvoir there are records of some correspondence between the Duke of Rutland and the Earl of Gainsborough as to the rightful ownership of a large caldron used for cooking the hounds' food!

According to T.F. Dale, from 1732 the Belvoir country began to acquire more defined borders. To the south, Lord Gainsborough hunted an immense territory including large tracts of Leicestershire, Northamptonshire, Rutland and Nottinghamshire.

This meant that the pack hunting from Belvoir was hunting the estates of the Duke of Rutland, and a large tract of Lincolnshire which was to be permanently part of their country.

The 3rd Duke's son, John Marquis of Granby (1721-70) loved foxhunting, but much of his life was spent in his great career as one of the leading soldiers and statesmen of the 18th century.

The 4th Duke was fairly indifferent to hunting, but he made an important link in the hunting world by marrying the beautiful Mary Isabella Somerset, daughter of the 4th Duke of Beaufort, thereby providing a link with a family which has been among the greatest foxhunters, and breeders of foxhounds, in the history of the sport.

During the latter half of the 18th century the Belvoir was increasingly hunting fox in the open in a similar manner, but appears to have had far less trouble from visiting thrusters, and the ducal Mastership held considerable authority over foxhunters who were mainly locally-based, but hunted as guests, not as subscribers.

The 4th Duke died in 1787 when his eldest son, John, was only nine years old, and for some years the Hunt continued to be managed on behalf of the Rutland family by dedicated foxhunters.

The committee appointed a new Master: Mr Edward Perceval, who took up

The Marquis of Granby (1721-1770), eldest son of 3rd Duke – a national military hero who adored hunting at Belvoir. Painting by Sir Joshua Reynolds.

residence at Croxton Park, and kennelled the hounds there. He was a brother of Mr Spencer Perceval, MP for Northampton and Prime Minister from 1809-12, until his assassination.

MR PERCEVAL AS MASTER

Mr Perceval MFH appointed a new huntsman, Tom Newman, who proved highly effective, introducing some useful blood into the kennels from other leading packs of the time: Lord Monson's, Lord Fitzwilliam's, and Lord Spencer's Pytchley pack, then hunted by the much-admired Dick Knight.

Perceval's huntsman, Newman, was said to have bred a 'small, sharp pack' for the 4th Duke, but his successor from 1804, 'Gentleman' Shaw, 'bred the hounds a deal higher than Newman,' according to the great hunting correspondent Nimrod (Charles James Apperley) who adored hunting with all the Shires packs, and indeed first spread their fame to London's early 19th century clubland.

It is probable the Belvoir extended their hunting fixtures from two to three days a week at this time. Much work was done to improve the pack and the kennel facilities before the 5th Duke (1778-1857) reached adulthood, and took over as an active Master in 1804.

He became a highly committed foxhunter, receiving advice and encouragement from his uncle, the Duke of Beaufort, as well as the strong team of senior supporters in his own country.

Foxhunting's golden eras were yet to be celebrated in the Belvoir and Beaufort countries — and for a ride across superb country in the wake of a great pack of hounds, the Belvoir was to shine as one of the finest in the Shires.

CHAPTER 2

Early Glory

The Coston Run...
For few the foxes who could stay,
Before the hounds who ran today...

Foxhunting entered the first of its golden periods in the early 19th century. The Belvoir was to emerge as one of the leading packs in Britain, and its hounds became the fountainhead of Foxhound breeding.

The combination of devoted continuity by the Dukes of Rutland, their staff and local followers enabled the Hunt to flourish in its wonderful natural setting for the Chase at its best.

The Belvoir Vale and surrounding countryside was ideal for the new style of hunting the fox in the open, enabling the mounted field to tackle fences used in the recent enclosures of farmland. From being a local Hunt, the Belvoir evolved as a pack which attracted visitors from far and wide, from royalty to the newly-emerging rich industrialists of the latter 19th century.

The 5th Duke of Rutland engaged as his huntsman a remarkable character known as 'Gentleman' Shaw who had already earned a reputation as an entertaining figure in the hunting field in the country now known as the Bicester with Whaddon Chase.

Shaw was quick and bold in his casts, with the drive and dash required to give the mounted field full value from the Leicestershire terrain. He was a consummate horseman, and in good scenting conditions showed excellent sport, no doubt much to the pleasure of his young Master.

GREAT HUNT: THE WALTHAM RUN, 1805

Shaw was huntsman when the Belvoir achieved a famous run on 10 December 1805. Hounds met at Waltham, and after a light snowfall, they found at Jericho covert, and ran towards Redmile, swinging towards Bottesford, crossing the Nottingham road, and the river Devon.

They passed Normanton on the right, and Kilvington on the left, made for Staunton, but ran to Cotham, Long Bennington, Allington, towards Sedgebrook and Barrowby Thorns. They passed Gonerby and ran to the wharf at Grantham where this strong fox ran the towing path and crossed over the bridge. He crossed the Melton road, passed Harlaxton Wood, to Stroxton, Great Ponton, beyond Bassingthorpe, and then ran towards Burton Slade Wood.

At this point, with only five or six riders still in the hunt, it was decided to stop hounds because the horses were exhausted. This was a hunt with a furthest point of 18

The Melton Hunt Breakfast, by Sir Francis Grant, painted for the 5th Duke of Rutland.

miles, in about three hours; hounds never entered any covert except Sir John Thorold's plantation. Nearly all the famous long runs in foxhunting history have ended with the fox given best.

THOMAS GOOSEY
Huntsman, 1816–42

Shaw was succeeded by an excellent whipper-in who had served his apprenticeship under him, Thomas Goosey. The 1816–17 season began disastrously when Belvoir Castle was severely ravaged by fire, the family losing some of their most precious pictures and furniture. The fire appeared to have started through new building works taking place on the Castle, but the Duke resolutely resumed the work afterwards.

Goosey had bad luck at the start, with poor scent in his first season, but he soon proved his worth as a highly effective huntsman, producing a great deal of excellent sport. Landowners and farmers were prospering before the repeal of the Corn Laws and there was money to spare for hunting and other rural entertainment.

The Belvoir, like its neighbours the

22

Early Glory

Quorn and Cottesmore, became increasingly fashionable. Princes, peers and foreign royalty were among the upper echelon visiting the country, often as guests of John, the 5th Duke and his Duchess who entertained on a magnificent scale. Beau Brummell, the Prince of Wales, the Duke of York, the Duke of Argyll, the Marquis of Lorne, Lord Alvanley, and Lord Jersey were among the aristocratic figures gracing the Belvoir hunting field, and staying at the Castle.

Let it not be thought the mounted field was entirely composed of the aristocracy and local gentlemen. According to the hunting correspondent who wrote as 'The Druid', one of the most regular followers at that time was 'Short Odds' Richards, a Croxton bookmaker, who carried an umbrella instead of a whip, and constantly nibbled pieces of stale bread, for which he had a passion.

The enjoyment of hunting by yeoman farmers was well established, and was the bedrock of hunting wherever it was practised throughout the British Isles, but no more so than in Leicestershire.

Farmers in 19th century Leicestershire learned a sporting culture which involved hundreds of riders from far outside the county, mainly from London and the south, annually riding over their land.

In crossing the country in great style, few could match the horsemanship of Cecil Forester, the first Lord Forester, brother-in-law of the Belvoir's ducal Master.

Hunting Scene near Belvoir Castle, by John Ferneley, 1828. The 5th Duke is in the distance on his grey horse, with his brothers, Lt. General Lord Charles Manners on the left, and Major General Lord Robert Manners in foreground.

The Belvoir

Forester was the son of the Duke's sister, the Lady Katherine.

Forester became heavily involved in the Hunt and took over management of the hounds from 1825, but he died three years later, leaving his son, John George Lord Forester to maintain the family connection with the Belvoir.

In 1830 the younger Forester was clearly so much valued in the Hunt that he was appointed Master, since the 5th Duke felt it was time to hand over; the Duchess had died five years earlier.

The second Lord Forester was Master from 1830–42 under an arrangement, according to the *Sporting Magazine*, whereby the Duke loaned the hounds, kennels and stables, and gave £1,200 a year towards expenses, a very considerable sum at that time. It was a step towards becoming a subscription pack, because Forester took a subscription of £1,000 a year from the Grantham side of the country, and found the rest of the expenses himself.

Forester apologises for his standard of writing in one letter: 'I have had a fall, and it was thought advisable for me to loose 12 ounces of blood.'

The new Master was fortunate in his huntsman: Goosey became a living legend in

The Duke of Rutland's Dog Pack, by Sir Francis Grant, depicts Thomas Goosey, huntsman 1816–42. The painting is displayed in the Duke of Rutland's apartments in Belvoir Castle, with Goosey's hunting horn attached to the picture frame.

Early Glory

the Shires. He was a meticulous kennel huntsman, keeping his hounds in wonderful order, and he was physically tough enough to withstand long winters in the hunting field, producing remarkably consistent sport, although inevitably he slowed down towards the end of his 26 years as huntsman.

Goosey was said to fortify himself with heavy draughts of alcohol, without faltering, nor showing any signs of drunkenness. He could drink of a bottle of brandy at a sitting, and was reported to have imbibed 13 glasses of hot whisky and water on one cold day without being any the worse for it.

His politeness in the hunting field was legendary. He said mildly to a young thruster: 'You jumped on that hound sir, and I beg leave to say that you buried him as well.'

On Goosey's retirement in 1842 he was presented with a silver cup and a testimonial. He died at Knipton and is buried in the churchyard.

Lord Forester's Mastership has been described as one of the most brilliant in the Hunt's history.

WILL GOODALL
Huntsman 1842–59

Goosey's successor as huntsman was William, better known as Will, Goodall who had been second whipper-in. Goodall established a great reputation in the next 17 years, some

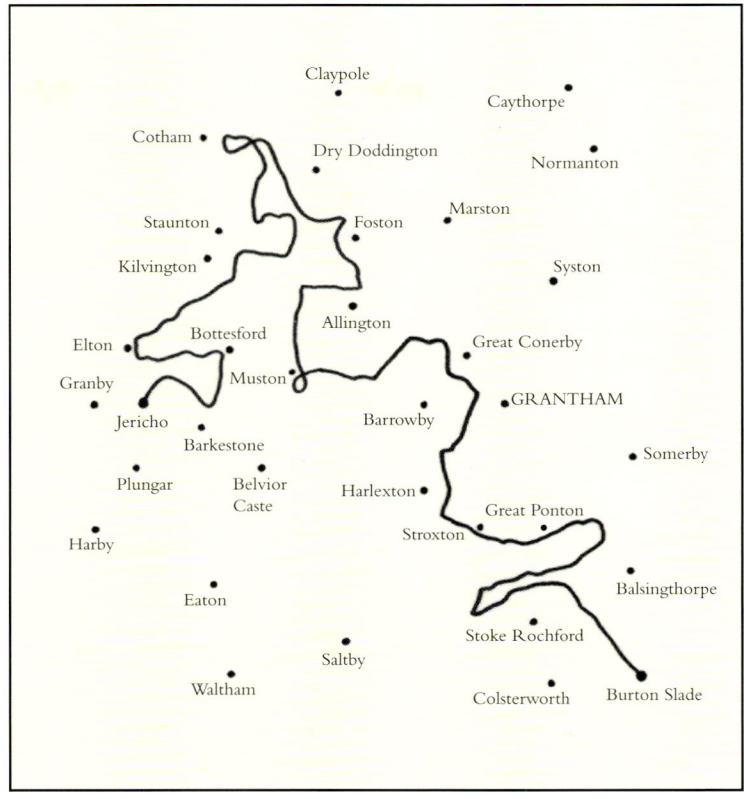

Route of the great Waltham Run of 1805, an 18-mile point in three hours.

said second only to Tom Firr, the Quorn's huntsman from 1872–99.

Goodall's career at Belvoir was described as a golden era for the Hunt; the country was wild, and well foxed; railways, canals and busier roads had not arrived. The huntsman earned a reputation among those at the pinnacle of the sport in the 19th century, much loved and admired in his own time, and revered ever since, according to Nimrod.

Goodall was the grandson of Stephen Goodall, reputed to weigh at least 20 stone, and therefore exceptionally heavy in the

The Belvoir

saddle, yet renowned as an excellent huntsman for the famous Mr Corbet in Warwickshire. Stephen later hunted the Pytchley and the Quorn in brief tenures.

Will Goodall learned his profession as second whipper-in to Tom Wingfield in the Bicester country, and the young man's talent and pleasant character earned him his place at Belvoir. He was educated enough to write remarkably expressive diaries and letters to the Duke of Rutland, reporting his sport and the work of the kennels.

Although adequate in the saddle, he was primarily noted as an exceptional hound man, taking a great interest in the breeding and presentation of his pack.

His introduction of Rallywood into the Belvoir kennel from the Brocklesby, secured one of the most influential foxhound sires in the 19th century. Rallywood is buried in the garden of the huntsman's house at the Belvoir Hunt kennels.

Rallywood is immortalised in the painting by Ferneley (1782–1860), son of a painter and wheelwright in the Quorn country, who became the greatest native painter of Leicestershire hunting and other aspects of rural life.

In Goodall's second season, in 1843, a great day, and a testing one for the huntsman, occurred when the Hunt welcomed as its guest Prince Albert, the Prince Consort. The major stress for all concerned was that the Prince was on this occasion accompanied to the hunting field by Queen Victoria who was not amused by hunting, although certainly not opposed.

Queen Victoria attended a meet at Croxton Park, accompanied by the dowager Queen Adelaide. They travelled in a carriage and four with the Duke of Rutland, escorted by outriders in livery. Carriages lined the route for nearly a quarter of a mile, and about 800 attended the meet on horse-back, with thousands in attendance on foot.

The Queen did not alight from the carriage, but hounds were brought to the window for her inspection. After a procession through Waltham, the Queen's carriage was halted on the high ground looking across to Melton Spinney.

Amid such a crowd it was amazing any sport was achieved, but hounds found a brace and a half which happened to have remained in the Spinney, and hunted one to

Will Goodall, renowned Belvoir huntsman from 1842–59; died aged 42 after a fall.

Clawson Thorns where the fox was headed by foot people and ran back to Melton Spinney, hounds catching him one field before the covert. After several abortive draws, hounds found in Newman's Gorse and ran to Sproxton Thorns.

The Prince was among the leaders in the mounted field, although both his equerries suffered falls which caused some local amusement. Everyone was relieved the Prince survived without harm, not least the Queen who was always most solicitous of Albert's health.

Afterwards the Prince Consort declared himself 'well pleased by a capital run'. Victoria reported on Albert's visit to the Belvoir in a letter to King Leopold of the Belgians: 'One can scarcely credit the absurdity of people, but Albert's riding so boldly has made such a sensation that it has been written all over the country, and they make much more of it than if he had done some great act.'

Goodall was now hunting the Belvoir hounds five days a week, and some 60 couples were kept in kennel. Additional kennels were established at Ropsley to assist the huntsman when hunting on the Lincolnshire side.

The 5th Duke died in his 80th year in 1857, and was succeeded by his son, Charles, who took the Mastership soon afterwards, and undertook to hunt the hounds at his own expense, which he did for over 20 years in great style.

He adored hunting, and was a bold horseman, suffering the severe falls which can be the lot of the best riders on the rare occasions when they occur.

The 6th Duke endured ill health later in life due to his hunting accidents, and suffered especially after a fall over a stake-and-bound fence during a run from Casthorpe in 1863 in which he received a head injury which impaired his riding ability thereafter.

The Belvoir enhanced its reputation for hard riding at this period.

James Cooper, the 6th Duke's huntsman from 1859–70, producing great sport.

Charles Manners, 6th Duke of Rutland (1859–88), bold horseman and great Master of Foxhounds. Hand coloured steel engraving by J. Hunt 1861; given to the 11th Duke by a friend who spotted it in a local shop in 2008.

In his youth as Lord Granby, the 6th Duke had jumped the Croxton Park wall on the south side where it was five foot high, with a big drop. He jumped the river Witham between Great Ponton and Grantham, at a very wide place, and swam the Nottingham and Grantham canal on horseback.

He was remembered fondly by Belvoir followers for maintaining authority in the field without using bad language, but he could call them to order 'in a determined manner', and on some occasions when he was not listened to, he threatened to take hounds home, according to the reminiscences of Frederick Stanley.

Near the end of the 1858–59 season, on 6 April, Goodall suffered a severe fall, near the Reeded House, from a horse he was trying. He had a habit of carrying his horn in his breast, and it was thought he fell heavily on to it. James Cooper, his whipper-in saw him, and was about to help him up, but Goodall got up on his own.

He suffered a chill afterwards, declined in health and died aged 42 on 1 May, the first day of the next hunting year.

A huge crowd attended his funeral before burial at Knipton. Goodall left a widow and 11 children, one of whom, Will junior, became a notable huntsman of the Pytchley. Will junior was educated at Guilsborough Grammar School thanks to support from Sir Thomas Whichcote of Aswarby Park who was a great admirer of Will Goodall.

There was a public subscription for the huntsman's widow, Frances Goodall, and the children, and their future was assured by the Duke of Rutland. Mrs Goodall lived to a great age in the redundant hunting lodge provided by the Duke at Croxton Park, who carried out a promise he made to the huntsman on his deathbed.

Mr Philip Shipman, who breeds magnificent Shire horses, is a direct descendant on the maternal side, of Will Goodall, and the fifth generation of the Shipman family farming at Croxton Lodge Farm, between Branston and Knipton. One of old Will Goodall's daughters, Frances, married a gamekeeper called Tom Dent, and their daughter, Lizzie Goodall Dent, married a farmer called Shipman who farmed at Croxton Lodge.

Philip Shipman and his wife, Margaret, are keen Belvoir supporters, and they treasure a fascinating collection of original diaries and letters written by old Will Goodall in impeccable handwriting.

JAMES COOPER
Huntsman, 1859–70

After Goodall's death, James Cooper was appointed in his place. He was a Scot, from Fife; a strong, wiry man, and a great horseman. He remained in office for the next

The 6th Duke, in old age, inspecting hounds in the Duke's Room at Belvoir Hunt Kennels, sitting behind a guard to protect his legs; illustration by Cuthbert Bradley, dated 1893, after the Duke's death.

decade, and achieved good sport, becoming a favourite of the Duke.

The Prince of Wales, eldest son of Queen Victoria (later King Edward VII) accompanied by the Princess, hunted with the Belvoir in February 1866, an event seen as being of much importance in the Hunt's history at the time. There was a huge crowd

29

at the meet at Piper Hole, on a day when the country was unfortunately very wet and deep.

There was a hunt from Hose Gorse in the Vale, and another over a stiff line of country from Harby Covert. Next day the Prince hunted from a meet at Weaver's Lodge, east of Grantham, again attended by a huge crowd.

There was a morning hunt from Sapperton, in which the Duke of Rutland had a fall. The royal party had lunch under the shelter of some stacks during hailstorms, and a good hunt was later achieved from Ingoldsby Wood.

On the way home to Belvoir Castle the Prince and his party stopped at the Angel Hotel at Grantham for refreshment. Mr Boyall, the landlord, informed the Prince that King John stayed at the Angel before he lost his baggage in the Wash, and King George IV had stayed there too. The landlord said in view of the latest royal visit, with the Prince's permission, he would henceforth rename the hotel the Angel and Royal – which he did.

Cooper's term as huntsman was a golden period of sport in the Belvoir's history. The 6th Duke was in his prime, and able to ride at the front of the mounted field, whereas at the end of his long term he was infirm.

Among Cooper's whippers-in had been Frank Gillard who was to emerge as one of Leicestershire's 'greats'. Born in Devon, Frank began service with a pack of harriers at Monkleigh, moving to Stevenstone as second whipper-in, before joining the Duke of Rutland's as whipper-in in 1860.

He recalled hunting five days a week, and on the sixth visiting a neighbouring pack. Seven years later he was promoted kennel huntsman at the South Notts where John Chaworth Musters was Master and hunted hounds. It was a fine opportunity for the young kennel huntsman to learn venery under a top-class hound man.

Gillard next moved to the Quorn with Musters when he took that Mastership in 1868, and in 1870 Gillard was promoted huntsman of the Quorn under the new Mastership of Mr Coupland.

Frank Gillard, Belvoir huntsman from 1870–96.

FRANK GILLARD
Huntsman, 1870–1896

Cooper resigned and the Duke of Rutland asked Coupland if he would release Gillard to return to the Belvoir. Coupland graciously obliged, and Gillard was installed at the Belvoir where he achieved a remarkable reputation as huntsman for the next 26 years.

At Belvoir, Frank Gillard's duties far exceeded hunting the hounds. According to his biographer Cuthbert Bradley: 'The noble Master placed the greatest confidence in Gillard's abilities, leaving it to him to carry on the correspondence and business generally of the Hunt. The whole internal machinery of so vast and important a Hunt as the Belvoir was practically worked by one man for a quarter of a century, and on such good lines that the kennel occupied the premier position by general consent.'

The 'Duke's Room', at the Belvoir Kennels, superbly refurbished by Mr Tony Fenwick in 2009 as a fascinating miniature museum, remains much as it was when Frank Gillard would show the 6th Duke the celebrated sires and favourites of his pack. Long discussions would take place over a railed guard, still in position, which prevented hounds touching the Master's gouty leg, aggravated by his hunting accidents. Pictures adorning the walls give a flavour of the Hunt's long history.

A supreme example of the 6th Duke of Rutland's transference of responsibilities to his huntsman Frank Gillard, occurred when the Empress of Austria visited the Belvoir in 1874, her first day's hunting in England. The Duke was away, and Gillard arranged a special 8am cubhunting meet at the end of September to suit the Empress.

They met at Three Queens, and hounds found in Herring's Gorse, providing a nice spin by Saltby to Hungerton, and finding again at Sproxton Gorse they ran hard over what was then heathland to Denton where they caught their fox after a sharp 25 minutes.

The beautiful young Empress, immaculate in close fitting side-saddle habit which her maid sewed on to her, crossed the country superbly. Afterwards Gillard was deputed to show her over the kennels and stables, the gardens and the Castle, and he and his wife were hosts to the Empress for luncheon in their parlour. Poor Gillard drenched the Empress when he attempted to open a fizzy bottle of soda water, but she laughed it off.

It was a happy occasion, and the Empress commissioned Gillard to buy her a complete pack of beagles to be shipped to Austria. His son, Frank, took them to Vienna and enjoyed a splendid week as the guest of Austrian royalty.

The agricultural depression caused the Duke to consider cutting fixtures from five to four days a week in the 1875–6 season.

Gillard begged him not to take this decision, and a solution was found when gentlemen supporters of the Hunt held a meeting at Belton Park, with Lord Brownlow in the chair. He offered the Duke a subscription of £1,500 a season to defray costs, with the proviso that Gillard was to continue running the Hunt in the same manner.

The Duke accepted the arrangement, and Gillard continued to hunt five days a week.

The 6th Duke died on 4 March 1888, having been Master for 30 years. Hunting stopped for eight days, and there had been 40 days lost through frost that season, but they had hunted 190 days and killed 42½ brace.

The Belvoir

The 7th Duke was the brother of his predecessor, and aged 70 when he succeeded. Gillard continued to run the Hunt, and it is clear that his burdens increased at this time, although he had his son Frank to turn hounds to him, and at last a Field Master was appointed: Lord Edward Manners, MP for Melton, second son of the Duke.

In 1891 the Belvoir reduced its fixtures to four days a week, owing to the agricultural depression causing the 7th Duke to cut his costs. He decided in the 1895–6 season to give up the Mastership. It was a major landmark in the Hunt's history.

Lord Brownlow, Lord Lieutenant of Lincolnshire, chaired a meeting at Grantham to express regret at the Duke's retirement, and to form a committee to make new arrangements for the Hunt.

It was also Gillard's final season as huntsman. His last Leicestershire day on 25 March 1896, saw a brilliant run of one hour and 20 minutes from Burbidge's, ending with a kill in Ranksborough Gorse, the famous covert in the Cottesmore country, near Oakham.

In Gillard's last season, 1895–6, the Belvoir pack killed 39½ brace, making a total of 2,709 during Gillard's 26 years as huntsman.

Gillard hunted hounds twice more on the Lincolnshire side, riding an old favourite, Farewell, at his last meet. Farewell was a half-brother to Playfair, a winner of the Grand National. Gillard had hoped to continue as huntsman for a while under the new Mastership, but it was not to be: understandably, the new Mastership wished to start a new era with a new huntsman.

The Duke gave Frank the horse as one of his retirement presents; a testimonial from the Hunt raised nearly £1,300.

Frank Gillard said in the preface to his biography: 'The memory of my hounds is very dear to me; their individuality has left a lasting impression on my mind, like those of human friends, which only death can cancel. It was beautiful to hunt such hounds.'

CHAPTER 3

Turning Point

*The Master who built railway
transport for his hounds...*

The year 1896 was a major turning point in the history of the Duke of Rutland's hounds. The Duke's decision to give up the Mastership caused great consternation in the hunting world. It seemed the end of an era, and no-one knew what lay ahead.

Lord Brownlow convened a meeting at Grantham to consider the future, and a temporary Hunt committee was formed. The Mastership was put out to tender, and a short-list formed.

The hot favourite was Mr Austen-Mackenzie MFH, Master of the Woodland Pytchley (1885-89), but he was turned down when he stated he intended to bring his own hounds and would hunt them. The very thought of an outside pack replacing the Belvoir's traditional pack, bred at Belvoir for generations, caused great concern in the country, and the prospect of an amateur huntsman was anything but popular at that time.

The pack was to remain in the possession of the Rutland family, and they leased to the Hunt the Kennels, the adjoining land and other Hunt buildings. The continuing connection with the Dukes of Rutland helped to give the Hunt stability amid the increasing pressures of the 20th century. Significantly, the Dukes insisted the pack continued to be bred on pure English lines, ensuring that it emerged into the 21st century as one of the very few packs left comprised entirely of these invaluable lines.

But from 1896 the Dukes did not figure in the Mastership, except for the perilous years of the second world war (*see Chapter 6*).

Sir Gilbert Greenall took on the challenge of succeeding the 7th Duke as Master in 1896. Sir Gilbert's father was an old friend of the Duke, and Gilbert was devoted to foxhunting.

He was the inheritor of one of the great brewing fortunes, Greenall Whitley and Co., started in the mid-18th century as a firm in the north-west, but growing to become the largest regional brewer in Britain, based at St Helens and Warrington.

Sir Gilbert was a 29-year-old bachelor when he was invited to become Master of the Belvoir. The country rejoiced when, in 1900, he married Frances, daughter of Capt. Edward Wynne Griffith, member of a keen hunting family from the Flint and Denbigh country.

Gilbert was already established as a man of considerable organising ability, and full of confidence in tackling a new project. No doubt he inherited these qualities from his father, also Sir Gilbert Greenall, the first Baronet and MP for Warrington, a formidable businessman and politician.

The younger Gilbert Greenall decided to be a non-executive chairman of Greenall Whitley and to devote himself to country life in which horses and hunting played a great part. He hunted enthusiastically with the North Cheshire and the Cheshire, and was mentioned by some as a future Master of the latter, but local gossip said the Cheshire considered itself too grand at that time to appoint a Master whose fortune was derived from 'trade'.

Sir Gilbert became honorary director of the Royal Show for 25 years, ensuring it became Britain's leading agricultural show. As a bloodstock breeder his greatest triumph was in breeding 'Love in Idleness', winner of the Oaks in 1921, and he bred and produced hunters, hackneys, cattle and pigs with equal enthusiasm and great success. He was ennobled as the first Lord Daresbury in 1927.

The Dukes of Rutland handed over the Mastership of their Hunt to an exceptionally capable individual. From the start, Sir Gilbert made it clear he was willing to dig deeply into his purse to ensure the highest standards at Belvoir.

Determined to provide good sport, Sir Gilbert bought an impressive array of Hunt horses, said to have been bought for £18,000 from Mr John Henry Stokes of Bowden.

In his first year Sir Gilbert erected a superb new Hunt stable yard on land given by the Duke at Woolsthorpe, to hold no less than 70 horses. It comprised a riding school, valeting rooms, a forge and cottages for the grooms – and suprisingly, it was completed in seven months, the bricks still smoking from the kilns when they were put in place.

Additionally Sir Gilbert built himself a Master's house by the stable block at Woolsthorpe cross-roads. On completion of the work he entertained 160 workers and members of his own staff to a 'thank you dinner' at The Chequers in early September 1896.

In May the following year Sir Gilbert was host at the first of the Belvoir Earthstoppers' Dinners, held at the Angel, Grantham for Lincolnshire, and another at The Peacock, Belvoir, for the Leicestershire side. Horse-drawn transport was provided to help those living in the outlying villages to get home afterwards, and outbuildings at The Angel were strewn with clean straw for those who

Sir Gilbert Greenall, Master of the Belvoir 1896-1912; created first Lord Daresbury 1927.

found themselves 'unable' to make it from the hotel to the waiting wagons. Apart from a brief period during the latter part of the second World War Earthstoppers' Dinners continued at various venues.

Sir Gilbert Greenall at a Belvoir Puppy Show talking to Mr Bemrose, a farmer in the country.

HUNTING BY RAIL

Local people were open-mouthed at Sir Gilbert's other major expense on behalf of the Hunt: he built a special railway siding which would enable rail transport for the hounds to their Lincolnshire meets, changing trains at Bottesford.

With liberal supplies of labour and material in later Victorian England, such enterprises could be undertaken by the wealthy leaders of industry.

The 'Hunt Special', organised to convey hounds and men to the distant fixtures to the east, replaced Gillard's system of a horse-drawn van which had been in use for some 25 years and had certainly outlived its usefulness.

The new train transport operated from Woolsthorpe wharf, close to the Master's own newly-erected house and stables, and joined the GNR line above Muston, where access to the rail network in Lincolnshire was gained.

The stations of Rauceby, Ancaster, Caythorpe, Leadhenam, Scredington, Billingborough and Rippingale stations were used as stations near meets, with Great Ponton useful for the more local Grantham meets. Stabling at each of these destinations was acquired overnight, or at least for the

The Greenall family and Hunt staff (left to right): whippers-in Herbert Norman and Jack Hewitt, Sir Gilbert Greenall, younger son Edward (Toby) Greenall, Lady (Frances) Greenall, huntsman Ben Capell, and Gilbert Greenall, elder son.

temporary accommodation of tired horses after long days.

There were drawbacks in transporting hounds by train: difficulties increased as the lines became more congested, and all too often time spent hunting had to be governed by the clock so that hounds could catch their train home.

Added time was needed in the morning for hacks to and fro from stables to the kennels to bring on and return the pack for the day, with hounds often coming home in darkness. During the Great War the problems grew even more when the lines were busy with movements of troops and munitions which had priority.

To ease matters during the September cubhunting, hounds and men were billeted at Aswarby Park for a week, through the generosity of Sir George Whichcote, which was not entirely popular with men and their families.

A regular problem encountered on the homeward journey awaited at Belvoir Junction where delays were frequent when the branch line to Woolsthorpe was occupied by an engine working the ironstone quarries.

Lord (Toby) Daresbury recalled: 'The special was the property of the railway company, and cost my father in the region of £500 for its use on five days per three weeks throughout the season.

'It consisted of one First Class and two Third Class compartments, four horse boxes (three horses to each box), a luggage van for hounds and men, and a guard's van. Space permitting, subscribers were welcome to make use of this facility, on payment of the first class fare for themselves and their horses.

'Lord Robert Manners was a regular traveller, and on these occasions I might find myself consigned with my pony to the luggage van among the hounds.

'I have travelled many miles since, but seldom in such joyful company.'

Foxhunting history relates that back in Cheshire some were wondering whether the local foxhunting grandees had not made a major mistake in rejecting the generosity of the young Gilbert Greenall who was already proving at Belvoir that his ambitions were backed by a generous commitment.

The new Belvoir Master ordained that the Hunt staff were in future to wear leathers instead of cord, and one man was employed full time during the season to keep the leathers clean. The quality of horseflesh

The young Frank Freeman, seen as first whipper-in at Belvoir from 1896 to 1902; later a renowned huntsman of the Pytchley (1906-31).

At Belvoir Castle, Lady Greenall centre, Sir Gilbert Greenall, their two sons on ponies, and huntsman Ben Capell right with hounds. left on the grey, Major Griffith.

in the Hunt stables had never been higher.

Sir Gilbert lavished expense on the Belvoir annual puppy show, making it one of the most popular and well-attended, and he gave splendid hospitality to puppy walkers and invited guests, being entertained to an excellent meal, with speeches at the conclusion of the judging at the Hunt Kennels.

As well as the customary spoon given to each walker, cups and other silverware were awarded to the walkers of winners and placed hounds. The Rev. Cecil Legard, a noted hunting clergyman of the day and an acknowledged expert on hound breeding, was a judge at each of Sir Gilbert's 16 puppy shows during his Mastership.

Maintaining foxhunting on a large scale was increasingly expensive, despite the major financial contribution of the Master. There had been a half-hearted attempt to start capping in the late 1890s, but in 1907 the Committee reintroduced a cap of £2 per day for visitors in the mounted field, and caps remained part of the Hunt's income thereafter.

Right: Edward (Toby) Greenall and his elder brother Gilbert Greenall on their ponies at the Belvoir Castle meet.

BEN CAPELL CARRIES THE HORN

It seems Frank Gillard was not ready to retire when the Mastership changed, but Sir Gilbert was keen to start with a new, younger huntsman. Gillard duly retired to the Red House at Knipton, and later ran a hotel in Oxford.

Sir Gilbert appointed Ben Capell as huntsman to succeed Gillard. Capell was the son of the stud groom to the Quorn's Master, Capt William P. Warner, and began his career in hunt service as second horseman to Capt Warner and the Quorn's Tom Firr. Capell was promoted to Quorn second whipper-in in 1878, and his early experience of Shires hunting under one of its greatest practitioners, was a major factor in his later appointment to carrying the horn at the Belvoir.

Capell also had experience of Hunt service with the Kilkenny in Ireland, with the Woodland Pytchley, and as first whipper-in at the Blankney from 1885, succeeding as huntsman two seasons later, until he came to the Belvoir in 1896, remaining throughout Sir Gilbert's Mastership.

In 1912 Capell returned from the Belvoir to the Blankney as huntsman for Mr R.C. Swan, and retired in 1914 to Bottesford until his death in 1919; he was buried in the parish churchyard.

Most of Capell's whippers-in were to score success at the top of their sport in the early 20th century. Initially Capell's first whipper-in at Belvoir was George Jones with Sam Gillson as second whipper-in. Later Jack Hewitt was first whipper-in, succeeding Capell as huntsman. Second whipper-in, from 1906, was Herbert Norman, later to become

The Belvoir

first whipper-in and kennel huntsman to the great amateur huntsman, Chatty Hilton-Green at the Cottesmore.

Capell's first whipper-in from 1898 was Frank Freeman, who had joined as second whipper in the previous season. Freeman, who left Belvoir in 1902, created a major reputation at the Pytchley as arguably the greatest professional huntsman of the 20th century. He was a reserved, obsessive personality, but the sport he produced transcended any personality defects.

In contrast, Ben Capell was an outgoing person, popular in the country, and eager to please. What sort of sport did Capell and his huge back-up staff produce at Belvoir?

Cuthbert Bradley, the hunting writer and artist, reported: 'Ben Capell is a Leicestershire huntsman bred and born, his methods of conducting a hunt being in keeping with modern ideas.'

This could be interpreted as a somewhat barbed comment, since Capell's past experience with Firr had certainly taught him how to 'keep the tambourine a'rolling' no matter what the fortunes of the day, and some of the older generation of hunting men in Leicestershire bemoaned the degree of lifting

Smartly turned out with cross-belts during Sir Gilbert Greenall's Mastership: the Belvoir Hunt second horsemen.

hounds and forward casting which this could sometimes entail.

The keenest riding members of the field had no complaint about the 'quick things' achieved across the vale by their huntsman. Pleasing everyone is impossible for any leading sportsman, especially a huntsman who cannot answer back, nor explain the particular difficulties he encounters in kennel and in the field. The Belvoir was providing great sport over grass and fences in the Leicestershire country, and the Lincolnshire side was a wonderful setting for longer, perservering hunts by the doghounds which should have satisfied any hunting purist among the numerous followers on horse and on foot.

Capell had the good fortune to be exceptionally well mounted. Cuthbert Bradley wrote that the Belvoir huntsman seldom rode the same horse for more than three seasons, observing that 'the constant change on to new mounts in the full vigour of life has probably reduced the average of falls taken by the Belvoir Hunt staff to a minimum.'

During Capell's 16 years, the Belvoir undoubtedly provided remarkable runs over their superb country: the Belvoir Vale was a sea of grass, some areas formidably fenced, and there was wilder country in the hills and beyond, with strong foxes abounding in a multitude of coverts. It was a challenge for any horseman to follow the famous Belvoir pack, soaring over their delectable country, usually well deserving the description of being able to cover them all 'with a table cloth,' and displaying their famous drive in hunting a fox.

GOOD SPORT INTO THE 20th CENTURY

The 1900-01 season was a special one for the Master. Sir Gilbert was married in London on 25 October to Frances Griffith. Major Longstaff, on behalf of the Hunt, presented two large silver cups to the Master at a celebration party at Little Ponton Hall.

Two serving officers who were Belvoir subscribers lost their lives during that season on active service in the Boer War in South Africa: Capt Gordon Wood and Lt. Alfred Millington Knowles. The Hunt also mourned the passing of Robert Parnham who had been the Belvoir's kennelman for 24 seasons, and died aged 56. He was replaced by Harry Edwards from the Blankney.

In the 1902-3 season, after the opening meet on 4 November. hounds hunted 71 days, with nine days lost due to the weather, and five days lost due to the death of Lord Edward Manners. Including cubhunting, hounds killed 71 brace throughout the season.

In the 1903-4 season, after meeting at Bescaby Oaks on 10 February there was a remarkable hunt into the Cottesmore country, with a nine mile point. After the meet on 19 March from Cotham Old Hall, there was a late hunt from Goddards Holt, with hounds running to the outskirts of Newark, but the most important incident was a severe fall suffered by the huntsman, Ben Capell, who had to be conveyed home, and hounds did not draw again.

Fortunately, Capell was not seriously hurt, and continued the tough regime of long days throughout long seasons in the Belvoir's very extensive country in Leicestershire and Lincolnshire, until Sir Gilbert Greenall's Mastership ended in 1912.

In the 1904-5 season they hunted 67 days, and were stopped on 17 days by severe weather, but it was a good season, and included a nine mile point in a hunt from Piper Hole Gorse to Wyville.

On Thursday 31 March 1904, following the last meet of the season from Rippingale, hounds ran from Kirkby Wood to Bulby Hall Wood and Breaches Wood, with the fox in view – until it was shot. The horror of such an occurrence in a hunting country hardly needs imagining. The fox was approaching Lord Ancaster's coverts at the time, and investigations disclosed one of his keepers as the culprit. A furious Sir Gilbert Greenall reported to Belvoir Castle on the outrage, and much ink flowed in correspondence between the Duke of Rutland and the Earl before an uneasy peace was restored.

Reports of the seasons up to Sir Gilbert's retirement from the Mastership all seem to indicate plenty of consistent sport, with most of the longer runs on the Lincolnshire side, as one would expect in that terrain, and plenty of action over the grass and fences in Leicestershire.

Sir Gilbert's final season, and that of Ben Capell at Belvoir, was reported as 'one of the best on record', with good scenting conditions throughout. Hounds lost only nine days to frost, and 67½ brace of foxes were accounted for, with the best run from Kaye Wood to Stathern on 16 March; it was a good 45 minutes, ending with a kill in the open. The season was marred on 26 January 1912, after the meet at Folkingham. Hounds had finished a busy day around Ropsley Rise, and as it was not customary to call for the use of the Hunt Special train when finishing near Grantham, they were hacking home.

Shortly before 6pm when approaching Denton cross-roads in the dark, the pack was struck by a motor vehicle being driven from Melton. One and a half couple were killed outright and a further four couple so badly maimed that some never hunted again. Almost a century later, the deceptive bend on the approach to Denton from Grantham remained an accident black spot. The 1912 accident was a grim reminder that in the 20th century motor transport would pose new dangers on country roads.

Sir Gilbert completed his Mastership, in which he had contributed so much to the Belvoir, and his last day was 6 April.

An accurate history of the Belvoir should relate that Sir Gilbert's Mastership, despite the excellent sport reported here, was marred by some published criticisms of his huntsman and his hounds, perhaps inspired by jealousy of the great popularity throughout the hunting world of Belvoir hound sires. Some of the rumours which had circulated widely about Frank Gillard resorting on occasion to hunting doped, or even bagged, foxes, began to haunt his successor.

These were put into print much later in 1935 in Guy Paget's Leicestershire hunting book '*Bad 'Uns to Beat*' in which he recounted stories about Gillard and Capell, purportedly told in local dialect by a Shires veteran, Dick Heathen. Since both had long since died, they could not answer these allegations.

However, Paget's book stated that if there were misdemeanours occasionally in the Belvoir's conduct of hunting, they were certainly not the fault of Sir Gilbert, nor of Capell, but of certain earth stoppers who had allegedly got into bad habits during Frank Gillard's reign as huntsman.

It is indisputable that during Sir Gilbert's Mastership a controversy erupted in

Ben Capell with hounds, and on foot (left to right): Gilbert and Edward (Toby) Greenall, Mrs Hardy and Capt Hardy, Lord Robert Manners, and daughter Betty Manners.

the foxhunting world concerning the Belvoir hounds, which was to have long-lasting effects on hound breeding later in the 20th century.

The late 19th century's emphasis on breeding traditional English Foxhounds of great substance had resulted in hounds in many leading kennels which were criticised as 'the Peterborough type' or more derisively as 'Shorthorns', comparing them to the girth and stance of beef cattle.

BELVOIR – THE FOUNT OF FOXHOUND BREEDING

The Belvoir remained the fount of much Foxhound breeding during the early period of the 20th century, although Sir Gilbert maintained the policy of the Dukes of Rutland in never showing them at Peterborough Royal Foxhound Show which started in 1878 and became the premier show of England. Despite this, many of the winning hounds every year at Peterborough were by Belvoir sires.

Frank Gillard's stallion hounds Dexter, Gambler and Fallible were among those much admired throughout the foxhunting world, and Ben Capell followed with other notable sires using the same lines.

A public row erupted when *The Field* published a letter from Capt. Charlie McNeill, Master of the Grafton, complaining that if the best Belvoir stallion hounds sired as many litters as they were shown to have achieved in the stud book, they could not have done much hunting.

This produced fury on behalf of staunch Belvoir supporters.

Perhaps the fulsome praise of the Belvoir hounds, and the criticisms, had both been over-stated. Certainly, the Belvoir pack continued to provide satisfactory sport for their devoted followers throughout this period. As we shall see, later Masterships were to obtain a more athletic type of hound whilst remaining loyal to the traditional breeding in the kennel, as ordained by the owners of the hounds, the Dukes of Rutland. Good noses, a great cry, durability, and an ability to work together as a pack are all virtues of the Belvoir hounds which have produced consistent sport, and earned the admiration of generations of foxhunters who have so much enjoyed following them.

The controversy raged on in the *The Field's* columns, but came to no conclusion. Capt McNeill responded to his attackers by writing that the Belvoir pack was a national institution, that hound breeding was of national importance, and therefore he was thoroughly justified in raising the matter.

Some criticisms of the Belvoir doghounds' performance in the hunting field were the usual stuff of hunting gossip, anonymous, and usually ill-informed. Even Guy Paget wrote that Mr Chandos Pole, a previous Master of the Meynell, had been 'very unkind' in describing the Belvoir hounds as 'a very beautiful summer pack'.

During the first quarter of the 20th century it was not unusual for over 100 couple of Belvoir pups to be sent to walk. There was a similar scale of breeding in other large-scale packs in order to combat the constant losses of young hounds to distemper, since there was no vaccine available at that time.

It was recorded at Belvoir that during the 1903 season which was exceptionally wet no less than 40 couple perished.

Of those who survived to be returned from walk to the kennels, perhaps no more than 15 couple would be carefully selected to make up the next season's entry. The remainder became the draft which at that period was considered to be one of the huntsman's 'perks'; the more hounds he had to sell, the more cash for his bank. It was also expected that Masters of visiting bitches to stallion hounds, should suitably reward huntsman and kennelman.

Some believed this constant stream of outside bitches to the Belvoir kennel contributed to a decline in the working capabilities of young doghounds. Major Bouch on his return from the first war was aware of the problem, and, anxious to restore both quality and numbers to the ducal pack, he reduced the number of visiting bitches to a minimum.

The ownership of the Belvoir hounds by the Dukes of Rutland ensured the whole pack was never sold, and was a major factor in building up the reputation of the Belvoir pack in the latter half of the 19th century, and well into the 20th.

After the 1914-18 Great War the new ideas about Welsh outcrosses became more popular – just one of many challenges the Belvoir was to meet, and to overcome in a century of overwhelming change which affected the hunting field as much as any other facet of country life.

During the 1898-99 season, on 4 December, Mr R.M. Knowles of Colston Bassett arrived at the meet in Elton by motor car. He was the first member of the Hunt do so – a more significant sign of a new century of major change than anyone could have imagined at the time.

CHAPTER 4

Surviving the Great War

Tommy Bouch's Great Hunt into the Fens...
...a point of 12 miles – and rather more than 17 as hounds ran.

There was great joy in the Belvoir country when Lord Robert ('Bobby' to his family) Manners, fourth son of the 7th Duke of Rutland, took on the Mastership in 1912. He was a hero in the Boer war, and was a delightful personality, wearing an eyeglass and speaking in a drawl, according to family history.

Sadly his Mastership was to be cut short two years later by the outbreak of the Great War, and Lord Robert, awarded a DSO for gallant service with the King's Royal Rifle Corp, was killed in action in 1917, aged 45. He had resigned from the Mastership in 1915, due to his war duties. His widow, Mildred, lived on at the family's Knipton hunting lodge, built by the 6th Duke, until her death in 1934.

Lord Robert's first choice as a Joint Master opted out at the eleventh hour, due to ill health. In his place Lord Robert approached Major Tommy Bouch, whose ready acceptance proved a happy decision for the Hunt.

Tommy Bouch was a devoted foxhunter who took a great interest in breeding and hunting effective hounds. Born in Warwickshire, Bouch served prior to the first world war with the 10th Hussars in India, and hunted with the Peshawar Vale. Resigning his commission, he returned in 1907 and hunted in Ireland, as Master of the East Galway, and later the Tipperary, followed by a season as a Master of the Atherstone before joining the Belvoir in 1912.

Jack Hewitt, first whipper-in since 1906, was promoted to huntsman for the 1912-13 season to succeed Capell, but from his appointment as a Master in 1912 Tommy Bouch hunted hounds on the Lincolnshire side two days a week.

The country was upgraded to five days a week with a bye-day frequently thrown in. Tommy Bouch kept at his own expense a private pack, which he brought from the Atherstone. These hounds included a mixed group of noted fox-killing hounds he had gathered from the Marquis of Waterford's pack in Ireland, plus drafts from the Burton and Woodland Pytchley.

Although they were not the most handsome, Bouch's own hounds showed great sport during their brief career in the Belvoir country.

GREAT RUN FOLKINGHAM 1914

Tommy Bouch's pack achieved glory in the run-up to the start of the war. Meeting at Folkingham on the Lincolnshire side on Friday 16 January 1914, hounds arrived after a journey on the 'hunt special' train to Billingborough where they were allowed to trot on to the meet.

Hounds found in Heathcote's new covert just before noon, and a brace of foxes broke covert. Hounds went away on the dog fox for Keisby Wood, Kirkby Underwood, over the Rippingale road, to Hacconby, and across the Bourne-Sleaford railway line. The remnants of the mounted field found their way barred by a locked level crossing gate, and time was lost until it could be opened.

The pack meanwhile ran on hard across the Morton and Dyke Fens, and came up to the imposing obstacle of the South Forty Foot Drain which forced water from the fens into the Glen river. It was protected by steep banks, but without hesitation, hounds slipped down the embankment and swam across, on the far side making for the Glen river.

The strung out field crossed the sluice by some rickety planks, but the pack was now swimming the 60 foot wide river. The only crossing was a narrow trestle footbridge, guarded by hand rails, 15 feet above the water. Mr F.G. Bowser of Swineshead on a sure footed Fen pony led the way over the unsteady structure.

Tommy Bouch took to his feet to follow, and on the far side Mr Bowser gallantly gave up his mount to the Master.

Mr Herbert Jones of Honington was next on the bridge, but his hunter slipped and with all four legs firmly wedged, the bridge was blocked for an hour before the

Major Tommy Bouch before the Great War.

sorry animal could be released by sawing the handrails, and the use of ropes.

Lord Robert Manners and a few others, including first whipper-in Jack Boore, could only ride along the bank of the river some two miles to cross by the next bridge at Pinchbeck West, leading the huntsman's tired horse.

Boore rode down the nearest fen lane, searching for hounds, and at Mr Frier's small farm at Pode Hole the whipper-in came across them, having just killed their fox in a reed bed in the water.

Tommy Bouch arrived on his borrowed mount to be in at the death, and though all hounds were on, and it was no more than two o'clock, he decided to end the day. They were some 35 miles from Belvoir, and six miles from any possible further draw.

Lord Robert Manners, Mr Cyril Greenall, the Hon. W.R. Wyndham and Mr James Knight were reported as having completed the run, and Mrs Brockton Wadsley from Dunsby was the only lady to finish.

Mr Bouch presented a pad to Mr Bowser as thanks for his selfless action at the bridge. This was a hunt of two hours and 10 minutes, with a point of 12 miles, and rather more than 17 miles as hounds ran.

It was the first time hounds had caught their fox beyond the Forty Foot since Will Goodall achieved it with his pack about 60 years earlier. Bouch achieved it twice more during the immediate seasons following the Great War.

At a puppy show much later Tommy Bouch said that at a meeting on his arrival in the country in 1912 a venerable fen farmer had wished him good sport with hopes that his hounds might one day run to Spalding.

Bouch replied: ' I like to think that but for one more mile we might have done so.'

The Duke of York, the future King George VI, with Major Tommy Bouch, Belvoir Joint Master and amateur huntsman from 1912–24.

WARTIME HUNTING

On the outbreak of war Bouch rejoined his regiment, and saw active service in France. He continued as sole Master from 1915, on the proviso that after the war he would be the sole huntsman.

During the war while Bouch was away, the Duke of Rutland approved the appointment as Acting Masters of Cyril Greenall, a cousin of Sir Gilbert Greenall, and Sir George Whichcote of Aswarby Park, a long serving member of the Belvoir committee, and a stalwart of the Lincolnshire side.

Like all Hunts, the Belvoir had to adjust to reductions in fixtures and standards during the 1914-18 war, with staff at the kennels and stables depleted, and hound meal strictly rationed. As the war drew on, food supplies for many of the civilian population in the towns became more scarce due to German blockages of the seaways.

Dick Woodward had been appointed huntsman in 1913 to replace Jack Hewitt who went to the North Cotswold; Woodward reported he had lost a finger in a shooting accident whilst ratting around the kennels, and was deemed unfit for military service when conscription was imposed to fill the terrible losses in the earlier great battles. Woodward had previously served with the Badsworth as first whipper-in and huntsman from 1911-13, and previously one season with the Meynell under Charles Gillson before coming to Belvoir. At the end of the 1918-19 season Woodward moved to the South Notts as huntsman, where he remained for three seasons before retiring from hunt service. Later he lived at Waltham-on-the-Wolds and was licensee of the George and Dragon for some years.

For the last year of the war George Purse from the Pytchley, and a very young Charlie Gosden helped the huntsman in the field, while Tom Hide, who had been coaxed out of retirement, and Tom Halls, the veteran flesh cart driver, held the fort in kennels.

Tom was to retire in 1924 after a remarkable 51 seasons at the Belvoir kennels. He began under Gillard, and held many positions at various times, such as kennelman, driver of the flesh cart, huntsman's valet and gardener, and summer grass cutter. For many years he was responsible for the transport of visiting bitches to and from Redmile station. He survived the second world war, and died in 1946 aged 93.

Another long-serving servant of the Hunt was William Burgess who came from Cheshire with Sir Gilbert Greenall.

Burgess rose to second horseman to the huntsman, and later to the Master; in 1929 he was promoted to stud groom, retiring in 1940 after 46 seasons at Woolsthorpe stables;

Tommy Bouch who hunted his own pack on the Lincolnshire side 1912–14, and was sole huntsman 1919-24; accompanied here by the Duke of York.

Lord Robert Manners, fourth son of 7th Duke, briefly Belvoir Joint Master 1912–14; killed on active service in the Great War.

he died within a year of retirement.

Hunting days were reduced somewhat, but the sport continued in a limited fashion throughout the Great War, as it would during the second war of the 20th century. In both world wars the governments of the day decided that foxhunting should continue as a contribution to pest control, in the interests of agriculture.

Despite all the limitations, and growing austerity, it is remarkable how much hunting took place during the Great War. Mr J.C. Mountain of Welbourn sent a report to the Acting Master Col. Swan of a day from Barnby Manor when the Blankney hounds met there by invitation, hunted by Joe Lewis who was serving on the Western Front a few months later. Col Swan missed the day through military duties.

A fox found in one of the spinneys near Barnby Manor was hunted to Stubton Gorse, to Hougham after several diversions, to Gonerby Moor, over the Great North road from Bee's Gorse, over the Allington road, to Sedgebrook, and on towards Casthorpe covert. They caught their fox in the open at the end of a two hour hunt with a point of 11½ miles, having run about 17 miles.

In the 1915-16 season the Belvoir were hunting Tuesdays, Wednesdays, Fridays and Saturdays, and some good days were achieved. For example on Friday 9 January, hounds scored a ten mile point after meeting at Weavers Lodge, and finding at Ropsley Rise, and eventually marking to ground at Cliff Hill near Rauceby Thorns. The comparatively small field who went to Long Clawson on 11 December must have enjoyed the 'very fast hunt', as recorded by the huntsman, over a delectable country of grass and fences, from a find at Sherbrookes, past Broughton, into the Quorn country, running to the Curate, down to Hickling village, to Kinoulton Wood, Blackberry Hills, on to Cotgrave Plantation and over the Broughton road where they gave the fox best.

In 1916 the Hunt Committee announced that due to the drop in subscriptions there was no funding to pay for the removal of wire.

Although more restricted, through bad weather as well as the war, the 1916-17 season saw hounds out 25 mornings before 1 November, although there was no formal opening meet. The accent officially was on 'vermin control', to assist agriculture, rather than runs in the open, but inevitably there was plenty of action outside covert. For example, hounds scored a five mile point after meeting at Eastwell on 2 December, finding in Hose Thorns, running down the vale to Clawson Thorns, Holwell Mouth, Little Belvoir and Marriotts where they marked to ground.

The 1917-18 season saw further cut-backs and the shortest season recorded up to then at Belvoir, hounds hunting 65 days, with a tally of 35 brace, some 12 brace

In the Vale of Belvoir: illustration of huntsman Nimrod Capell with hounds and the field.

caught before November. Cubhunting began on 11 September, and the end of season was 2 March.

Tommy Bouch managed to hunt hounds on 6 February when on leave from his service with the County of London Yeomanry. Hounds found in Newmans, ran to Garthorpe over the Wymondham Road, through Garthorpe Plantation, and killed by the Stonesby road at the end of a fast 25 minutes.

Shortly after the outbreak of war, Lady Robert Manners, who would become a war widow, opened a fund within the Hunt to buy and equip a new motor ambulance for the troops on the continent. By the end of hostilities two 'Belvoir Hunt ambulances' were fully operational in France, due mainly to her energetic campaigning. As soon as possible after the Armistice, Major Bouch returned to live at Woolsthorpe, and immediately resumed his role as Master and amateur huntsman. He wasted no time: although he had missed the cubhunting, he was sole huntsman from 30 November 1918. It was the first time the Belvoir pack had been hunted solely by an amateur huntsman; a similar appointment did not occur again until the arrival of Rupert Inglesant in 2006.

The 1918-19 season was inevitably difficult in many ways, but finished well.

Due mainly to the rationing of hound meal imposed earlier in the war it was generally accepted that the young entry fell below the usual Belvoir standard. Mr William Wroughton, former Master of the Pytchley, and Mr Edward Barclay, Master of the Puckeridge, judged the puppy show on 5 July with Alfred Earp, huntsman to Lord Harrington's.

There was a depleted entry of four and a half couple of doghounds, and seven and half couple of bitches. Considering the huge impact of the Great War on British life it is surprising that such annual functions as puppy shows had survived, although it was a shadow of the magnificent events held by Sir Gilbert Greenall before the war.

POSTWAR RECOVERY

Tommy Bouch attempted to upgrade the Hunt's performance immediately after the war. He bred a somewhat lighter, more athletic type of hound in the Belvoir kennel, although he was firmly forbidden by the Duke of Rutland to introduce Welsh outcrosses, nor use any other sires which might produce hounds of any other colour than the celebrated Belvoir black, tan and white. The problems of breeding from hounds closely related in traditional line breeding had to be overcome without recourse to the outcrosses which were to become so prevalent in other kennels later in the century, especially after the 10th Duke of Beaufort followed suit with Welsh outcrosses at his influential Badminton kennel.

The return of Fred Wright and Charles Peacock after Christmas provided much-needed experience and stability in the field. From the 1919-20 season Ned Friend was Bouch's first whipper-in and kennel huntsman, and Fred Wright was second whipper-in. With the steady return from military service to the Woolsthorpe stables of the grooms, more horses were available for work in the hunting field, and a fuller programme was attempted in the New Year.

After four years of hardship, and immense loss of life, it was cheering for everyone, including returning servicemen able to hunt again, that the Belvoir pack produced some fine sport in the second half of the season.

The hunt of the season followed the meet at Newton Bar on 21 March. A fox found at Newton Wood was viewed away by Mr Anyan's farm at Haceby, crossing the Bridge End road to Nightongale, and running on strongly for Oasby Mill. The quarry ran over the High Dyke, ran on to Minetts Hill, crossed the Sleaford Road to Spellar and the East Coast railway above Whitehalls, and was given best near Dry Doddington after two hours and 10 minutes, a hunt with a remarkable point of 13 miles.

The Master readily agreed to extend the season to end at Rippingale on 25 April.

A true foxhunter, gallant and extremely enthusiastic, Bouch took some following in the hunting field. He was a bold rider, as well as an excellent hound man, who used to say that if you went fast enough at wire, you generally got over it, or it broke. Barbed wire had become an increasing problem in the early 20th century, and Sir Gilbert Greenall had started an area plan for Hunt representatives to take down as much wire as possible at the start of a season, and erect it again in the spring.

Early in the postwar period, Leicestershire resumed its role as a magnet for visitors from far and wide. There was a major increase in women riding to hounds, astride as well as side-saddle.

For the next 20 years, Shires foxhunting saw another period of hectic sport, and an equally frenetic social whirl off the hunting field. Many spent the winter in Melton Mowbray as part of the 'the Season', some renting houses, others staying in the town's hunting lodges where parties were abundant.

In the immediate postwar years there were considerable difficulties in the Belvoir country, as elsewhere.

In 1919 a serious outbreak of rabies hit the dog population in Britain, said to be caused by dogs being smuggled from the continent by returning servicemen. Many kennels suffered serious losses from distemper and the 'yellows' just after the war, and there were several outbeaks of foot and mouth disease in farm stock. The 1923-24 season was ruined for the Belvoir by foot and mouth, which meant that sport was largely confined to the Lincolnshire side.

Probably due to the restrictions during the war, and the difficulties thereafter, fox control in some areas had been taken on by gamekeepers and farmers. In 1921 Tommy Bouch offered his resignation from the Mastership because he was not happy with the shortage of foxes, and the level of sport achieved. The Belvoir committee and followers reacted with concern, and there was a rush to coax Bouch to stay on in the Mastership.

Efforts were made by landowners throughout the country to give maximum cooperation in fox preservation in coverts,

While others try to open a gate, Major Tommy Bouch, Master and huntsman, sails over the adjoining rail, an admiring illustration by Cuthbert Bradley.

and sport improved markedly.

Tommy Bouch retired from the Belvoir in 1924, having made a great contribution to the Hunt as a highly effective Master during the challenging period before and after the Great War.

Later he became a Joint Master and amateur huntsman, with Lord Bathurst of the VWH from 1933-35, and latterly hunted with the Warwickshire up to his death in 1963. He deserves a special place in the 20th century history of the Belvoir, helping to lay the foundations of good sport yet to come.

CHAPTER 5

Between the Wars

The Great Hunt from Long Clawson…
Alone with hounds – 'a slight, pretty girl of 20…'

From 1924-28 the Belvoir Mastership was filled by Capt. Marshall Roberts, an American by birth, of Holme Pierpoint, near Nottingham. He had been badly injured while serving in the Grenadier Guards in the Great War, but made a remarkable recovery to be able to resume the sport he adored. He rented Easton Hall, home of the Cholmeley family, and devoted himself to the Hunt, spending generously, and appointing Nimrod Capell, Ben's son, as huntsman, with Fred Wright as first whipper-in, and Jack Singleton as second whip.

An indication of how hunting was conducted in the 1920s when Leicestershire was a sea of grass, was a notice in the Belvoir's entry in *Baily's Hunting Directory*: 'It is requested that motors be sent straight home from the meet.'

Nimrod had served nine seasons at the Quorn as a whipper-in and latterly as kennel huntsman. He had suffered a bad fall which kept him out of Hunt service for three years, before joining the Belvoir.

Hard-working and devoted to his craft, Nimrod was criticised by some as being less successful in producing sport than his father Ben Capell, but it has to be remembered that he had to meet very high expectations for almost guaranteed sport in front of large, fashionable fields on the Leicestershire side.

Nimrod bore no responsibility for the breeding of the hounds in the pack he inherited, still of the heavier stamp produced during Frank Gillard's term as huntsman, but hunt reports of that period indicate they continued to produce plenty of good hunts.

Nimrod was popular with mounted followers, and many others throughout the country. He played a key role in ensuring the Belvoir remained among the most popular packs in the land, attracting visitors from far and wide.

– AND ONLY ROSEMARY FINISHED

In the 1925–6 season, Nimrod Capell and the Belvoir hounds scored a remarkable hunt on Saturday 9 January, from a meet at Landyke Lane, attended by Edward, Prince of Wales, his brother the Duke of York, later King George VI, and Prince Henry, later Duke of Gloucester. The run was acclaimed and reported widely in the sporting and the national press.

A Meet of the Belvoir at Staunton Grange in 1926. Left to right: Miss Betty Manners, Mrs Marshall Roberts, Miss Payne Gallwey, Miss Hester Swan, Captain Marshall Roberts and Mrs Edward Greenall.

Among the exalted throng was a 20-year-old girl, Rosemary Laycock, who became feted as the only rider to finish the great run of some 35 miles as hounds ran, with a 14 mile point.

Below: Nimrod Capell, huntsman 1924-28, with hounds in Belvoir Castle park.

Rosemary was described in the *London Evening News* as 'a slight, pretty girl of 20, and though obviously a dashing rider to hounds – she rides astride – as shy as a schoolgirl.'

Rosemary hunted from Newport Lodge, a hunting box at Melton Mowbray taken by her father Brig-Gen. Sir Joseph Laycock of Wiseton, Nottinghamshire. Rosemary was the elder of two daughters of Sir Joseph who also had three sons. Rosemary Laycock married Arthur Baillie, and today her grand-daughter, Sarah Fountain, lives at Hose Lodge, Harby Lane, with her husband, Johnny Fountain, keen members of the Belvoir field.

The huntsman's official report of that day said hounds drew Old Hills blank, but found in Holwell Mouth; the fox was repeatedly headed, and went to ground. At Clawson Thorns hounds found again, and settled to run at a great pace over the Shilcocks' farm, as for the Harby Hills, but the fox turned right-handed and ran to Landyke Lane, continuing at a great pace for Holwell Mouth where he was headed on the right.

He went away from Clawson Thorns again, running down to Clawson village, turning right over Mr Shilcock's farm again, and straight to Piper Hole Gorse, and away as for Goadby Bullimore. He turned left-handed and ran straight to Harby Wood where there were several foxes afoot which caused complications.

Then hounds went away on their fox, running away down the Vale towards Harby village, crossing the Eastwell and Harby

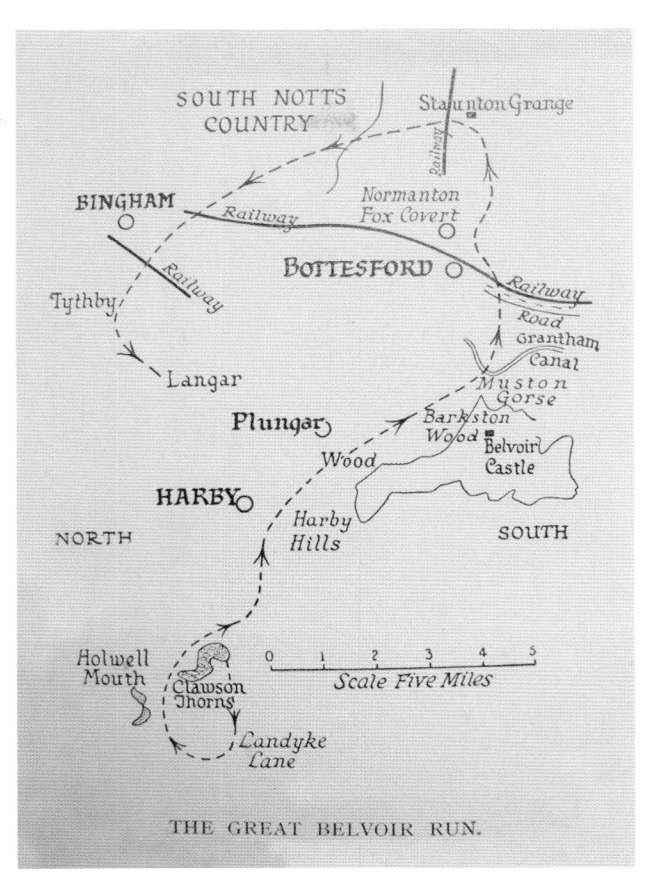

Route of the Great Run on January 9th, 1926, when the Belvoir hounds ran 35 miles, with a 14-mile point.

road, leaving Harby village on the left, as if for Granby Gap.

On reaching the canal, the fox turned right, and ran over the Plungar road as if for Barkestone. Then he turned right to cross the Harby and Redmile road, as if for Belvoir Woods, but short of the Woods he veered left-handed, crossed Bissill Hill, straight through Muston Gorse, towards the Stainwith. Hounds hunted their quarry on towards Easthorpe, and turned right to run the ironstone railway to Muston Gap, and over the L. and N.E. railway.

Above: Press picture at the Landyke Lane meet before the 1926 history-making 35 mile run: l.to r. Mr Peter Laycock, and sisters Miss Joyce Laycock and Miss Rosemary Laycock (the only rider to finish the run out of a field of 300), Capt and Lady Kathleen Rollo and Lord Francis Hill.

Rosemary Laycock's account of the day, recalled:

'Hounds crossed the Nottingham-Grantham main road, and the railway. They ran on towards Staunton, short of which we were all held up by locked railway gates.

'By the time a key was produced, or the padlocks were broken, hounds were out of sight. There was a covert on ahead which everybody expected them to run to, and they galloped towards it.

'I was about to do the same, when Bill Rollo shouted that he had seen some cattle hunched on the left, and was sure hounds had gone that way. I think about half a dozen of us went with Bill Rollo, but I can only definitely remember him, my brother Peter, and Fred Cripps.

'Very soon we saw a tail hound or two, and knew we were right, but the going was very deep, and being now in the South Notts country there was a good deal of plough, which eventually stopped all of our party except me.

'I can't remember how long the others carried on, but I do remember Fred Cripps coming to a grinding halt in the middle of a beanfield, his horse standing absolutely stiff with all its legs stuck out, and Fred still smoking a cigar.

'Having caught up with hounds by now I just carried on with them, as I had no idea where I was. They apparently ran close to Aslockton, then turned up the hill again to Langar, where the hunt came to an end.

'The fox must have got in somewhere in the village, as when I got to them they were casting about on the road, and round some hen houses close by. There was a culvert under the road, but it was full of water, and the fox had obviously had a look at it, and then gone elsewhere.

'For the last half mile or so I had realised that my mare was beat. At the last two fences I dismounted and managed to pull down, and drag her through, and when hounds crossed the Langar-Bingham road I turned up that road, leading her on foot. Hounds were just on my right, and when I followed the road into the village they had checked, and could not account for their fox. I tried to cast them on foot, but they paid no attention at all, and I could not even collect them up.

'I was wondering what on earth I should do, when by the grace of God, Nimrod Capell the huntsman, Alba Paynter, and Gill (Gilbert) Greenall, elder brother of Toby Greenall, all turned up. They collected the hounds and then Gill helped me with my mare.

'There were no motor horse boxes in those days, and we were 12 miles from Melton. It was

George Tongue, huntsman 1928–56.

obvious the mare could not walk back there that night. Gill knew the Parson who had a stable of sorts.'

Rosemary Laycock records putting up her 15.1 hh mare, named Beauty, in the parson's loose box at Langar, giving her some chilled water with sugar in it. Roberts the second horseman from Newport Lodge arrived with clothing and mash, and made the mare comfortable. He rode her back to Melton the next morning, none the worse. Rosemary says she hunted her again the following Saturday, as they were short of horses at the time.

Beauty had been intended as a polo pony, but was no good at polo, and Rosemary's father bought her as a hunter.

The mare was the third horse Rosemary rode that day, having first been mounted on an old Flat racehorse, then

Nimrod Capell, described by Lionel Edward as a 'most graceful horseman and accomplished horseman... to hear him cheer hounds was inspiring...'

The Belvoir

changing to a horse provided by 'old Harry Beeby' who 'had pity on me, and gave me one of his horses 'til I could find the second horseman.'

Rosemary's account pays tribute to Bill Rollo... 'it was cruel that his weight stopped him from getting to the end.'

Bill Rollo, a lawyer, was a keen hunting man who lived in the Cottesmore country. His step-sons, Billy and the late Robin Abel-Smith, were well-known foxhunters with the Leicestershire packs.

Below: Joint Master Peter Ackroyd with Payne Gallwey and Charles Tonge.

1925–6 SUBSCRIPTIONS

Rosemary Laycock's father, General Laycock, is listed in the Belvoir subscription list for 1925-6 as having paid £100, one of the major subscribers. He was also hunting with the other Leicestershire packs, in common with most people in the Shires hunting set at that time. The 1925-6 Belvoir subscription scale was £50 per day per week, or £75 per three days per fortnight, but for those hunting regularly with the Belvoir only, the subscription was £35 per day per week. The official scale of subscriptions stated 'If a gentleman is accompanied by ladies of his family, then in addition to his own subscription, £30 per day per week, or £45 per three days per fortnight for each lady of his family who hunts regularly.' Regular Belvoir-only male subscribers were charged only £25 per day per week for each lady of the family hunting with them. No subscription was levied on landowners, covert owners, or tenant farmers, but they were invited to subscribe voluntarily. Regular serving officers, quartered in the Hunt country or hunting solely with the Belvoir, were charged a minimal subscription of £5 per horse. Those hunting only part of the season were charged £35 for each month, or part of a month, or alternatively £20 for each horse kept for hunting.

Despite the above scale, there were in the list of 1925-6 subscriptions. numerous sums of only £5, £10 or £15. Flexibility has long been a key requirement of a Hunt Secre-

'In the Vale near Jericho Gorse' by Lionel Edwards 1924. Hounds hunted by Nimrod Capell, with Capt Marshall Roberts as Master. There was doubt about the identity of the faller, and surprise that the Belvoir was painted jumping into plough. Hounds are running parallel to the railway and canal, with Redmile Church and Belvoir Castle beyond.

tary in any hunting country in extracting money from those who hunt.

The cap for non-subscribing visitors was £3 per day, although landowners 'within five miles of the Belvoir Hunt boundary' were not capped for their first three days' hunting in each season. Guests of owners

Above: Another very large Belvoir mounted field – believed to be near Scalford Hall in 1926.

Below: Miss Monica Sheriffe of Goadby Hall, a prominent Belvoir hunting personality.

Below right: The new regime after 1928 (left to right): 1st whipper-in Frank Anyan, huntsman George Tongue, Joint Master and amateur huntsman Charles Tonge, and right, 2nd whipper-in Bert Rawlings. Charles Tonge's grandson is Tim Hall-Wilson, Belvoir Hon. Secretary 1988–96.

A huge Belvoir field, with George Tongue in front, and in the centre at the head of the field senior Joint Master Charles Tonge.

of 1,000 acres, or covert owners in the Belvoir country, or a subscriber of not less than £100, could hunt two days in a season without being capped. All subscriptions were required by 1 December.

In the 1925-6 season the Belvoir's income from subscriptions was £7,159, and from caps £220, total income from all sources amounting to £7,681.

1928–9 SEASON: A TIME OF CHANGE

Although it was to be a comparatively short Mastership, from 1928-31, the appointment of Major Charles Tonge proved to be another landmark in the Hunt's inter-war history.

Feeling in the country was in favour of some changes of emphasis in the breeding and handling of hounds, and in the way the country was run. A tendency to 'guarantee sport' for hard-riding fields on the Leicestershire side had put great pressure on all concerned. Some believed the pack was not always working at its full potential at this time.

One of those keen on radical change was Hunt Committee member and Chairman of the Point-to-point Committee, Col. Robert (Bobby) Clayton Swan of Barrowby Grange who had been a Master

The Belvoir

Lady Violet Manners, third daughter of the 8th Duke of Rutland, changing horses, with the aid of a second horseman in livery.

Below: Royalty in the mounted field: Edward, Prince of Wales, later King Edward VIII, and his brothers Prince Henry, Duke of Gloucester, and Prince George, Duke of Kent.

of three packs, the Morpeth, Sinnington and Blankney, and was Belvoir Field Master from 1921-4. Hester, the youngest of four daughters of Col. Clayton Swan was married to Major Charles Tonge who was an experienced and effective foxhunter, interested in hounds and their breeding. Tonge was Master and an amateur huntsman of the Newmarket and Thurlow from 1919-27. Tim Hall-Wilson, who was Belvoir Hunt Secretary from 1988-96 is a grandson of Major Tonge, and a great-grandson on the maternal side of Col. Clayton Swan.

An eccentricity of Charles Tonge was keeping two honey bears as pets at the Hunt stables at Woolsthorpe.

Col. Gordon Colman left, Joint Master from 1930-39 with Charles Tonge.

'They were kept on leads, but allowed off sometimes to exercise by climbing the trees. I can't think how they got them down again,' former Belvoir Joint Master Ann Reid Scott recalls. 'Charles Tonge's chauffeur was expected to drive them about in the back of the car sometimes, but I believe the bears tore the leatherwork terribly. I was a schoolgirl at the time and I thought the bears were lovely.'

At the Belvoir Charles Tonge continued Tommy Bouch's practice of hunting hounds himself two days a week on the Lincolnshire side. His brother Maurice Tonge, although not a Master, contributed considerably to the Hunt's finances, which could be a heavy burden on a Master's purse in those days before Acting Masterships and 'open ended' guarantees came in.

Masters in most packs were given an annual fixed guarantee by a Hunt Committee, and all expenses above that figure were borne by the Masters. Costs could expand rapidly when unexpected items occurred.

The Belvoir's annual running cost at that time was between £15,000 to £20,000, a considerable sum translated into 2010 money. Tonge's Joint Master for two seasons, 1928-30, was Peter Ackroyd, a serving officer with the Welsh Guards, who lived at Scalford.

In 1928 the Belvoir type of Old English Foxhound was still dominating the top placings at Peterborough Royal Foxhound Show, and other hound shows, and could be seen in Hunt kennels throughout the land. However, the American-born hunting man Ikey Bell became Master and huntsman of the South and West Wilts in 1925, and was persuasively spreading his view in English hunting circles that an improved 'modern Foxhound' could be achieved by using Welsh

The Belvoir

outcrosses. His views gained ground in more Hunts before 1939, although the greatest switch to 'modern hounds' was to occur in the postwar years, led by the Portman, Beaufort, the Curre and others.

While retaining the Old English bloodlines, the aim of Charles Tonge was to breed a lighter, more athletic hound in the Belvoir kennel, through judicious selection, and this trend succeeded, with the cooperation of his Joint Masters in the 1930s. Ann Reid Scott says that for a while Charles Tonge used to run a group of cross-bred hounds in the hunting field with the Belvoir hounds, but he adhered to the ducal edict that they were not bred into the Old English pack.

One of two honey bears kept as pets at the Hunt stables at Woolsthorpe by Charles Tonge.

THE GEORGE TONGUE REGIME

The most beneficial decision for the Belvoir made by Charles Tonge was to engage as a new huntsman, George Tongue, at that time carrying the horn with the East Essex.

George was born in 1891 at the Grafton kennels, the son of a huntsman of the same name, who hunted the Essex Union, the East Essex and the Garth hounds.

George junior began his career as spare second horseman at the East Essex while his father was huntsman.

In 1908 young George moved to the York and Ainsty as a second horseman, and two years later he was appointed second horseman to the Essex huntsman James Bailey who promoted him to second whipper-in in 1912.

Joining the Army on the outbreak of the Great War in 1914, George Tongue showed his mettle in arduous service with the Army Veterinary Corps attached to the Royal Horse Artillery in France and Belgium. Promoted to sergeant, he was awarded the Distinguished Conduct Medal for coolness, gallantry and devotion to duty under fire.

His citation said that on 17 October 1918 his unit came under heavy shell fire while moving through Zandvoorde, near Ypres, causing casualties to men and horses.

George Tongue 'took charge of the situation' under the heavy fire, ensuring the drivers of the teams were sent to a place of safety.

He emerged with honour from the horrors of 1914-18, to return to the Essex Hunt for the 1919-20 season, serving again under James Bailey. George was promoted to first whipper-in under Bailey's successor,

*The Belvoir Puppy Show 1930 attracted an influential gathering of Masters and huntsmen, representing both sides of the Old English versus Welsh-cross 'Modern' Foxhound controversy:
Standing: W. Wilson, H. Lord (Blankney), Tom Down (Earl of Harrington's), Mr 'Chatty' Hilton Green MFH (Meynell, later Cottesmore), Capt Hodgkinson MFH (Mendip), Lt. Col. Lockett, Fred Holland (Old Berks) George Barker (Quorn), George Tongue (Belvoir), Will Morris (Berkeley), and Tom Newman (Duke of Beaufort's).
Seated: Mr Ikey Bell MFH (S. and W. Wilts) 'Master', the 10th Duke of Beaufort MFH, Countess of Harrington MFH, Col. Gordon Colman MFH and Mr Charles Tonge MFH (Belvoir), HRH the Duke of Gloucester, Lord Conyers, and Capt. Freddie Horton.*

After the 1930 Puppy Show, huntsman George Tongue shows older hounds to (l.to r.) Belvoir Joint Master Charles Tonge, 'Master' the Duke of Beaufort, Mr Ikey Bell MFH, and Mr 'Chatty' Hilton Green.

Harry Speake, and also Jack Boore. In 1923 George joined the ranks of huntsmen, being appointed by Eustace Hill, Master of the East Essex.

Benefitting greatly from his family background, his thorough training, and his Army experience, George showed his abilities in the field, and in the kennels where he was notably firm but fair with his staff. He earned an excellent reputation at the East Essex for five years, justifying his appointment to the major Shires pack kennelled at Belvoir Castle.

After Charles Tonge in 1931 gave up his Mastership and his role as huntsman in Lincolnshire, George Tongue hunted both packs with distinction until his retirement in 1956, when he had completed 28 years as Belvoir huntsman.

He was remembered by those who served under him as a man of great strength and resilience, able to stand up to the rigours of long days in the hunting field in the years when hounds often hacked to fixtures far from kennels.

His strict discipline in kennels enabled

the Belvoir to keep very large packs of hounds at a high level of performance, and his excellent horsemanship allowed him to cross the Belvoir Vale and High Leicestershire day after day in front of large, extremely well-mounted fields.

The youngest of George Tongue's three daughters, Doris, was born in the huntsman's house at the Belvoir Kennels in 1933, and recalls cycling to Woolsthorpe to catch a bus to attend school in Grantham. On one occasion she missed the bus, and had to walk all the way from Grantham to Belvoir. She recalls that as well as the Kennels, the huntsman's house was lit by oil lamps, and the bedrooms were 'freezing cold' in winter.

The Belvoir's mounted 'terrier boy' Neville Watchorn, raising his cap to signify he has seen a fox in the hunting field, c. 1930. He later became huntsman of the Essex where he was known as Tom Watchorn.

'But it was a wonderful life at the Kennels, in such a beautiful setting, and I loved the hounds and the horses.'

She learned to ride as an infant, and from an early age she helped her father, riding out with him on hound exercise, and accompanied him to meets.

'On exercise I didn't wear a cap, and I only had sandals on my feet. No Health and Safety regulations in those days!

'We used to hack many miles to meets, for example it was eight to ten miles each way to Cotham Thorns. When we were passing Normanton after a day right up the Vale, Alice Lovett always used to invite us in for cups of tea and delicious cakes.

'My father ran the kennels very efficiently. He did exercise discipline, and he was a bit a slow to give praise,' she recalls.

'On one occasion as a schoolgirl I jumped an iron gate behind him, and he turned and said, 'I didn't know you could jump that high.'

'That was high praise indeed!'

On leaving school, Doris worked in the Hunt stables for about 18 months before helping with the brood mares belonging to the Duke's sister, Lady Isobel, at Burton Marston, and then she worked for the Duke and Duchess of Gloucester at Barnwell, before employment with Barclays Bank in Newark. She continued to hunt after her marriage in 1960 to Belvoir farmer Brian Knight, of Fen Farm, Long Bennington, where they have lived ever since.

Doris's parents were living at Long Bennington when George died on 18 January 1970, aged 78.

George Tongue's first whipper-in at Belvoir for the initial season was William Lawrence from the Grafton; followed for the next season by James Goddard from the Old Berks.

Tongue benefitted for the next eight seasons 1931-38, having a settled arrangement with Frank Anyan as first whipper-in. Frank went to the Blackmore Vale, to be replaced in the 1939-40 season by William Biston from the Woodland Pytchley; then Harry Evans for a season, and for the rest of the war, from 1940-45, Harry Morris. Richard Perkins was first whipper-in from 1946-49; Arthur Onions 1949-50; Harvey Andrews 1950-51; and Jim Webster from 1951 until he succeeded as huntsman in '56. Henry Holland, kennelman, came to Belvoir with Charles Tonge in 1928, and stayed ten years, continuing part-time thereafter. He was a son of the old Bedale huntsman, and his brother Fred hunted the Old Berks with success. Harry was a very experienced kennelman and George Tongue rated him highly. When he retired he went back to Yorkshire, but was bombed out early in the war, and came back to Knipton where he continued to help George on a part-time basis.

Frank Anyan, who came from the Newmarket and Thurlow, was second whipper-in for George Tongue's first two seasons, and the Hunt staff formed an effective team, with George very much in charge.

George Tongue's first season at Belvoir, 1928-29, was hit by severe weather, with some 27 days lost to frosts and snow. Scent improved after the first frosts, and good days were enjoyed in Leicestershire and Lincolnshire.

The doghounds, hunted by Mr Tonge, after a meet at Stubton Hall, achieved a splendid hunt of some 2½ hours, with an eight mile point, and 16 miles as hounds ran. They found their fox above Gelston, running by Hougham station, past Spellar and Brandon for Shields Gorse, and continuing over Court Lees farm to turn by Stubton to Fenton.

The fox ran by Torry's Plantation and Stragglethorpe before hounds were stopped in the dusk by Willson's. Hounds hunted 117 days, and caught 31 brace of foxes, marking another 16 brace to ground, before the season closed on 16 April, so much later than is possible today in modern farming conditions.

Peter Ackroyd retired from the Mastership in 1930, and Charles Tonge continued in office, with Col. Gordon Colman as his Joint Master. Colman's family firm made the famous mustard, and his family home was at Epsom. He used to say his fortune was made by the fact that 'people always leave a portion of mustard on their plate, and soon need more...'

Born in 1881, Eton-educated Gordon Colman proved to be a keen sportsman who adored hunting. As a young man he hunted with the Brookside Harriers and the West Surrey Staghounds, and the Crawley and Horsham, becoming a Master of the Surrey Union at the age of 23, from 1904-10.

In the Great War he saw arduous service on the Western Front with the Surrey and Sussex Yeomanry, and later in Salonika, and was twice mentioned in dispatches. After serving as High Sherriff for Surrey in 1924 he was awarded an OBE.

Gordon Colman's move to Leicestershire coincided with his marriage in 1930 to Peggy Brocklehurst, daughter of Mr and Mrs Alfred Brocklehurst, of 'The Spinnies', Melton Mowbray. Col. and Mrs Colman made their home at Burton Lazaars, and later at Scalford Hall. On joining the Mastership he took over the management of the

Lincolnshire side of the country.

Gordon Colman was a popular Master, with a particular interest in hound breeding, and his contribution to the Belvoir was immense, since he served as sole Master from 1931-34, following the resignation of Charles Tonge.

Colman continued as Joint Master until 1940 when war service intervened again, but he resumed hunting with the Belvoir after the war, continuing until shortly before his death on 23 February 1969.

A great mainstay of the Hunt for 30 years Mr William Newton of Old Hall, Barrowby, retired in 1932 after 30 years as Hunt Secretary, mainly on the Lincolnshire side. Mr Newton had succeeded in 1902 another Barrowby hunting man, William Pinder, who served as Hunt Secretary from 1900 to 1902 when he died in office. Mr Newton stepped in as Secretary from November, 1902, and rendered great services thereafter. He was succeeded by Mr H. Garner Bellamy on the Lincolnshire side, and Col. W.J. Lockett for Leicestershire. (See Appendix 2, List of Hunt Secretaries)

TOBY DARESBURY GIVES A LEAD

From 1934 Gordon Colman's Joint Master was one of the most remarkable personalities in foxhunting. He was the Hon. Edward (Toby) Greenall, heir to the first Lord Daresbury who had made such a crucial contribution to the Belvoir as Sir Gilbert Greenall.

The future Lord Daresbury was an elegant horseman who gave a great lead over Leicestershire on superb horses which he rode with great flair. The Belvoir was well able to entertain the pre-war fashionable throng

The Hon. Edward (Toby) Greenall, later Lord Daresbury, Joint Master 1934–47, superb horseman who gave a great lead as Field Master in the 1930s.

who came to Leicestershire in the winter, many quartering themselves in the hunting lodges in and around Melton Mowbray.

Edward, Prince of Wales, who was to reign briefly as Edward VIII before his abdication to marry Mrs Simpson, relished Shires hunting in the 'twenties and 'thirties, and thoroughly enjoyed the social life of Melton Mowbray, often staying at Craven Lodge, the residential club set up by General Vaughan.

The Prince of Wales' royal brothers, Prince George (Duke of Kent) and Prince

Henry (Duke of Gloucester) also hunted from Melton Mowbray, although the Duke of York, later King George VI, hunted from Melton less often, basing himself in the Pytchley country at Naseby after his marriage to the future Queen Elizabeth.

As referred to previously in the great run from Clawson Thorns, the royal brothers all hunted with the Belvoir frequently. The 1925-6 subscription list is headed by the Prince of Wales who paid £150, and the Duke of York and Prince Henry are listed next as paying £100 each. Only one subscriber is listed that season as paying more: Mr F. Ambrose Clark paid £200.

The Duke of Gloucester was especially fond of the Belvoir. He married on 6 November, 1935, Lady Alice Montague-Douglas-Scott, who shared his sporting interests. They included a hunting tour in their honeymoon arrangements, visiting a number of packs, including the Belvoir who put on a special meet at the Hunt kennels for the royal pair.

Fancy dress balls, pageants and other jollifications filled the Melton Mowbray season off the hunting field. As often reported, the Prince of Wales first met Mrs Wallis Simpson at Burrough Court in the Cottesmore country. His previous love for 16 years, was Winifred May Dudley Ward, wife of the MP for Southampton, a Nottinghamshire personality who hunted regularly with the Shires packs, including the Belvoir.

As well as local businessmen and landed gentry who hunted, and the social set, including some genuinely knowledgeable foxhunters who visited Leicestershire, there was always staunch support from the farming community. Despite a constant influx of large mounted fields, the Belvoir was especially fortunate in a high level of cooperation from farmers throughout the hunting country in Leicestershire and Lincolnshire.

This was to be a major factor in the survival of the Hunt through the war, the austerity postwar years, and into the 21st century and the arrival of Labour's iniquitous 'hunting ban' from 2005.

In the somewhat feverish atmosphere of the social scene of the 1930s, when farming was in depression and war began to loom again, the Melton Mowbray area benefited economically from the annual arrival of hunting visitors who spent heavily in the area on accommodation, replacement and care of hunting dress, and the purchase of horses and their keep. Dealers' yards included plenty of 'rough riders' who made horses in the hunting field before they were the mounts of hunt subscribers. Sales of hunters at Leicester before and after the season were a major part of the local rural economy.

The Belvoir retained its position as one of the most popular Hunts in the land, and the pressure was considerable on Masters and staff to maintain consistent sport before the large, well-mounted fields who flocked to the Shires.

When he became Joint Master, the future Lord Daresbury was 32-years-old, and already a seasoned foxhunter, with a dry sense of humour and a *sang froid* which enabled him to cope with triumph or disaster. As the Belvoir's Field Master he wore a top-hat instead of a hunting cap, and was always immaculately turned out.

'If anyone in the field could not recognise me in a top hat he had no business hunting with me,' he used to say.

Toby Daresbury rode as many as three horses a day in the Leicestershire country.

Lord (Toby) Daresbury and his second wife, the former Joyce Laycock.

He was keenly interested in hounds, and was famous in the hunting world as a lifelong admirer of the Belvoir's old English type of Foxhound for its hunting abilities, and especially the pack's drive in front of hard-riding mounted fields. Later he was to describe the modern Foxhound with Welsh outcross as 'barking dogs', and he proved the pure English Foxhound's versatility by taking a pack of Belvoir-bred hounds to hunt in Ireland after the war.

A man of great charm, he maintained his popularity, and the discipline of the field. This helped to create an excellent working relationship with his huntsman. The Hon. Toby Greenall succeeded his father as Lord Daresbury in 1938. Toby's elder brother, Gilbert, would have succeeded, but died in 1928 in a car accident, while driving to Windsor for duty with his regiment.

There were other family tragedies to endure. Toby Greenall's first wife, the former Joan Sherriffe, sister of the popular Belvoir hunting personality, Monica Sherriffe, of Goadby Hall, Goadby Marwood, died in March 1926, only seven months after their marriage, from injuries received in a fall while hunting with the Quorn.

Two years later Toby Greenall married Joyce Laycock, sister of Rosemary Laycock; Joyce bore him a son, the Hon. Edward Greenall, but she predeceased her husband in 1958.

Throughout his long hunting career, Toby Daresbury became renowned for meeting disaster with equanimity. After falling in the River Smite during a hunt, he was given a bottle of whisky by a hunting farmer. To the farmer's amazement the Master poured one half of the whisky into one hunting boot and the rest into the other.

'That will keep me really warm,' he said.

He was featured in the social columns of the national press when he engaged in a bout of fisticuffs with Capt. Billy Filmer-Sankey, Master of the South Notts Hunt.

Filmer-Sankey was well known as a light-hearted poacher of sport from the Belvoir's coverts.

'Hands up who'd like to draw the Belvoir today?' he would ask his mounted field when they were hunting near their boundary. This caused a great deal of mirth among the South Notts field, but became less of a joke in the Belvoir country.

According to an account in the *Daily Sketch*: 'The two Masters met by Blackberry Hill fox covert on the border of the South Notts country…Filmer-Sankey wore a low-neck jersey, flannel trousers and tennis shoes.

But Greenall contemptuously retained his collar and tie.

'They set to with a will. Weight and experience were in Greenall's favour and he looked to be winning when Filmer-Sankey landed a punch between 'wind and water' in the Derby Kelly (old style slang for belly).

'Though Mr Greenall's heart was willing, previous digestive trouble had made his stomach weak. The fight was ended.'

However, the Belvoir Master had made his point, and incursions by the South Notts when they were not actually pursuing a fox, became less conspicuous after the pugilistic encounter on the border.

The future Lord Daresbury suffered from an ulcerated stomach, needing major surgery. After his operation, for the rest of his long hunting career, he made a point of providing sandwiches and a bottle of milk for his huntsman during the break for second horses, because he was sure this would prevent ulcers which he believed could be caused by long days in the saddle without anything to eat.

Toby Daresbury's organisation of hounds and horses in Leicestershire, and later in Ireland, was impeccable. He was to prove himself a most effective huntsman during the greater part of his 30 years' Co. Limerick Mastership (1947-77).

There was always a twinkle in Toby Daresbury's eye, and he enjoyed making many friends through hunting. A young lady in the hunting field once asked him: 'Lord Daresbury, what do you do with your old hunting clothes?'

He replied: 'I take them off, then I fold them up and put them on the next day.'

George Tongue and later Jim Webster were regular postwar guests at Lord Daresbury's Irish home in the Limerick country.

The 1920s and '30s in the Shires Hunts reflected the hectic gaiety seen in most sports and pastimes at that time – a means of forgetting the recent horrors of the Great War, and giving some respite from the series of financial crashes and depressions in the 1930s leading to the threat of another world war.

All too soon the Belvoir would have to face up to a time of immense change in retaining its place in the countryside.

Edward Prince of Wales with veteran rider to hounds, Mr David Ward, at Bescaby House before a day's hunting with the Belvoir on February 18th, 1925.

CHAPTER 6

Second World War Challenge

'Charles Rutland, the 10th Duke, took over as Master...'

Britain's entry into the Second World War on 3 September 1939 brought to the surface a 'lack of communication' between Col. Colman and Lord Daresbury.

It led to a temporary resignation of Toby Daresbury from the Mastership before the opening meet, and Gordon Colman only continued in office until the following year when he resumed military service with his regiment. After the war Colman resumed hunting regularly with the Belvoir, until shortly before his death in February 1969, having made an enormous contribution to the Hunt. He and his wife made their postwar home at Scalford Hall.

One of the issues of contention in 1939 was whether, and when, to reduce the size of the Belvoir pack, and by how much. The MFHA was urging Hunts to make such reductions, by cutting back breeding programmes and retiring older hounds. There was confusion at that time as to whether Britain was in for a long war, and what the implications would be for everyday life, but Hitler soon settled any doubts.

In the countryside during the 'phoney war' period of 1939 a few Hunts over-reacted and put down nearly all their hounds, losing valuable breeding lines, whilst some others made no changes at all. Matters were not resolved until the wartime Ministry of Agriculture made decisions in favour of limited foxhunting continuing.

The Belvoir's 1939-40 season had a semblance of normality, with the Hunt still managing to fulfil four-day-a-week fixtures. Hounds were out on 92 days and lost 27 days, the season finishing on 30 March 1940.

The end of the brief 'phoney war' period in the spring of 1940, when Germany invaded Belgium and France, concentrated minds on reality.

Britain was in for a long, hard struggle for survival, with a real threat of invasion, and bombing of civilians a certainty.

As owners of the Belvoir pack, the Rutland family stepped into the breach, and made vital decisions which helped to ensure the future of their pack, and the Hunt.

Although only 20 years of age, Charles Rutland, the 10th Duke, took over as Master in 1940, having succeeded when his father died on 21 April. He was serving as a subaltern in the Grenadier Guards when he

The Belvoir

Presentation to Lord (Toby) Daresbury, left, on his retirement as Belvoir Joint Master in 1947, by Hunt Chairman Capt Sir Hugh Cholmeley, centre, with the new senior Joint Master Lt.Col. James Hanbury, right.

succeeded as Duke; he stayed in the Army, rose to the rank of Major, and then, having been wounded in France, was sent home in 1945.

His distinguished military service meant that he could devote little time to the Hunt during the war, but by resuming Mastership and overall responsibility, he played a key role in the Hunt's survival, and he continued in office until 1952 when the Hunt was already set on postwar recovery.

He continued to maintain close interest, and a vigilant eye, on the Hunt's affairs, and was just as firmly committed as his forefathers to ensuring the pack retained its Old English breeding.

He was held in great respect in Leicestershire as a County Councillor, and from 1976 he led much of the opposition to the National Coal Board's plans to extract millions of tons of coal from part of his estate and other areas of the Vale of Belvoir, all rural districts of outstanding natural beauty. He famously announced, 'I shall put up a great fight, and I shall lie down in front of the bulldozers.'

T-shirts were printed with the slogan 'I'll lie down with the Duke', and many of his supporters, including some pretty girls, wore these for a press demonstration which was widely reported.

Fortunately, mining operations at the new pit, very expensively started at Asfordby, Melton Mowbray, were to be abandoned because it was proved that coal excavation from the Vale was uneconomic.

Charles Rutland died on 1 January, 1999 and his son, David, succeeded as the 11th Duke. He has continued to maintain the family policies in ensuring that their famous pack of hounds continues to be bred on Old English lines, and is supported in all his endeavours to maintain the Belvoir estate by the Duchess who is a keen advocate of country life, and farming. The Duchess enjoys riding, and in the early years of their marriage was warmly welcomed when she appeared in the hunting field with the Belvoir hounds.

WAR-TIME SPORT

Toby Daresbury resumed his Mastership in 1940. He had joined the Lifeguards, but for health reasons spent most of his service on the home front. He was determined to ensure the Belvoir survived the war, and travelled from London to Leicestershire as often as possible to hunt, and to ensure the management of the kennels and country. He took some of the Hunt horses into his own stables at Waltham.

George Tongue was keen to rejoin the Army, in which he had served with such distinction in the first war, but he was over-age for call-up, and continued to run the Belvoir kennels with a much reduced staff of older men, and some youths awaiting call-up. Both whippers-in, Evans and Perkins, and Reg Bell were called up. Jim Webster, who had joined the kennels as a 16-year-old whipped-in with Harry Morris.

Jim remembered his first stint at the Belvior as: 'Very hard times; the kennels still had no mains electricity, so we used oil lamps; discipline was tough under George Tongue, and it was really a seven-days-a-week workhouse. We started at 4am during the cubhunting season, and during the season proper there were often long hacks to the meets in all weathers. Exercising the young hounds in the park could be a problem; they would get away into the trees, and I had to go up there to find them and bring them back.'

The 1939-40 season saw a surprising amount of sport, with hounds out 82 times, although losing 22 days due to hard weather. In the new regime Harry Morris ran the stables, which had to be moved to the kennels from Woolsthorpe, commandeered by the Army. George Gale, an excellent man, was kennelman.

Remarkably, foxhunting continued on a limited scale throughout the war, the government accepting that it contributed to pest control, aiding a swiftly growing farming industry, recognised at last as a vital asset, following the major slump in the 1930s when cheap imports wrecked home farming. Free range poultry was still the main method of egg production at that time, and foxes had to be culled to reduce predation.

The emphasis in the war was supposed to be on holding up coverts as much as possible, to ensure maximum fox control.

Such strictures did not prevent some good hunts in the open, and foxhunters in the Forces who could manage a day or two with their home pack were able to taste the sport which they so much wanted to preserve for their full return to the hunting field postwar.

War Agricultural Committees were formed to step up production, and many farmers played a key role in assisting the survival of their local Hunts, by providing flesh from fallen stock, unfit for human consumption, for hounds.

The Belvoir's fixtures reduced to two a week, Saturdays and Wednesdays usually, and soon hunting on the Lincolnshire side was abandoned completely, due in part to the lack of petrol for transporting hounds and horses.

The growth of emergency airfields, and huge increase in intensive farming, made the Lincolnshire side of the country less practicable for wartime hunting, although the support and interest in the Hunt from Lincolnshire remained as strong as ever.

George Tongue hacked hounds to meets on the Leicestershire side, and had to return to kennels well before dusk set in, due to lighting-up restrictions. Keen local

George Tongue continued to hunt the Belvoir hounds throughout the second world war, and afterwards until retirement in 1956.

foot-followers gave much needed help at the kennels during the war.

Hounds were out on 43 days in 1942-3, and lost three days; in 1943-4 hounds were out 54 days, and lost three fixtures; in the 1944-45 season hounds were out 55 days, and lost seven. In 1944 George Gale returned to the Percy and was replaced by Duncan Grieve.

As the war drew on, Hunts everywhere were discouraged from hunting after January, and conditions for sport became ever more stringent. Huge swathes of the famous Leicestershire grass went under the plough for the first time in many year, and the vastly increased use of tractors saw arable farming become far more intensive. However, there was still plenty of grass in the Belvoir Vale, and on the Leicestershire uplands at the end of the war.

There was considerable evidence foxhunting would receive the fullest support in the countryside again, after peace was declared.

When victory came, there was immense cause for rejoicing, although in the first postwar season the Belvoir suffered an untimely setback. In the autumn of 1945 George Tongue broke his leg, especially unwelcome when hunting was beginning to start a build-up to 'normal' conditions.

Lord Daresbury hunted hounds himself during that season, which saw more than a few returning servicemen in the field, and some good sport was much enjoyed. Sport resumed on the Lincolnshire side one day per week; hounds were out 69 days, with four days lost.

Thanks to all the dedicated hard work of the hunt staff, and volunteers, and the guidance of the Masters, the Belvoir pack had survived the war in remarkably good order, and was able to expand to cope with peacetime hunting surprisingly quickly. Some limited hound breeding had continued throughout the war, with small entries of young hounds entered each season. The great lines of pure English hounds going back over 200 years were intact.

As in the previous war, many horses were requisitioned by government for military service. Among the wartime staff at the Melton Mowbray re-mount depot was a young horsewoman from Scotland, Margaret ('Migs') Crawford.

Second World War Challenge

'We had to convert hunters and other horses from riding to harness work, pulling wagons of coke,' she recalls. 'It was something that had to be done for the war effort.'

Fortunately, she found time occasionally to enjoy some hunting with the Belvoir. It was there that she became acquainted with Lord Daresbury, and in 1952 she married his son, the Hon. Edward Greenall who later lived in Jersey. For many years the Hon. 'Migs' Greenall, a superb horsewoman across country, has been a popular figure in the Belvoir field, one of the Hunt's strongest supporters, and a great benefactor through keeping her land at Waltham-in-the-Wolds among the most rideable in the country.

Her eldest son Peter, the present Lord Daresbury, served the hunting world as chairman of the MFHA, has been Joint Master of Sir Watkin Williams-Wynn's since 1991, and has earned praise for his contribution to National Hunt racing as the chairman of re-developed Aintree Racecourse.

Lord (Toby) Daresbury concluded his Mastership of the Belvoir in 1947 when he decided to make his future in Ireland, acquiring an estate near Adare, where he became Master of the County Limerick foxhounds for 30 years until 1977, hunting hounds himself until 1971. He formed his own pack of Belvoir-bred English hounds, and proved they are as effective over the great banks of Ireland as they are in the vastly different terrains of Leicestershire and Lincolnshire. Miss Meriel Atkinson, short in stature but large in personality, and dauntless riding across country, the daughter of a doctor in the Vale of Belvoir, went to Co. Limerick to assist Toby Daresbury as housekeeper, and breeder and sustainer of hound puppies and foals on his estate.

Charles, 10th Duke of Rutland, stepped into the breach to take over as Master of the Belvoir in 1940, having succeeded as Duke in April that year aged 20.

In 1966 Toby Daresbury married Lady Helena Hilton-Green, known as 'Boodley' throughout the hunting world. She was a devoted foxhunter, and an elegant horsewoman, daughter of Earl Fitzwilliam and a former wife of 'Chatty' Hilton-Green, famed Master and amateur huntsman of the Cottesmore (1931-46).

In 1947 the Belvoir found its next Master from the Cottesmore country, and he proved to be one of the most popular and effective in the postwar years.

The Belvoir

Lt.Col. James Hanbury, the Squire of Oakham, and owner of the notable country house, Burley-on-the-Hill, was born and bred in the traditions of Shires hunting. His grandfather, Evan Hanbury, was Master of the Cottesmore at the beginning of the 20th century (1900-07) and achieved great sport with the renowned Arthur Thatcher as his huntsman. James Hanbury's son, Joss, has earned a remarkable reputation as a Joint Master and popular Field Master of the Cottesmore, and latterly the Quorn.

James Hanbury was a good horseman, and gave a great lead as Field Master. He was soon earning a reputation for creating a happy atmosphere in the hunting field.

'James was very easy-going as a Field Master. He was never in a bad temper, always enjoyed himself, went well, and was fun to hunt with always,' remembered Ulrica Murray Smith, the Quorn's Master for 25 years (1960-85), in her memoirs Magic of the Quorn.

Despite the austerity years which hit Britain immediately after the war, foxhunting at top levels resumed remarkably quickly in peacetime.

Leicestershire saw the start of the change to arable farming during the war, but immediately afterwards retained large areas of grass and fences. The Belvoir Vale remained a magnet for foxhunters who liked to gallop and jump, and soon visitors arrived each season to augment the mounted fields of all the Shires packs.

The Belvoir was facing a buoyant period of sport in the remaining years of the 20th century when many more would thrill to the challenge of following pure-bred English hounds as they soared across one of the finest foxhunting countries in the world.

Lt.Col. James Hanbury, right, senior Joint Master 1947-64, with Lance Newton, founder of the Melton Hunt Club.

CHAPTER 7

Post-war Triumph

'the best all-round, old fashioned sporting day I've had since 1938...'

George Tongue was rejoined in 1946 by Dick Perkins, returned from the war to serve as single-handed first whipper-in. The following season Brian Gupwell, son of the Fernie's huntsman Walter Gupwell, joined the Belvoir as second whipper-in. Brian Gupwell later went from Belvoir to the Brocklesby under Ron Harvey; then he hunted the Eridge with much success, before going to Badminton on the retirement of Bert Pateman. Especially noted for his skills in showing hounds as well as hunting them, Gupwell served a distinguished term as huntsman of the Duke of Beaufort's from 1967-84.

Dick Perkins first saw service under Arthur Thatcher at the Atherstone, and after riding second-horseman for two seasons he became second whipper-in under Nimrod Capell who succeeded Thatcher at the Atherstone. Perkins came to the Belvoir in 1937 under George Tongue, with Frank Anyan as first whipper-in.

According to an interview he gave Kenneth Ligertwood for his book *Huntsmen of our Time*, 'Belvoir was very hard on hunt servants before the war, they had only oil lanterns. It was an unhandy kennel in which to work, with the boiler house on one side of the yard, and the feed house on the other side, and it was surrounded by those huge Belvoir Woods into which hounds always seemed as if they must escape!'

'Despite all this, Belvoir did him a lot of good. During the war he served as a gunner in an anti-tank battery, mostly in Burma.'

Dick Perkins left Belvoir in 1950 to go to the Meynell, and two years later went to the Grove and Rufford as a successful huntsman. He was pleased to say he modelled his style on that of George Tongue, from whom he had learned so much in handling hounds in the field, and in kennel management. The Duke of Rutland remained in office for seven years after the war as Joint Master with James Hanbury.

Maurice Davies, known to all as Mo, came to Belvoir as kennelman in 1951 from the Bicester, and stayed for 28 years. He had learned his trade under Joe Wright senior at the Cheshire before the war; a quiet and hardworking kennelman, he was considered top notch at his job.

Col. Francis Bowlby, of Culverthorp Hall, joined the Mastership from 1952-4, being responsible for the Lincolnshire side, later with Major George Pretyman,

George Tongue's last opening meet, in Croxton Park 1955, with Jim Webster as first whipper-in leading hounds.

of Ponton House. He had hunted with the Belvoir regularly in the 1930s, and he and his wife, Camilla, were among key figures in re-starting hunting on the Lincolnshire side after the war. Camilla acted as a Field Master in Lincolnshire in the 1945-47 seasons. Major Pretyman served in the Mastership from 1953-54, and 1955-56.

The *Field*'s hunting correspondent, John Smith Maxwell, reported a visit to the Belvoir on 21 March 1956 as 'the best all round, old fashioned sporting day I have had since 1938.' It was a deserved tribute to Masters and staff, and the farming community, who had resurrected the Belvoir as a highly popular Shires pack in the early postwar years.

The day began with the first cross-country ride run by the newly created Melton Hunt Club, over four miles of natural country from Freeby Wood to Wymondham New Plantation, on land farmed by Lance Newton, Hon. Secretary and founder of the MHC, and Mr Bartram and Mr Mountain. The field of 48 riders met at Waltham House, home of the Hon. Edward Greenall, son of Lord Daresbury, and Mrs 'Migs' Greenall. The ride was run in three sections, for ladies, gentlemen, and members of the Army Saddle Club. The winners respectively in the sections were Miss Pat Newton, Col. Frank Bowlby and Lord Patrick Beresford.

Hounds met at noon at Buckminster where the hosts were Mr and Mrs Dick Black. Col. Hanbury and Major Pretyman were the Joint Masters at the head of the field, and hounds were hunted by George Tongue who was fulfilling his final fixture on the Leicestershire side before his retirement at the end of the 1955-56 season. Jim Webster, who was to succeed him, was first whipper-in, with Jim Browning as second whipper-in.

Finding in Coston covert, hounds ran towards Marriott's, then went swinging left as if for Gunby Gorse. Smith Maxwell reported the mounted field 'sat down to ride

James Hanbury, the Hon. Ursula Rank (later Mrs Lance Newton) and Lord (Rupert) Manton.

a lovely country to Sewstern village, which hounds left on the right, running straight through Coston covert as if for Garthorpe, swinging sharp right-handed short of Coston Lodge. They killed their fox in the open after a run of 50 minutes, the first 20 minutes very fast.'

The Field's hunting correspondent paid tribute 'to George Tongue DCM for taking the rough with the smooth, just as he did as a soldier in the First World War, and continuing to be, as always, a very great ambassador for the foxhunting world'.

In the 1955-56 season hounds were out 96 days; 22 days were lost through weather; the fox tally was 29½ brace. At the Belvoir point-to-point at Garthorpe in May 1956 the Duke of Rutland presented to George Tongue a cheque for £5,500, contributed by followers in Leicestershire and Lincolnshire, and 'including members of the Royal Family and many farmers from both countries'.

Michael Saunby reported an excellent day on the Lincolnshire side in Jim Webster's

Lord Belper, Joint Master twice: 1955-65 and 1976-78. He said he wore a top-hat in his second term 'because I am now an Acting Master!'

first season, from Aslackby on 15 March 1957; from the meet, hounds found at Heathcotes, on the airfield, and went away for Folkingham. They crossed the Bourne road (A15) to Folkingham Little Gorse, and ran the brook to Piper Dam, where he crossed the Billingborough road.

Running on over the hill, with Stowe Green and Threekingham wide on the left, they crossed the Bridge End road (A52), and running on past Spanby and Scredington to the Burton Plantations on the Aswarby Estate, where fresh foxes were in evidence. Hounds were stopped after a seven mile point, and eleven as hounds ran.

A popular, although sadly a short-term, Joint Master in the postwar period was the noted 'chase rider and amateur huntsman, Major James Seely (1954-55), of Ramsdale House, Arnold, Notts. He had succeeded his brother, Lt.Col. W.E. Seely as Master of the South Notts in 1944 whilst also serving with his regiment in Germany. After ten seasons at the South Notts., James Seely joined the Belvoir Mastership, having hunted regularly with the Belvoir since the 1920s. It was agreed he would hunt the Belvoir doghounds in Lincolnshire, but his one season in office was spoiled by ill health, and the effects of a fall at Cheltenham. Sadly, he died in 1956 aged 54.

A brilliant rider over fences, and a memorable character, the 4th Lord Belper, of Kingston Hall, Derbyshire, joined the Belvoir Mastership in 1955, and made a significant contribution to the Hunt for the next decade. He was more than qualified to give a great lead to hard-riding mounted fields on the Leicestershire side, even though he lost the sight of one eye in a shooting accident in 1957. As the Hon. Ronnie Strutt, he was one of the most successful amateur steeplechase jockeys of the inter-war years.

Riding Crown Prince, owned by his step-father, the Earl of Rosebery, he won the Cheltenham National Hunt Chase in 1934. Two years later he rode Crown Prince to finish fourth in the Grand National. He served during the war in the Coldstream Guards, and was wounded in action. In 1951 he was appointed sole Master of the Quorn, with George Barker hunting hounds. In the post war years he was a shrewd owner and backer of flat race horses, and according to an obituary in The Daily Telegraph 'he confided to a friend that he met the heavy costs involved in being Master of the Quorn entirely out of the profit shown by his betting'.

Ronnie Belper rode superb Thoroughbreds as a Field Master, and helped to bring to the hunting field more than a flavour of pre-war sporting Leicestershire. His obituary in *The Daily Telegraph* said: 'Lord Belper was a strong personality; in all spheres of his life he had definite opinions about how things should be done. He had little time for people whom he found unsympathetic, but there was also a most generous side to his character; many found him to be an extremely kind friend.'

Lord Belper returned for a short second term as Joint Master of the Belvoir from 1976-78. He wore a top hat as Field master this time, and when asked why, he replied, 'Because I am now an acting Master'.

The author of this history visited the Belvoir in 1976, when Ronnie Belper was much in charge, but the excellent Field Master was John Parry, also wearing a top hat.

At the meet, as Editor of Horse and Hound, I was introduced to Lord Belper. On being told I was from Dorset, he barked with a suspicion of a smile, 'Well, I should go back there! Hunting up here is just a racket! Just a racket!'

We had an extremely enjoyable, and hectic day, starting at Holwell, and swooping down into the Vale late. Ronnie Belper, then a senior figure, was at the front of the field, and going well. At end of day I approached the Master to thank him 'for a very good racket'.

'What did he say? What did he say?' rejoined the Master, as I rode off.

One of the most important decisions taken in the 1950s was the appointment of Jim Webster to succeed as huntsman when George Tongue retired in 1956.

As recounted, George had served the Belvoir remarkably as huntsman for 28 years, maintaining an excellent working pack during the difficult war years, and managing a large kennels and staff, all the while retaining the confidence of the Belvoir's hosts, the widespread farming communities in Lincolnshire and Leicestershire.

The Belvoir

Continuity is a great benison in foxhunting. There had been ten changes of Mastership during George Tongue's period as huntsman. The Belvoir was to benefit from another long term huntsman: Jim Webster would stay in his post in fast-changing times, through another ten Mastership changes.

Below: Map showing the country around Belvoir Castle in the early 20th century.

CHAPTER 8

The Webster Way

'...the Belvoir hounds is very inclined to explore the Quorn country...'

When Jim Webster died, on 13 September 2008, aged 85, there were warm tributes from many in the Belvoir country – and from far beyond. His continuity, his dependability, and his durability, all contributed to the stability of the Hunt at a time when the countryside was under increasing pressure.

There were increasing changes to arable farming from the traditional stock farming in Leicestershire. Towns, villages and roads were all becoming much busier. More followers were able to drive up to Leicestershire from the South. There was a waiting list at one time of subscribers to the Belvoir's Saturday meets in the Vale country. Because more men followers were free at weekends, there was a strong competitive element in the mounted field, with a notable contingent of well-mounted thrusters at the front. It was rather over-stated, but someone described the most crowded Belvoir Saturdays in the 1970s and '80s as 'rugby on a horse'.

None of this makes a huntsman's life easier, but Jim was imperturbable and well understood that his role was to produce enjoyable sport.

Visitors came to hunt with the Belvoir from all over the world during Jim's remarkable 28 seasons (1956-83) in one of the most arduous roles in the sport: a historic, four-day-a-week country undergoing major changes, with vastly different types of hunting in Lincolnshire and Leicestershire. There was a regular challenge of hard-riding fields on the Leicestershire side, seeking maximum sport across grass and fences, especially on Saturdays which were the Mecca of foxhunters from far and wide. Most of them brought two horses, ensuring that home was rarely blown until the light was failing, so that Hunt staff were involved in very long days at the height of the season.

Apart from his physical endurance, and his equable temperament, plus a dry sense of humour, James Harry Webster benefitted from a true foxhunting birthright. He was born of a remarkable family of professional huntsmen, going back to his great-grandfather, Harry Judd, huntsman of the Lanarkshire and Renfrewshire at the end of the 19th century. Jim's grandfather succeeded as huntsman of that pack.

Jim was the eldest son of Arthur Webster, huntsman of the Taunton Vale, and the Essex Union until he retired in 1951. There was no question as to Jim's path in life.

He was born at the Taunton Vale kennels on 26 February 1923, and began hunt service at the age of 14, working under his father at the Essex Union. Jim's younger brother, Clarence, had a similar start later; his hunt service culminated in 24 years as huntsman of the Warwickshire.

Above: Jim Webster, huntsman 1965-83, with the Belvoir hounds by the lake in Belvoir Castle park.

Below: Jim Webster with hounds on his last day in the Vale of Belvoir as huntsman – 10th March 1983.

Jim recalled his father as a stern disciplinarian: 'He was a great schoolmaster, but I was pleased to get away from him.'

At first Jim applied for a job at the kennels of the Brocklesby, the other great home of pure English packs belonging to a titled family. 'But they said I was too weak to lift the heavy iron bed frames in the lodges, so I didn't get that job,' Jim recalled.

Instead, in 1939 at the age of 16, he succeeded in being appointed second whipper-in to George Tongue at the Belvoir. As related previously, the Army call-up of Dick Perkins meant that despite his youth Jim was put on as sole whipper-in for the 1940-41 season. He had great respect for

First whipper-in Ron Stouph leads hounds, followed by the Master, Lord King, huntsman Jim Webster, and Graham Roberts second whipper-in – near Long Clawson on December 13th, 1969.

Tongue, but the young whipper-in clearly had a difficult working life in a kennel still lit by oil lamps, with a greatly reduced staff, yet was expected to hack long distances to meets in all weathers.

The following season Jim moved to the Grafton to whip-in to their famous huntsman, Will Pope, but at 18 he was due for military service, and joined the Essex Yeomanry.

'I never found discipline in the Army any trouble at all after the sort of military discipline I had in hunt kennels,' Jim remembered with a grin.

In September 1942 his regiment, the 14th (Essex Yeomanry) Fd. Regt. RA, was stationed at Nawton and Gilling in Yorkshire.

'Some of the officers wanted to hunt with the Sinnington, but they were shorthanded. They were only going out occasionally on fox control patrols because they only had one old kennel huntsman still on the staff,' said Jim.

'The Hunt said if the Essex Yeomanry could provide some help they would be willing to do some more serious hunting. So I was asked to send home for my hunting kit and my horn. I got back to the barracks one day and found it all laid out on the bed. So I started hunting the Sinnington hounds and we had quite a bit of fun.'

Jim's hunting horn became even more famous in the Regiment on D-Day when he drove the commanding officer's tank ashore from its landing craft. As soon they were on dry land on the beaches, Jim produced his hunting horn and blew 'Gone Away' as they drove up the beach. His co-driver, Wilf Allen, and he then shared a large tot of whisky before proceeding to the battle.

Jim's hunting horn was a precious family treasure, inherited from his grandfather. He drove the Commanding Officer, Lt.Col. R.A. Phayre, in his tank throughout the Normandy campaign.

They narrowly escaped capture when enemy fire hit one of the tank tracks. Gunner Webster and his crew escaped, and as the battle ebbed, they were able to return to the tank. It had been ransacked by the Germans, but to Jim Webster's relief he found his precious horn tucked away inside.

At the end of the war he became batman to his CO, now a Brigadier at Headquarters in Schleswig Holstein. Jim recalled having had 'a great time there, duck shooting and riding', before he accompanied the Brigadier

Below: The Hon. Migs Greenall and Mrs Ann Reid Scott, Joint Master 1972–78, followed by Mr Nick Playne MFH 1980-83.

The Webster Way

Mrs Di Turner, Mr Nick Turner (Joint Master 1972–74 and 1980–83), Mr Richard Henson and the Hon. Mrs "Urky" Newton.

for a stint in North Italy which also had its compensations.

Immediately after the war Jim returned to Hunt service, whipping-in to Jack Simester at Sir Watkin Williams-Wynn's, one of the most beautiful hunting countries on the Welsh Borders, where he met and married Sheila – who proved to be one of the most supportive wives for a huntsman, always popular and capable of dealing with visitors and telephone callers.

After two seasons they moved to Cheshire, where Jim was put on as first whipper-in to Arthur Redfern, but although the hunting in the lovely Cheshire grass country was fine, the accommodation for a married whipper-in was far from suitable, and after another two seasons Jim moved again – this time back to Leicestershire, whipping-in again to George Tongue.

Jim served as Belvoir first whipper-in for five happy seasons, sometimes hunting hounds when George was unwell. When George retired Jim took over at the age of 33, considered young in those days for a huntsman of a premier four-day-a-week pack.

'They had put in electricity at the kennels at last, and it made such a difference,' Jim recalled.

His first whipper-in was Bill Lander (1956-7), who was first whipper-in to Capt

The Belvoir

Above: Lord King as Belvoir Joint Master in 1969. Below: Jim Webster and hounds at Friars Well, home of Lord and Lady King.

Ronnie Wallace at the Heythrop, and later a highly effective huntsman at Sir Watkin Williams-Wynn's. Bill nowadays lives in retirement in Melton Mowbray, and is to be seen at Belvoir puppy shows and other events.

Jim Webster's later first whippers-in were Dennis Boyles (1957-9) who became huntsman of the Devon and Somerset Staghounds for 20 years from 1971; Charles Appleyard (1959-62) who went to the Morpeth; Geoff Harrison (1962-65), later huntsman of the North Staffs and the Portman; Ron Price (1965-67) who hunted the Mendip; Ronald Stouphs (1967-70) who went to the Hurworth; Robin Foster (1971-74) who also went to the Hurworth; Malcolm Wing (1974-76) who went to hunt the Co. Down Staghounds; Graham Roberts (1976-80), who hunted the Meynell & S. Staffs; and Stuart Coley (1980-83) who went to the Bramham Moor. Godfrey (Goff) Berry, who was second whipper-in from 1965-68 later hunted the East Sussex and Romney Marsh. Mindful of his own early experiences, Jim's working relationship with his whippers-in was excellent, although he made sure they knew the standards they had to reach.

Above: Jim Webster in Hunt kennels with hounds.

The virtues of the pure English hound in thinking alike during a hunt, and running in a pack 'as if covered by a blanket', as Surtees put it, were often demonstrated during Jim's long stint as Belvoir huntsman.

The pure English hound is notably bold in approaching horses in contrast to some modern hounds who can be shy of clattering hooves.

When necessary Jim could summon his pack into a biddable group, and take them back swiftly through a large mounted field so that he could cast back with little time lost, to get on good terms with his fox again.

Huntsmen, and especially Leicestershire huntsmen, are like other leading sportsmen in having to endure the comments and criticisms of the uninformed, or plain ignorant, who seldom realise the many challenges facing the man carrying the horn in the modern countryside, where foil of all kinds is likely to spoil scent, roads and lanes are much busier, and villages tend to sprawl into the surrounding fields. Not least is the far greater likelihood of a fox being headed, either by outside forces or even by Hunt followers!

When Jim retired in 1983, he was 60-years-old, a good age for a huntsman who had missed very few days in the hunting field throughout a long career. In his last five years he was inclined to look after himself more

Racehorse trainer Barry Hills who hunted frequently with the Belvoir.

After overnight snow, Jim Webster and hounds at Garthorpe, with Ron Stouph left, and Lord King.

on the most hectic Saturdays, which was a sensible course of action.

A huntsman of the Belvoir has to jump first over daunting hedges and timber, often with a front rank of thrusters, all too close behind. Crossing country in this manner for season after season is a major challenge. Jim had remarkably few falls and accidents, and had the knack of making an obstacle look a great deal easier to jump than in fact it proved when the mounted field arrived.

He was quite happy to let the field overtake him at times in his last few seasons, waving them on, and shouting, 'Go on, Sir. Don't worry. I shall catch you up.'

His hound control remained as sure as ever. He would get to the end of a hunt, and would be in the right place at the right time when it was necessary.

Jim and Sheila Webster were among the huntsmen and other hunt servants entertained regularly by the Prince of Wales at Highgrove in recognition of the huge fun the Prince enjoyed in following their hounds. The Websters were among huntsmen and their wives who attended by invitation the marriage of the Prince of Wales to Princess Diana on 29 July 1981.

The Belvoir

ROYAL FOLLOWER

The Prince's first day with the Belvoir was from Goadby Hall in January 1977, and he continued visiting the Belvoir until the mid-1980s. Although he was an experienced rider on the polo field, the Prince had to adapt his riding style considerably to cope with cross-country riding in the hunting field.

He described his first impression of being among the mounted field in Leicestershire when the fox goes away (*Prince Charles – Horseman*, by Michael Clayton, 1987):

'It is like the start of the Grand National. I had never seen anything like it, everyone pushing and shoving. It was terrifying to start with…going for a fence you get knocked over. Now I know nearly everyone, and I know how to cope. Initially, if you are not used to it, and you haven't much experience, it is terrifying. I wouldn't recommend anybody to go anywhere near until they have done a lot.'

One Saturday afternoon the Belvoir hounds were running hard in the grass vale below Long Clawson. It was possible to jump most fences on a wide front, but on Lord King's land near the Smite there was a jumping place, a set of rails installed by the Hunt.

Members of the mounted field surged forward one after another to jump the rails. Prince Charles was in the melee, and tried several times to take his place. Each time he was baulked by a queue-jumper.

Far ahead, hounds were running on. The hunt was getting further away every second. The Prince turned his horse and trotted to the back of the queue once more.

'Ah well,' he said with a rueful smile. 'I can't do anything about it. I just wasn't brought up to barge.'

When Jim Webster retired in the spring of 1983 there had been a great deal of exceptionally wet weather. It was a tribute to the high regard in which Jim was held by the farming community that they insisted that his last meet in the Vale take place in March, despite the deep going. They assured the Hunt that the huntsman and mounted field could 'go anywhere'. It was all part of the legacy left by Jim Webster: an open country full of goodwill, and an excellent pack of hunting hounds.

I reported it at the time: 'With the ground so wet, there was a tremendous scent, and the Belvoir hounds did their huntsman proud. We had a series of storming hunts up and down the Vale in the morning. A field of 104 riders had a marvellous time, and for many the morning session was enough. They went home after expressing warm thanks to the retiring huntsman.

'There was a group of only 34 remaining after second horses were taken late. Rain fell steadily from low grey clouds, and visibility was not good, as Jim put hounds into Hose Thorns for the last time.

'Hats were up as a fox stole from covert, to cross Mr Jack Palmer's grass, and Jim's unmistakeable 'Gone Away' signalled our Field Master, Robert Henson, to lead the field across the grass in pursuit, and over the stiff in-and-out across the Green Lane. They ran on over Richard Chandler's fields, swinging right over Mr Sneath's land, and over the Canal Lane.

'We jumped on to the verge, clattered across the lane, and over the next hedge, with hounds screaming on our left. We galloped on, and tackled a formidable cut-and-laid with sold timber on top, and then on to Mr John Doubledays' farm. It was still all grass,

Above: Prince Charles out with the Belvoir on his mare Reflection, with Robin Jackson.

and hounds were hurtling ahead.

'We turned right to leap perhaps the biggest fence of the day, with a dyke rather than ditch on the landing side. I spot a top hat lying on the brink, and there is a rending crash as someone lands in the ditch, but the pace is too good to enquire.

'We gallop on in the wake of hounds, across Mr Ken Egglestone's and Mr Brian Wiles's farms, crossing the Clawson-Hickling lane, and going on to Sherbrooke's.

'Hounds hunt their fox into the dense covert; the fox is given best. We stand in the rain, as dusk descends.

'Time: just under 30 minutes; a classic Leicestershire 'quick thing'. How do you measure the pleasure in terms of minutes?

'Better one hour of glorious life, than half an age without a name…' says the poem.

'Robert Henson turns to the field, and takes off his cap. 'Three cheers for Jim Webster!' he commands.

'We cheer as loudly as we can amid

The Belvoir

the dripping fronds of Sherbrookes. Jim just takes off his cap, says thank you, and without any fuss trots off with hounds. A great huntsman's career was over, and so was a sizeable chapter of the Belvoir's history.'

In retirement, Jim and Sheila lived on the Belvoir estate at Croxton Kerrial, fortified by their family, and by so many local friendships. Jim appeared at puppy shows and other Hunt functions, and was never anything but supportive of his successors hunting the Belvoir hounds.

On 29 May 2009 Jim attended the funeral in Melton Mowbray of his great friend, Michael Farrin, retired huntsman of the Quorn for 30 years, who died at the early age of 65.

Jim, in his 85th year, was becoming frail, and passed away that year on 13 September. Warm tributes were paid in obituaries in *The Daily Telegraph* and *Horse and Hound*, as well as the local press. At a funeral on 20 September at St Botolph and St John the Baptist Church, Croxton Kerrial, former Belvoir Joint Master Nick Turner praised Jim Webster's great contribution to the Belvoir Hunt and to country life.

Sheila Webster, and their son and daughter, Richard and Diane, and their families, led the mourners in the packed church.

'Gone Away...' was blown by the Belvoir's Master and huntsman, Rupert Inglesant.

Left to right: Lt Col. James Hanbury MFH 1947-64, Lord Belper MFH 1955-66, Jim Webster, and Lord King MFH 1958-72.

CHAPTER 9

20th Century Sport

'Being Chairman of British Airways was nothing compared with being Chairman of the Belvoir.'

Although there was much good hunting in the 1950s and '60s, aided by the great swathes of grass country still surviving in Leicestershire, British society in general was struggling with post-war austerity.

Money was short in hunting, as in other rural sports. In 1957 the Belvoir Hunt Chairman, Lt.Col. W.E.H. (Ted) Garner, father-in-law of Dr Tom Connors, sent quite a stern appeal to the Hunt's subscribers to pay more. He pointed out: 'It has been the country's own wish to continue as far as possible to maintain pre-war standards, and keep the Duke of Rutland's Hounds one of the premier packs.'

But he warned that subscriptions had not advanced in proportion with the increased cost of running the Hunt since 1939. The Hunt Committee appealed for an extra 20 per cent on subscriptions to balance the budget. Mr Garner said the Committee considered that instead of what has so often been thought 'How little can I get away with?' the attitude should rather be 'What is the most I can afford to give?'

Somehow, Hunts throughout Britain survived the postwar austerity years, and thrived later in the 20th century, but increased wealth in rural areas brought another problem, a permanent one: busier roads and more building on rural land.

So those who hunted in the 1950s and '60s were able to look back on a postwar golden patch when the East Midlands countryside was under far less pressure from development, and changes in agricultural practice to arable farming, than occurred later. In those two decades it was possible to achieve long runs, and stay with hounds, in areas which by the end of the 20th century were under the plough, or bricks and mortar.

Joint Master with Lord Belper from 1956-64 was Lt.Col. Hugh Beddington, a bachelor who hunted regularly with the Belvoir. He was still holding office when he died suddenly, aged 67, at his home near Newark on 28 May 1964, following a visit to York to see his horse Aviator run. His brother, Mr Thomas H. (Tommy) Beddington, who was Hunt Chairman from 1963, died in office while out hunting in 1967.

A leading figure in this Mastership, from 1958, was John King, knighted in 1979, and made a life peer in 1983, choosing the title Lord King of Wartnaby, taking his title from the village just inside the Quorn border where he lived. He was a national figure as the highly effective Chairman of British

Airways (1981-93), and he was chairman of the engineering company Babcock and Wilcox from 1970-94.

Previously living in Yorkshire, John King was a keen hunting man in the Badsworth country, and served as a Badsworth Joint Master from 1949-58. One of his reasons for buying the Wartnaby estate, just to the west of the Belvoir boundary in the Quorn country, was his passion for hunting.

His first wife, Lorna, who died in 1969 after a marriage of 28 years, shared his keenness for the sport throughout his Masterships. His second wife, the former Hon. Isabel Monkton, daughter of Viscount Galway, was a well-known hunting lady. With his first wife he had three sons, and a daughter, Rachel, who was an exceptionally stylish horsewoman, and a popular member of the Belvoir field. She became a leading judge of ridden and in-hand stock at many horse shows.

John King made a huge contribution to the Belvoir, serving as a Joint Master from 1958-64, and as Hunt Chairman for 25 years, from 1976–2000, a crucial period of pressure on modern foxhunting.

An outspoken personality, with a sometimes caustic sense of humour, Lord King was a formidable Master and Chairman, and he was committed, as with all his enterprises, to ensuring the Belvoir was run successfully. He could be a tough opponent in business or leisure, but he was known by many as a warm and generous friend.

A great many kindly acts were performed quietly without fuss. He was a good friend of Charles, Duke of Rutland, and always understood the absolute importance of farmers and landowners to the Hunt, making sure their needs were at the forefront of the Hunt's priorities. John King's

Below: Mr John Richardson, Hon. Treasurer, with (right) Lord King.

displeasure if things were not done as he deemed correct, was a powerful incentive to ensuring that everything ran smoothly in all his enterprises; inevitably he was known as King John to some.

He used to say mock seriously, that being Chairman of British Airways was 'nothing compared to being Chairman of the Belvoir... I've had to break out of business meetings at British Airways to deal with a problem involving split rails in the Belvoir country.'

In the hunting field Lord King rode very large hunters, with plenty of bone. They were well kept and schooled for him for many years by Tom Barlow. It was unwise to get in front of the Master, and later the Chairman, in front of a fence until you were really going because his horses, once committed, would surge on at the obstacle no matter what, or who, was in front. His Lordship loved the hooroosh of the chase, and I recall him shouting to me as we galloped up the Belvoir Vale in an especially good hunt, 'Don't ever forget this. Remember it always. They can't take this away from us!'

As Master, John King was exceedingly loyal to his huntsman, Jim Webster. In the middle of the afternoon, if it had been a less than brilliant day, King would turn to the huntsman and say in front of the field: 'Come on, Jim, do something to astonish us!' Jim would smile, and hounds would be taken to the nearest 'sure find' he knew.

Latterly, one of John King's rules about making a success of every enterprise, included ploughing up a considerable portion of his estate, most of it in the Quorn country, when the economics of farming dictated. However, he owned some land which remained on the Belvoir side of the Hunt border, and did not complain if the Belvoir field sometimes galloped over his arable land on the eastern side of Little Belvoir.

'Come on, let's give the Chairman's seeds a bit of a dusting,' said one Belvoir Field Master as we set off across the Wartnaby estate in the wake of hounds running hard up the hill.

Mrs Victoria ('Tor') Owen, whose husband Barry performed great services for the Hunt as its Hon. Treasurer, succeeded John King as Hunt Chairman. She wrote a generous tribute to her predecessor, noting that his very busy professional life 'did not preclude him from starting up the Belvoir Charitable Trust in 1978, and succeeding Lord Belper as Chairman of the Hunt Committee in 1977. John King's ability to chair meetings was legendary, and the skill with which he and the late Duke of Rutland skipped through a tricky Hunt AGM was an education in itself. Fortunately he is kind enough to pass on a few tips to the incoming Chairman.'

Mrs Owen, having served as a Joint Master from 1990-99 – in which she gave great services to the Lincolnshire side as a Field Master and organiser of the sport – took on the chairmanship at what was to be the most challenging period in foxhunting history, the run-up to the imposition of the Hunting Act in 2005.

Looking back on her long association with the Hunt, Mrs Owen says she especially remembers a hunt in January 1971 during John King's Mastership, reported in the sporting press:

The bitches were in good form on 9 January from Hose. A fox from Mr James's Quarry on Penhill set off for Hose Thorns, but bore left to Strouds' and, leaving Kinoulton Grange on the right, swung back to Penhill as for Harby Lodge, short of which he was lost. Hose Thorns quickly responded and this fox was hunted well to Mount Pleasant. After a check here they hunted more slowly to the old siding at the foot of Harby Hills, where they were beaten – a nice hunt of 40 minutes, the first part fast.

A hack back to Sherbrookes was rewarded with a grand hunt of over an hour. This fox set his mask for Hickling Standard, but was headed on the Broughton Lane, turned left and ran to Newcome's Parlour. He bore right here to Bleak Hill, but, failing to get over the Nottingham turnpike, went down the hill through Shelton's and on for three miles, to be lost on foiled ground short of Hickling village – a grand hunt some ten miles as hounds ran.

Conqueror (pen name of Brig. Cooper)

Michael Saunby reported two exceptional days in December 1972, one the Lincolnshire side, the second in Leicestershire:

From Barkston le Willows the dog hounds had a good hunt from Reeve's Gorse, running straight for Leadenham Low Fields below the Heath, crossing some of the best grassland in Lincolnshire. Turning away from the Newark-Sleaford road (A17) they kept left-handed towards Willson's Osiers, over the Fulbeck lane and Mr Cottingham's land and on over the hill to Caythorpe. A good hound hunt lasting 75 minutes and covering nine miles as they ran.

The next day at Saxby the hounds found on the brook, first running back towards Saxby and the crossing the Garthorpe road, running up the Freeby brook and up past Keeper's, crossing Freeby Lane and over towards Bell Plantation. Here they swung right-handed up the gated road through Brentingby Wood and over the Golf course (ignored by the players!). Unfortunately the fox was headed on the main Melton-Grantham Road, so the hounds ran on over Mr Spencer's land to Thorpe Arnold where he got to ground. A hard hunt over beautiful country, with a six mile point, but eight as they ran.

Tom Hudson, Hunt Secretary and well-known show commentator.

Mrs Fiona Gibson and her parents, Mr John Parry, former Hon. Treasurer and Joint Master 1987–9, and Mrs Parry, one of the last side-saddle riders with the Belvoir.

One of the Belvoir's most distinguished subscribers, Major General Sir Brian Wyldbore-Smith in 1971 joined Lord King in his Mastership for his final season, 1971-2, and remained in office a year longer.

A lifelong hunting man, and a keen polo player, the General had a remarkable war career in the Middle East and European campaigns, being awarded a DSO in 1943, OBE in 1944 and CB in 1965. He was Colonel of the 15/19 Kings Royal Hussars from 1970-77. Later he was to be a leading fund-raiser for the Conservative Party.

The Belvoir was fortunate to have the General as a member of the Hunt Committee, and he served as an assistant Hunt Secretary in 1970. His Mastership provided a much-appreciated link between the reign of Lord King and the new Mastership formed with Nicholas (Nick) Turner, who farmed extensively at Ropsley, and Mrs Ann Reid Scott, who was a keen follower and supporter of the Hunt since her parents, Major and Mrs Freddie Horton, moved to Easthorpe in 1928.

The mounted field in action after the opening meet on 16 October, 1986.

Mrs Reid Scott, one of the most popular personalities in the Hunt, has very happy pre-war memories of the Belvoir. Shortly after the war she married Major Alexander Reid Scott MC of the 11th Hussars who shared her fondness for hunting and country life. They moved to their home 'Ravenholt' in Scalford, where Ann Reid Scott has lived ever since. Her husband, who had an arduous war, passed away in 1960, aged only 41, being survived by Ann and their daughter Fiona who inherited her parents' love of hunting and country life.

Joining the Mastership in 1972, Mrs Reid Scott worked hard for the Hunt during a period of great change throughout her Mastership until 1978. Nick Turner retired as a Joint Master in 1979; he had formed a particularly constructive relationship with Jim Webster which was beneficial to the Hunt. Nick later dedicated a new covert on his estate to the huntsman, called Webster's, and at Jim Webster's funeral Nick was invited to make an address in tribute. Nick made a substantial contribution to the hunting fraternity as long-time chairman of the Melton Hunt Club.

Mr John Hine, an entrepreneurial Midlands businessman from the Derbyshire borders, had a brief but memorable Mastership of the Belvoir.

He learned to ride across country as an adult, but he was a natural athlete, having been a successful rugby player. Taking on the Belvoir Mastership, and serving as Field Master on the Leicestershire side was a major challenge, but he tackled it with great enthusiasm. There was always an excellent atmosphere in the hunting field when he was Field Master, and there was no question of him not giving a good lead. He mounted himself well, and essentially, made sure Jim Webster and the whippers-in were well mounted.

Unfortunately, for business reasons, he was a Joint Master for only two seasons, 1974-6, but sport was excellent during that period.

BELVOIR 'AT THE PICTURES'

A tremendous day scored by the Belvoir hounds near the end of that season was to be seen by huge national audiences. Part of the run was recorded in a film (voiced and scripted by the author of this history) which was probably the only modern documentary hunting film to gain viewing on the national cinema circuit as a supporting film to the main feature film. Entitled *Wednesday Country* the film was directed and produced by a former BBC TV sports director Alan Mouncer who had been responsible for much of the TV coverage of showjumping when it was gaining major national audiences.

The film showed the Melton Hunt Club's ride in the Belvoir country, at Scalford on 28 February 1975. Fortunately Mouncer included shots of the Belvoir hounds in kennels and in the hunting field, to show the connection between competitive cross-riding and the hunting field. The Masters of Foxhounds Association and the British Field Sports Society were pleased, because it was the sort of message vital to convey to the general public at a time when the anti-hunting lobby was gaining more strength, although still a long way from gaining legislation.

The film showed the mass cavalry charge of the field of 70 after the start of the Ride, organised as usual by Urky Newton.

Tom Hudson and his team created the route which crossed Mr Ted Atkinson's farm towards Scalford, over the Melton Brook, and behind Scalford to Clayfield Farm, over Holwell Back Lane to Old Hills, and back by Scalford Ashes to Scalford Hall.

Belvoir mounted followers were renowned for their ever-ready appetite for fences, and there was extra zest when they tackled their own country against visitors from far and wide.

On this occasion the winner overall was Richard Aston, a successful point-to-point rider from Cheshire, riding a Thoroughbred. Second was Suzanne Lumb, later to marry Chris Collins, the top-class amateur rider and event rider; and third overall was Marietta Fox-Pitt, a superb rider across country, and mother of the world class event rider, William Fox-Pitt.

As evidence of the widespread appeal of riding over Leicestershire, the first heavyweight was Capt. Sandy Maxwell Hyslop,

Mr James Knight MFH 1983-90 and Mrs Knight at a Puppy Show.

from the Portman country in Dorset.

Another redoubtable ex-soldier was first mounted infantry rider home, Major Charlie Humfrey, Hon. Secretary of the Quorn. The Quorn won the team competition that year, represented by Sally Everitt, Jennifer Phillipps, and Chris Barclay.

The day's hunting which followed proved one of the most memorable in the Scalford area in the postwar years. Here is Foxford's report in *Horse and Hound (7 March 1975)* which gives some flavour of a great performance by the Belvoir hounds and their huntsman, Jim Webster, with an especially hard-riding field in pursuit, and a huge following in cars and on foot, making it exceedingly difficult for a fox to get away. There was also foil on the land caused by the Melton Ride.

'In the interests of farming, in the current sticky going, there was some limitation of visitors, but it was still a large mounted field following Joint Masters Mr John Hine and Mrs Anne Reid Scott to the first draw, at Old Fields.

Hounds found immediately, and we had an eventful ride round the covert, but the fox was headed on the road twice.

'This problem did not arise when hounds drew Melton Spinney, and a strong fox went away smartly. Jim Webster did extremely well to get hounds settled on a difficult early line over plough, but then hounds worked up to their fox, the pace accelerated, and, my goodness, one had to ride on a bit to stay anywhere near the pack.

'They went up to Hindles, leaving Thorpe Ashes on their right, running down to Chadwell, over the road by Wycomb to Scalford brickyard. Here they swung left-handed by Langdyke lane, through the Willows and across the quarries to Old Hills, and on through Scalford Ashes.

They crossed the main Melton Road by Framland Farm, going on over the old railway line, and returning to Melton Spinney. Then they ran back towards the Hindles, left handed by Debdale Lodge and Goldsmith Grange, eventually running their fox to ground on the old railway line by Wycomb.

As you may deduce, this was roughly two enormous loops, which included part of the Melton Hunt Ride line. Altogether, hounds had run up to 15 miles in less than two hours. Only 22 of the mounted field were with hounds at the finish, and the entire field had lost touch when hounds had swung right on the way back from Old Hills.

We had ridden across some superb grass and fences, and many a horse was running out of fuel long before the run was over.

After we lost touch, I had partaken of liquid refreshment at the pub in Scalford, and was wending my way home outside the village when I heard hounds speaking beautifully. Riding towards them, I caught sight of a brown shape along the hedgerow. Some car followers arrived and holloa-ed.

The Belvoir hounds spoke again and ran on strongly, with their huntsman and a very small mounted field still following, led by John Hine. With the evening sun a big red ball in a hazy evening sky, the Hunt was a stirring sight as it surged across the Leicestershire grass, and right glad I was to join them again until Jim Webster blew for home.

It had been a brilliant performance. The Ride had been enormous fun, an annual event well worth doing, but here was regular cross-country riding in its proper context — following hounds.'

Sadly, John Hine had some temporary,

and much publicised, business problems, and resigned from the Belvoir in 1976, much to the regret of the mounted field on the Leicestershire side. He was Master of the High Peak Harriers, and proved that he could hunt hounds successfully, showing great sport over the Derbyshire walls and grass.

Others who served as Masters during the 1970s and 80s (*see Appendix 1*) were Robert Henson, John Blakeway and John Parry, all mainly concerned with the Leicestershire side of the country, plus Nick Turner, and Marjorie Comerford. In charge of days on the Lincolnshire side were Philip Watts, Charles Harrison, James Knight and Nick Playne.

Philips Watts and Charles Harrison had acted as Field Masters on the Lincolnshire side for a decade before they served as Masters, and they virtually ran the country in that area, where the Belvoir doghounds provided so much fun for the devoted following east of the A1. Philip Watts died in office in 1979.

After John Hine's departure, Lord Belper returned to fill the breach from 1976-78.

Robert Henson's Mastership, from 1978-87, was a great boon to the Hunt, and he formed an especially effective partnership as Joint Master with John Blakeway, Joint Master from 1983-92, who came up from Gloucestershire to show Leicestershire that he could give them a great lead across country. Due to a circulatory problem in his legs, John used specially-made large stirrups. He was already well into middle life, aged 58, with grey hair showing below his peaked cap.

'Do you think he'll be able to keep in front?' asked one doubtful Belvoir follower when John first appeared in Master's rig.

I assured him, 'Just you wait and see. I've tried to keep near him across the Berkeley reens, and all I can say is 'you ain't seen nothing yet'.'

In his youth John Blakeway was a successful amateur rider in NH racing, winning the Kim Muir at Cheltenham in 1946. His father was one of the founders of the Cotswold Vale Farmers' pack, and John served as a Joint Master of the Croome. He adored Leicestershire, and combined his Mastership with leading roles in the horse world, including Chairman of the BSJA, and Hon. Director of the Horse of the Year Show.

Robert Henson was brought up to hunting by his father Gino Henson, one of the great characters of the Lincolnshire

Robin Jackson, huntsman 1983-92.

The Belvoir

sporting scene, a Master of the Blankney, and a well-known breeder, producer and dealer in horses. Robert's elder brothers Richard and Bill were excellent across country in the hunting field, and Bill was a great success as Director of Burghley Horse Trials.

Robert Henson and John Blakeway always exuded cheerfulness and bonhomie as Field Masters, and the atmosphere on Wednesdays and Saturdays was often electric as they gave a great lead across the country, no matter what obstacles were encountered.

There were some great runs into the Quorn country to the west; the Belvoir hounds seemed to put on an extra spurt after crossing the Smite, and went on to hunt their fox over The Standard and beyond in some of the Quorn's most hallowed grassland. One day I recall hounds running three times over the Green Lane into the Muxlow Hill grass and fences so carefully nurtured by Dr Tom Connors. Fortunately, the doctor was out with us at the time, and urged Robert: 'Go on, go on.... don't waste a minute.'

We had an especially exciting ride jumping the Green Lane as an in-and-out on the return, after the Belvoir's fox headed back home towards Sherbrooke's.

At first, Robert was not so well mounted, but with the cooperation of his wife Sarah, former leading event rider, this was remedied. He maintained his *sang froid* in all circumstances, an especially testing task when the Belvoir was attracting Saturday fields of

Joint Masters at the 1986 opening meet (left to right): Mr John Blakeway, Mr Robert Henson and Mr Charles Harrison.

Marjorie Comerford, leading event rider – and MFH 1988–92.

visiting male foxhunters from the south who were usually very well mounted, and eager to show their prowess as thrusters, just behind the Field Master. As always, the Hunt owed everything to the Belvoir farmers who tolerated these large, hard riding fields throughout some of the best scent seasons since the war, when hounds ran especially well.

The atmosphere at the meets and at the first draw on the Saturday fixtures was often electric. Keen, well-mounted fields were raring to go, and the riding was often highly competitive when hounds went away on their first fox, perhaps swooshing down in the Vale, or finding in the Vale and immediately tackling a line of fly fences.

In 1983, after Jim Webster's retirement, Robert Henson, and his Joint Master, Charles Harrison, a shrewd Lincolnshire farmer who has done so much for eventing, made a good decision in appointing a young Scots huntsman, Robin Jackson, to carry the horn.

ROBIN JACKSON'S SEASONS

Robin was only 27-years-old, but he had already earned a good reputation as huntsman of the Lanarkshire and Renfrewshire, and at the Grove and Rufford where Robert's brother, Bill Henson, was a Joint Master.

His career had started at the Eglinton Kennels in 1970 when George Orr was huntsman. For two seasons from 1974 Robin whipped-in to the late Jack Howells who he rated as 'a very good huntsman, a lovely horseman'.

He went to the Lanarkshire and Renfrewshire in 1976 as whipper-in, but was promoted to huntsman the following year when he was only 22-years-old. It was an important year: he married his wife Dorothy in 1977.

In 1980 he came south to be appointed huntsman of the Grove and Rufford. He described the country as 'very hard to hunt' but clearly made a good impression, because he was recommended to hunt the Belvoir from 1983.

The Belvoir

Mr John Blakeway, Joint Master 1983-91, gave a great lead as Field Master.

He paid special tribute to Jim Webster and his wife Sheila: 'good friends who made the takeover as easy as possible.' Robin praised his 'super Masters' during his nine seasons with the Belvoir.

Robin recalled, 'When the Belvoir huntsman's post came up, I thought I was a bit young, but as the job might not come up again for 25 years, I thought I would have a go.'

He confessed his first Saturday opening meet at Long Clawson, when the world and his wife habitually turn up, was 'the most frightening experience ever'.

It did not show at the time; the Belvoir hounds performed superbly, and everyone had an enjoyable day. Robin was fortunate with hunting conditions through the early years of his decade at Belvoir (1983-92).

Michael Saunby reported an excellent day in January 1988 on the Lincolnshire side:

From Tennant Baxter's meet at Ingoldsby, hounds found a good fox in Ingoldsby Wood, and came quickly away to the Arc, and on to Humby, swinging left through Parsons Wood to Boothby Little Wood. They ran up the brook towards Old Somerby, right-handed to Hern Wood, and the Ropsley sewage works before heading up to the Grantham main road (A52) which they crossed towards Dembleby Woods.

Belvoir Puppy Show 1980 (left to right): Mr Nicholas Playne MFH, Mr Robert Henson MFH, Lord Daresbury (who was judging hounds), Prince Charles (co-judge), the Duke of Rutland, Lord King, and Mr Nick Turner MFH.

Fortunately former Master Nicholas Playne viewed them towards Oasby, and onto Welby, where this good fox was left in the village. A seven mile point, 15 as hounds ran, in under two hours.

In Robin's first season, his first whipper-in was Stuart Coley, who had whipped in to Jim Webster since 1980, Stuart having come from the South Notts.

Philip Lucas was second whipper-in. From 1984-87 the first whipper-in was Ralph Mankee who came from the Heythrop, and left the Belvoir to join the Portman.

Second whipper-in from 1984-7 was Roy Hart, succeeding as first whipper-in from 1987-89. The first whipper-in position was filled from '89 by John Holliday, from the Braes of Derwent, for three seasons, having been promoted from second whipper-in where he had served for a couple of seasons under Roy Hart. Gary Joynes from the Portman joined as second whipper-in 1989, remaining for two seasons before departing to the Zetland, to be succeeded at Belvoir by Julian Brewitt in Robin Jackson's last season, 1991-92.

John Holliday was a significant appointment as whipper-in because in the 2010-11 season he was to return to the Belvoir as huntsman, having achieved a fine reputation as huntsman of the Ledbury. He earned much admiration in many quarters of the hunting world for his part in the famous 'interruption of business' achieved by Otis

Prince Charles (right) with Robin Jackson and hounds.

Ferry and friends in the House of Commons on 15 September 2004, in protest at the impending Hunting Bill, then being debated in Parliament.

In Robin Jackson's second season there was a truly memorable hunt on the Leicestershire side on 3 December 1984. Hounds hunted in the Quorn country by invitation, owing to the Quorn hounds suffering kennel cough.

Soon after the meet at Hickling hounds found a brace by the Old Grantham Canal, killed one and hunted the other straight back into the Belvoir country. They ran to Pen Hill, and ran down past Hose Thorns towards Kay Wood, losing their fox over Home Farm.

The afternoon saw a tremendous hunt into the heart of the Quorn country, after hounds found in Curate's. Their fox ran past Folly Hall and Wolds Farm, and surprised everyone by crossing the busy A46 Fosse road. The Prince of Wales and Michael Farrin jumped a stiff iron gate by the road, and then politely held up traffic briefly as hounds crossed. Those drivers who suddenly recognised the Prince looked amazed.

Hounds hunted westwards as far as Broughton Lodge and the lovely grass and fence country near Willoughby. The great hunt, which had been a marvellous ride for a steadily depleted field, ended near Wysall in dusk as fresh foxes intervened.

It was one of the most enjoyable rides because the pace allowed the Field to see hounds working, and to tackle each fence, and the run had that special quality of all good hunts in that they had no idea where they would go next.

It says much for the professionalism and generosity of Michael Farrin that he confirmed to me afterwards the exact line the fox had taken because Robin Jackson did not know the Quorn country well enough to be able to advise me in such detail. He had been guided across the Quorn country by Farrin during part of the run, once we had crossed the A46.

On 2 December 1989, the Belvoir hounds, hunted by Robin Jackson, achieved a hunt worthy of comparison with any of the great runs of the past. I reproduce here my report as 'Foxford' in *Horse and Hound*. I was out that day, but riding a young horse new to the hunting field, and with much regret I confess to pulling up fairly early in this hunt, and not completing the run. However, the huntsman and the Field Master, John Blakeway, gave me all the news of the great hunt afterwards. I recall all too many Belvoir followers waiting by their horse boxes on Langar airfield for 'hounds to come back' – but they didn't, for a very long time indeed, and by then the day's sport was over.

'The Belvoir bitch pack achieved a remarkable hunt from their meet at Plungar on Saturday 2 December reflecting great credit on their huntsman Robin Jackson and his staff. The pack completed a hunt of 18 miles as hounds ran, with a seven-mile point, catching their fox.

'Carried out in modern conditions, this hunt certainly ranks alongside the greatest hunts of the past achieved by the Duke of Rutland's famous pure English-bred hounds.

'After we had been well entertained by Mr and Mrs Michael Chatterton, hounds quickly found near Merrivale Farm, and some local hunting ensued around Plungar. Then hounds found a brace and a half of foxes outside Langar village. They hunted one for four fields, and caught it.

'They quickly found again in the covert below Langar Hall, and ran to Langar Lane covert, and on towards Tythby where, after only 10 minutes, they change foxes. A large, powerful dog fox got up on the plough.

'Hounds hunted their new pilot to Wiverton New Plantation, Wiverton Hall, across the River Smite, over the old Nottingham railway line to the Whatton Manor coverts. They ran on towards Whatton village, but swung left on the A52 and ran parallel to the main road for about two miles towards Bingham. Then they re-crossed the Smite on to Mr Page's farm, over Mr Bernard Parker's Northfield Farm, to Barnstone Station, and over Mr Sam Lee's farm at Granby.

'From Granby hounds ran almost straight for two miles, passing Granby Gap and on to the old railway line to Stathern Lodge where they caught their fox at 3.05pm, having hunted for two hours 40 minutes; all but ten minutes on the line of the same fox.

Only a handful of the mounted field completed the entire hunt, well-led by Joint Master Mr John Blakeway.'

In the 1991-92 season, Robin Jackson made a firm decision to give up his career as huntsman at the age of 36, after nine seasons at Belvoir. His change of lifestyle was his personal choice: 'If I don't make the change now, I think it will be too late in a few years' time,' he said.

He and his wife, Dorothy, and their children settled in the Belvoir country, and Robin became a salesman for a horse feed company, and later worked with horses in the Royal Mews at Buckingham Palace, and in private yards. He is a welcome visitor to Belvoir puppy shows and other Hunt events.

On 13 March 1992 the Belvoir paid tribute to Robin after a final hunt on the Leicestershire side. An excellent day's hunting was achieved, despite gale force winds and driving rain. Prince Charles rode with Robin and the whippers-in throughout the day.

After sport in the vale, with hounds hunting round Hose Thorns, and catching a fox in Clawson Thorns, the afternoon hunting was mainly on the hill, where hounds found in Melton Spinney and hunted locally. The day ended with a hunt from Goadby Gorse towards Melton Spinney, left over the Hindles to end the day at Thorpe Ashes where we were hit by a sudden, fierce hail storm.

Joey Newton, Joint Master and Field Master paid warm tribute to Robin Jackson's record at a packed supporters' tea party in Hose village hall, after hunting.

It was the end of a decade of excellent sport, achieved at a time when agriculture was beginning to accelerate to more arable farming. John Holliday left the Belvoir to go to the Quorn, and Julian Brewitt was promoted to first whipper-in for the incoming huntsman, with James Pearson from the Exmoor as second whipper-in.

Fortunately, one of the most successful terms as a Belvoir huntsman was about to start, with the arrival of Martin Thornton. He demonstrated how to produce excellent sport, with high standards of venery and patience in sticking to the line of a hunted fox in all conditions, in a country where the plough advanced still further, even into the heart of the Belvoir Vale.

Off the hunting field there were many distractions, for these were the difficult and turbulent years leading to Labour's iniquitous *Hunting Act* in 2005.

Left to right: Mr John Martin MFH, Mr Joey Newton MFH, Mr Steve Taylor MFH and Martin Thornton with hounds.

CHAPTER 10

Recollections of a Master 1978–1987

'...the first person who went over that Hunt jump, goes home NOW...'

Robert Henson, Joint Master from 1978-87 here provides his own memories of a period notable for good sport. He says that in recalling events, people, and incidents, he is attempting to describe 'what makes the incredible love affair with hounds, horses and hunting.'

MY APPOINTMENT TO THE MASTERSHIP FROM 1 MAY 1978

The appointment took a long time with endless meetings at The Red House, now The Manners Arms. Poor Jim Smith, the publican, had to keep climbing the stairs to summon me from the bedroom where I was posted until required, while various members of the Committee, under the Chairmanship of Sir John King, as he was then, discussed every aspect of my antecedents, my previous experience, and my likely ability to do the job.

I gather one very wise gentleman commented: 'He may have a bit of money now, but it will soon run out.' (How right he was.) Eventually I was appointed after at least three committee meetings. And although very excited, after such a gruelling introduction, I was nervous to the extent that I spent a large part of that summer visiting the Hunt Kennels and stables, seeing the incumbent staff, Jim Webster, the huntsman, and Paddy Elliott, the stud groom, seeking to glean as much information as I could on what the job was really about.

Although they were always pleased to see me, in reality they wanted to part with as little knowledge as possible. Once, when I was particularly pressing Jim about why a very odd practice should be followed, he replied: 'Well, I know something, Sir, that you don't know.'

So, I was none the wiser!

FIRST SEASON AS MASTER

We had arranged a very early autumn hunting meet near my home on the Tuesday side, so that I could 'find my feet', but these early mornings were not sufficient preparation for the traditional Opening Meet on a Wednesday at Croxton Park, home of the incumbent Belvoir Agent; at the time, Andrew and Billie Thompson.

Robert Henson Joint Master 1978-1988: 'life for a Master is busy...'

It was always difficult to have a hunt from the Park coverts, but it did provide an opportunity for 'everyone to settle down' – including those with very fresh horses being ridden for the first time that season, which included mine.

Much to everyone's surprise, after that particular Opening Meet, foxes were flying about all over the Park, and hounds ran between the coverts very well. Being very keen on my first day as Field-Master, I felt I should show that I meant business.

Whereas, at this stage of the season, one would have normally opened the Park gates when going from one area to another, on this occasion, with hounds in full cry, I decided to make sure my mount, Likely Lad, was as good as my father had told me. So I rode fairly hard into a medium sized five barred gate. My horse did not in fact take off at all, and all five bars lay in pieces on the ground. At a post-hunting tea, of more of which later, all the Hon. Mrs Ursula (Urky) Newton had to say was, ' Well, at least he tried!'

It proved to be a somewhat difficult first season in terms of my mounts, some of which were too green for the job, and others, never having had experience of going first, initially found it tricky. However a few weeks later from the meet at Landyke Lane we had an incredibly good hunt, fully written up in *Horse and Hound*. After that both horse and rider began to settle down a little. But to show how unconfident I was still, having enjoyed the hunt immensely, with hounds marking at Kenwyn Wright's land at Saxelby in the Quorn Country, on hacking back to second horses I had to ask my huntsman, 'Jim, that *was* a good hunt wasn't it?'

It was shortly after that, on a Wednesday, that we were honoured with the presence of our neighbouring Master of the Quorn, Capt Fred Barker, with whom I did not get off to too good a start – for two reasons. Firstly, on this particular day, as we were approaching a covert from the Melton Mowbray direction, Fred asked me the name of the covert (unpardonable sin for a Master not to know the name of every covert), to which I could only respond by saying I had never approached from this direction before,

Recollections of a Master 1978–1987

so could not recognize it. It just happened to be the most well-known covert in the whole of the Wednesday country, Melton Spinney!

The other incident probably happened after the Landyke Lane day. It was one of those days when afterwards we retired to High Leys at Knipton, the official residence of our Hunt Secretary, namely Tom Hudson, ably assisted by his wife, Sally. It was the custom, and still is, that should you run into your neighbour's country you should telephone the Master concerned to explain what had happened and apologise for the intrusion. I was a little nervous about this, and in spite of reminders from Tom Hudson to make the call, I kept having another cup of tea, or something stronger, and had just sat down in a large armchair, when I heard Tom approaching me with a 'phone in his hand saying, 'One moment Captain Barker, I have Mr Robert Henson for you, the new Master of the Belvoir.'

I leapt to the 'phone and gave what explanation I could, and as briefly as I could, before finding a reason to end the call.

The next Monday at the Quorn's Hickling meet, the same Capt Barker was overheard to say, 'Had a call from the new Master of the Belvoir. Bit of a rum chap, gets his butler to make his calls for him.'

Robert Henson crossing country.

SEASONS FROM 1978

Apart from the hunting, life for a Master is busy, and all the year round. There is money to be raised, so participation is essential in a number of events, such as the Point-to Point, Hunt Ball, Kennel Open Days, Puppy Show, Farmers' Dances/Dinners, Keepers' night out, to name but a few.

These were all social affairs organized by members of the Hunt or officials, and in the main they helped create a great spirit of friendship, sportsmanship, and comradeship, which goes some way to explain why, when our way of life is attacked, there is such a forceful reaction from our own people.

I found a Master's non-hunting activities took up as much thinking time as the hunting itself.

Robin Jackson bringing hounds to the opening meet in 1986.

Over the years I gained a reasonable reputation as a Field Master, but some said, 'He neglects the farmers.' I would contest this only in that my approach was not as clinical as other Masters may have been, whereby they visited very often and on a set day. I tended to go when needed, and not so much at other times, but certainly a lot of visiting went on in the summer months.

One of my most cherished compliments came from a man who had made a number of complaints during my tenure, but when I came to retiring, Garth Doubleday, of Long Clawson renown, said to me, ' I'm sorry to hear you are going. You have just started to do some good!'

APRÈS-HUNTING

In terms of social activities within the hunting season, during these years *après-hunting* was extensive. I do not think there is so much these days, with everyone so busy, and needing to get back home to work, cook supper or even do their own horse. In the '80's, tea after hunting was an important part of the day, and although a bit of a toll on the host/hostess, did provide for a good post-mortem of the day. I confess that in those seasons of being Field Master twice a week, as I was in the first part of my Mastership until I became ably assisted by John Blakeway, the opportunity to wind down was very welcome, and on some occasions I was too frightened not to be present!

In those days there were some notable places for tea, but to my knowledge only one person had two locations, namely Urky Newton who, on alternate Saturdays entertained at her home, Church Farm, Saltby, or in the washroom at her Garthorpe stables on Wednesdays. It was usually pouring with rain as about twelve to fifteen people tried huddling up to the little open fire at the far end of the room in the washroom.

It was on those occasions I probably learned more about the day's hunting, since going through each hunt in detail was *de*

Brothers Roger and Mike Chatterton in action during Jim Webster's last day in the Vale in March 1983.

Robert Henson as Joint Master and Field Master on grey, centre, with l.to. r. The Hon. Mrs Ursula (Urky) Newton, John Blakeway MFH, Dr Tom Connors, Graham Vere Nicoll and John Baggaley.

rigueur, with all hunt staff present, as well as a few hardened, dedicated subscribers.

It would be remiss not to mention a few other hosts and hostesses for after-hunting teas:

Friar's Well (the Kings), a little formal, but popular with Prince Charles, and other royalty; Waltham House (Hon. Migs Greenall), less formal, but with the advantage of a resident butler!

Another after hunt venue was High Leys, previously mentioned, the home of Tom and Sally Hudson, and although no longer with us, I use this opportunity to record what an enormous help Tom was to me in my first few seasons. Later on I once had the temerity to complain about him to the Hunt Chairman. I asked him, was he going to do anything about it? He, the Chairman, replied, 'If I had done anything about you every time someone complained about you, you would have been fired years ago!'

Moving on to the other side of the country, the so-called less fashionable side, there the thoroughly enjoyable teas were longer and more sociable. For instance, there was the Bagley family at Normanton; the Chattertons at Plungar; Millers and Fitzherberts at Barkestone-le-Vale... and there were many others.

The intensity of these teas did come under scrutiny, after I was admitted to Grantham Hospital following three such teas in one day. The sharp bend at the end of what is known as the 'Long Lane' did not come onto my screen at all, somewhat similar to Likely Lad at the gate in Croxton Park.

Some time after the ambulance had taken me to Grantham, the local constabulary arrived and looked into my car in the bottom of the ditch. All he had to say was, 'He's had a bit of pop'.

Mentioning the Chattertons earlier allows me to observe that the two brothers Roger and Michael in many ways represented what the Belvoir hunt was all about. Both were always competitive in the field.

'Who won the hunt' had nothing to do with killing foxes, but was much closer to whose horse went the best over the country, and ended up first at the end of a hunt.

Roger and Michael were very good hosts to visitors to the Hunt, particularly in the morning, and then they showed them 'the way to go' in the afternoon. They were always helpful to fellow members of the mounted field.

Roger broke his nose when helping me and my horse out of a ditch on the landing side, in which we had inadvertently found ourselves. My horse repaid him by kicking him on the nose.

The Chatterton brothers have a love of the sport second-to-none, and consequently have played an active part over many years, Roger on the finance committee and Michael and his wife Anne running the point-to-point. Michael has remained a life-long friend and we still meet, whether for lunch or skiing, to do some serious reminiscing... 'not like the old days.'

The Hon. Mrs Ursula (Urky) Newton and her daughter, Mrs Carol Taylor.

Belvoir Hounds running well on the line of their fox...

PUPPY SHOWS

Breeding hounds and preparing the Young Entry, puppies going into their first season's hunting, is an important part of the hunting calendar, and therefore the annual Puppy Show takes on a number of important roles, not least of which is to thank those who undertake the critically-important task of walking the puppies. If only it was just walking!

It also provides the opportunity for the Kennels and stables to have a make-over. It ensures all the Young Entries' names are known by all the Hunt Staff by Puppy show day, sometimes having to learn up to 50 to 60.

It is a learning curve not just for the young puppies, but for all new staff who have joined for that season. Of course, it is a social occasion for the lucky few, although not all subscribers can be invited. The day is primarily for the Puppy Walkers, some farmer subscribers, and Hunt officials plus committee members.

However, the Puppy Show for my second year was somewhat different, in that Prince Charles had accepted to judge, and had asked that Lord Daresbury should be his co-Judge. The Prince in his reply to our invitation to judge, thought it would be a good idea to have the Puppy Show earlier in the day (it had been at 3pm for the last 150 years), and thus lunch would be provided for everyone.

I don't know to this day whether he was aware it was the Masters' responsibility to foot the bill for the Puppy Show, but it went ahead as requested, and it was a great day.

One small anecdote which amused the audience at the Puppy Show was my story concerning a hunt away from Scalford Ashes, when a member of the mounted field cut a corner, then jumped a hunt jump into a field of new seeds, and found himself in front of hounds. I lost my cool, and shouted: 'The first person who went over the hunt jump goes home NOW! A regular aide on such occasions, Marjorie Comerford, came up alongside to advise: 'You do know who went over first, don't you?'

It didn't take me long to work it out (because Prince Charles was out that day), so I shouted even louder, 'The *second* person over the hunt jump is to go home NOW!'

SUMMING UP

These recollections are not meant to be a detailed catalogue of nine years in Mastership, naming everyone who was involved, because it would have been too long, and in the main, boring. It is sad that a number of those who feature are no longer with us, but their contribution and exploits live in our memories.

The fact is that over the period a very large number of people contributed to the success, or otherwise, of what at the time was a popular Leicestershire pack of hounds, and still is. Before the Lloyds disasters, and other recessionary factors, we would regularly have over 200 mounted followers, mainly on alternate Saturdays, at such meets as Holwell, Landyke Lane, Hose, Wartnaby (by permission), Colston Bassett and so on. There were many regular, experienced foxhunters out on Wednesdays which were well supported by farmers, both those not hunting, and those who were mounted. Much credit for the goodwill in this area, at the time, was down to my first season Joint Master, Mrs Ann Reid Scott who along with Ronnie Belper gave me great support from the start.

From 1983 I was joined by John Blakeway, a great horseman, who shared the Field Mastering with me at a very high standard; he was always a stalwart help and friend during our time together.

That, however was just the input of the Mastership. What made this four-day-a-week pack really work was the contribution of everyone else involved. Obviously at the head of the list was the Hunt Staff, absolutely pivotal to the running of the Hunt. I was lucky enough to have known and worked closely with both Jim Webster, whose wife Sheila is still living in Croxton Kerrial, and Robin Jackson. Their support staff in Kennels, and in the stables, worked tirelessly in some very unsocial hours, to ensure the entire system ran smoothly.

On hunting days further people became involved; the previously-mentioned fencing men; the terriermen, valuable not just for working their terriers, but their great knowledge of the location of foxes, and where they went; and the amateur 'second-whips' whose role is a little technical in that it covered a multitude of tasks, from being sent on to a covert corner, to helping round up a few stragglers, and all sorts in between. The car followers played a role, often viewing a fox when hounds were out of touch, or *not* getting ahead of the game and potentially spoiling the scent. Keepers on all the shooting estates and syndicates were a part of the machinery and although not always easy, since they had their sport to look after, it was essential we maintained a good working relationship with them.

The Belvoir

Robert Henson with his Joint Master Charles Harrison at a Belvoir meet, looking forward to a good day's sport.

And, lastly, only because they were the most important, came the farmers over whose land the sport was pursued. This is probably the single most difficult factor about hunting for non-hunting, or anti-hunting, people to understand. Throughout the winter months, and very occasionally week after week, the landowners and farmers would welcome the Hunt and its followers on to their land, the majority doing so enthusiastically, some tolerantly, and a very few not at all. It was a main task for the Masters to maintain good relations with *all* farmers, and so therefore we needed to work out solutions in the farmers' best interests, on the roads as well as in fields, and using courtesy as well as minimizing damage, enabling the sport, regardless of politics, to continue into the next century and beyond. These goals, I feel sure are still the main task of any Master of Foxhounds today.

I shall finish where I started, which was with Likely Lad at the opening meet breaking a five barred gate. I went on to say my first two seasons were made a little more difficult due to lack of experienced horsepower. If you are to go first, there is no saying so true as 'you are only as good as your horse'.

The person who shared and supported my experiences as a Master, and did more by way of ensuring what success I had in the hunting field, was my wife Sarah. She found horses enabling me to do the job of Field-Master, and helped look after them when they returned home, for which I have always been most grateful. It was more than sad she could not have enjoyed more seasons in the saddle.

CHAPTER 11

The Fateful 1990s and into the 21st Century

'...extremely fortunate when Martin Thornton was appointed...'

The Belvoir was fortunate when Martin Thornton was appointed huntsman in 1992. A Lincolnshire man, he was born in the Brocklesby country where his father worked as kennelman for the Brocklesby Hunt, and looked after horses for Lord Yarborough's Joint Master, Laurence Kirkby.

Martin started in hunt service, as second horseman to Ron Harvey, huntsman of the Brocklesby, the other great family-owned pack of Old English Foxhounds. In 1971 Martin was appointed second whipper-in to Michael Farrin at the Quorn, then whipped-in to Geoff Harrison at the Portman in Dorset, followed by a move to the Eridge in Sussex, and then north to the Zetland from 1978-82. He began his career as a huntsman at the Bramham Moor in 1982, and returned to the Zetland to hunt hounds from 1984-88. He went south to the Bicester with Whaddon Chase from 1988-92.

Martin gained much from his career in widely-differing countries, from superb grasslands to mixed arable terrains. He had handled hounds of varied types, and he knew a great deal about the challenges of hunting hounds in modern conditions. The Bicester with Whaddon Chase enjoyed much support, but hunted an area not far north of Greater London, where roads and towns were increasingly busy.

In his stint in the Quorn country, Martin met Sally Christian, a keen rider to hounds whose father farmed at Walton-on-the-Wolds. She is a direct descendant of the famous Shires rough-rider of the early 19th century, Dick Christian, whose daring exploits were immortalised in the famous hunting book *Silk and Scarlet,* written by *The Druid.*

Martin and Sally married in 1974, and with such ancestry, it is no wonder their son, Robert 'Chocolate' Thornton, has become one of Britain's leading jump jockeys, with a huge following. Belvoir followers remember him as a schoolboy, riding with his mother across the Vale with remarkable skill and dash.

'Who is that child?' some of us asked in Martin's early seasons when the boy appeared riding near the front on 'adult' days. The pace was too good to enquire, but we soon learned that he was the huntsman's son – and since Martin himself could clearly cut

The Belvoir

Martin Thornton, huntsman 1992-2006.

out the work riding in front with hounds, it was clear his wife and son were among those able to follow him the best.

From the start of Martin's 14 years' carrying the horn for the Belvoir, it was evident that he was a huntsman with a special persistence and skill in ensuring that runs had a beginning, a middle and an end where the fox was either caught or marked to ground. He was never content with a hunt which ended because hounds had 'run out of scent...'

Casting brilliantly, and encouraging his hounds to pursue the line in all conditions, he conjured remarkable hunts out of days when conditions were far from ideal, and earned the admiration and support of true foxhunters who liked to see hounds working at the top of their ability. He could certainly make the most of the 'quick thing' when appropriate, but he was skilled in achieving long, slow hunts in appropriate conditions. He was as much appreciated in Lincolnshire as he was in Leicestershire.

Martin's persistence and drive as a huntsman was especially well-suited to a period when the terrain throughout Leicestershire was changing more rapidly to major increases in arable farming over grassland, as grain crops became more profitable, and stock farming less favourable.

Although brought up in the Brocklesby country, this was his first experience of hunting Old English hounds.

The Bicester with Whaddon Chase pack is an example of 'modern' breeding, with some broken coated hounds showing signs of their Welsh outcrosses, introduced in that pack during the Mastership of Capt. Ian Farquhar.

'I had hunted Welsh-cross and modern English hounds and so the pure English were something new,' Martin said. 'They needed a bit of patience at first, but I've grown to love them. I have the highest regard for the pure English now.'

Some indication of Martin Thornton's prowess as a huntsman is contained in the tally for the 1992-93 season when hounds caught 78 brace during cubhunting, and 107 brace by the end of the season, despite very patchy scenting conditions.

The 1993-94 season was a desperately wet and heavy season throughout, with scent moderate before Christmas, but improved in the second half when there was some good hunts, especially in January and February. Hounds accounted for 78½ brace overall.

Michael Saunby reported a really good day on the Lincolnshire side in January, 1994 with Martin hunting hounds:

A field of over 80 greeted the Masters for the Pony Club Meet at Aswarby Park. Drawing Aswarby Thorns, hounds spoke at the Willoughby end, and hunted the length of the covert before pushing their fox away towards Aswarby village, running nearly as far as Osbournby, before returning to Aswarby rectory. The hounds pushed on to the Drove and over the Mareham Lane to Scredington, and back through the Burton Woods to the Thorns. With scent beginning to fail, the fox was reluctantly given best on Mr Darley's, after a three and a half mile point, 10 as they ran.

After the wet season of 1994-95, the following season started with a drought and bone-hard ground. This was followed by severe cold weather causing many lost days. Both packs contracted a kennel virus on 28 February and did not hunt again that season. Hounds were out 92 days, losing 17, and their tally was 79½ brace.

Mr Joey Newton Joint Master 1989-2000 and Field Master thereafter.

The 11th Duke of Rutland, President of the Hunt and owner of the pack, with hounds in front of Rutland Castle at the pre-Hunting Act meet.

Giving a lead – Mr Joey Newton.

Much more grassland went under the plough including large areas of the Vale of Belvoir, during Martin Thornton's time as huntsman. His high standards of venery and hound control ensured consistent sport, with persevering hunts on any type of going that a hunted fox crossed.

Julian Brewitt and James Pearson remained as first and second whipper-in respectively for the first two seasons of Martin Thornton's term. For two seasons from 1994-96, first whipper-in was Ian Jones from the Berkeley. From 1996-2002 Richard Markham from the HH formed a good working relationship with the huntsman as first whipper-in. Mark Winter was second whipper-in from 1994-96; Michael Woodhouse from the New Forest for the next two seasons, from 1996-98; Edward Irving from the Portman 1998-2000; Michael Little, 2000-2003; Roderick Wilson 2003-2004; Oliver Harding, from the Berkeley, 2004-2005.

Richard Markham left the Belvoir in 2002, to be succeeded by Philip Stubbings from the Ledbury who performed well, and went on to become huntsman of the Blankney from 2004. He was succeeded at Belvoir by Jack Bevan from the Waveney Harriers for the 2004-2005 season, with Oliver Harding promoted to first whipper-in for Martin Thornton's final season, 2005-2006.

Millennium hunting – new Chairman Mrs Tor Owen.

From 1991 the Belvoir team was greatly strengthened by the appointment of George Grant from the Berkeley as an effective kennelman. He remained in kennels until 2002 when he was appointed as 'countryman', working in the hunting field where he followed hounds on a quad bike. George was appointed non-riding kennel huntsman under Capt Rupert Inglesant when he succeeded Martin Thornton from 2006-2010.

As the millennium approached, there was sadness in the Belvoir country over the passing of the 10th Duke. The October issue of *Belvoir Tan*, the Hunt Supporters' magazine, carried a message from David, 11th Duke of Rutland, pictured with His Grace's hounds at the 1999 Puppy Show:

Masters and staff at the Hunt Kennels March 2000. Left to right: Martin Thornton, Mr John Martin, Mr Joey Newton, Mr Richard Morley, Mr Sten Bertelsen, and Edward Irving, whipper-in.

Below: Richard Morley, MFH 1998–2006, fought the battle for hunting.

The Hon. Vicky Westropp MFH 2003-06.

Mr Bill Bishop MFH 2000-06.

'For me, rather like hunting, we have had an immense year. My dear father has died (on 1 January 1999), and I have taken over the estate. I have entered the House of Lords, for how long, who knows? Likewise in hunting we have seen a change of government. All agendas moved, and Bills to ban hunting have come and gone.

'We do all live in a changing world. We fight to maintain all that we know and love. We hope with strength in numbers we can outweigh the urban vote. For how long, is up to us, to show the powers-that-be that without the rich tapestry of countryside their lives will be that much poorer.

'So, like the House of Lords, we will not go down without a fight.

'I believe we will still have a long future in hunting in this country with all your support.'

Joey Newton, as senior Master, gave a similar call for unity and strength in the face of the political challenges ahead: 'The future seems to be a roller coaster of uncertainty, but the bigger the ups and downs, the more we need to stick together, and try to carry on as normally. Therefore, the strength and the unity of subscribers, farmers, foot followers and supporters must be maintained...Just remember, we are not working for a lost cause, and we will not be dictated to by little towns people in suits!'

Joey's Joint Master Richard Morley and friends went to the Labour Party Conference in Bournemouth in the summer of 1999 to make a truly remarkable sea-borne protest on behalf of hunting.

They towed a 16 foot boat from Richard's Redhill Marina all the way down to Poole in Dorset. Philip and Caroline Henson joined the crew, and next morning they sailed from Poole to Bournemouth Bay, joining other boats manned by hunting people off the Pier. They displayed pro-hunting messages from their boats, and these were conveyed to millions on TV that night.

Afterwards they rushed to the Conference Centre in Bournemouth to join in a mass protest directed at Labour Party delegates, shouting down a few anti-hunting sabs, with the message: 'What do we want? Freedom!' and 'Listen to us!'

Foxhunting, deeply embedded in the British countryside, had its share of stress from February 2001 when foot and mouth disease suddenly appeared in virulent form, first identified in Essex, but spreading widely. Millions of cattle and sheep were slaughtered in the north and west of Britain. Farmers in the East Midlands were spared the worst excesses of the outbreak, but it was a time of great pressure throughout the British countryside. Some hunt staff were among those who worked in the north-west helping with the immense task of slaughtering sheep from the Cumbrian hills.

Mr Harry Westropp and the Hon. Vicky Westropp.

Hunting stopped immediately, even before a DEFRA order cancelling sporting activities in the countryside was announced. The remainder of the 2000-1 season was lost; many activities involving animals were cancelled or curtailed throughout the summer, although racing survived, and hunting only resumed on 17 December 2001, operating under a special 'permit' conditions imposed by DEFRA, whereby those out with hounds had to sign compliance forms for procedures such as dipping one's feet in disinfectant before and after a day's hunting.

Above: Mr James Henderson MFH 2000-06.

Below: Mr John Martin MFH 1991-2004, whipper-in Tim Coulson, and Mr Michael Bell, Field Master, and Joint Master from 2010.

The Fateful Nineties

The Duke and Duchess of Rutland and children at the Belvoir Castle meet on 17 February, 2005.

The Duchess of Rutland, on a hunter given to her by the Duke as a wedding present, at the opening meet of the Belvoir in 1992.

The Duchess of Rutland, during autumn hunting near Garthorpe.

Above: Mr David Bellamy, MFH 2001-2, Field Master, and Joint Master again from 2010.

Below: Veteran followers: Mr Simon Brodie and Mr Don Field.

Mr Martin Brown MFH 2003-06, and again Joint Master from 2010.

Hunt members and supporters were ready to take part in the Countryside Alliance's planned Liberty and Livelihood March, but it had to be postponed because of the foot and mouth outbreak.

As Mrs Tor Owen, Hunt Chairman, wrote in *Belvoir Tan*, 'It is a bitter blow. Our buses were full, and we had more on standby, so let us hope that our opportunity to show the present government what we think is not denied.'

It had been a difficult first season of the new century even before foot and mouth arrived, with long spells of wet weather, but a newly-formed Mastership had coped well, with Martin Thornton and hounds producing some excellent days up to the sudden stoppage.

Mrs Owen wrote: 'Martin Thornton and his staff in the kennels and stables deserve our special thanks in maintaining the high standards of sport to which we have become accustomed, at a time when their future is being kicked about by Mr Blair for his own political convenience. I am quite confident that hunting does have a future.

'Our first thoughts now must be with any farmer who has lost his livelihood

Lady Sarah McCorquodale, Joint Master from 2010.

through foot and mouth, and our vigilance is essential to ensure that it does not come any closer.'

When hunting resumed, from 17 December 2001 the Belvoir pack showed their resilience, and were soon producing consistent sport again. But the foot and mouth episode was a disastrous blow to the countryside in general, and with the Blair government still squaring up for legislation to ban hunting, Masters and staffs running Hunts were bearing a heavy burden.

There were many new problems to be solved for Hunts; one of the most acute was the problem of collecting fallen stock from farmers to feed hounds. By 1998 the Treasurer, Rob Gardiner, was reporting that it was costing the Belvoir £30,000 a year to collect dead stock free of charge to the farmers, but the BSE crisis had caused all sorts of problems in disposing of the flesh not fed to hounds, which amounted to about 300 tons per annum.

The government had taken away the subsidy to renderers for disposing of carcase material not consumed by hounds. Charges

Mr David Bellamy and Mr Michael Bell, Joint Masters from 2010 – at the meet at Belvoir Castle on 13 March, 2010, to end the season.

were now from £80 to £120 per ton, increasing the annual cost to about £35,000. The Hunt could not afford these sums, and was charging farmers fees on a 'headage' basis, but even so there was a shortfall of £10,000 which the Hunt had to meet.

In 1998 the Belvoir Hunt Committee decided on a major reinvestment in vehicles, horses and equipment at the kennels having deferred any expenditure for the previous two seasons because of the political uncertainties caused by the Foster Bill to ban the sport, but the defeat of this Bill produced fresh confidence.

In '98 they installed a new horse-walker at the kennels, purchased a new Land Rover, and other material, positive signs that the Hunt was going to dig in to fight to protect its long term future.

Contributions to the Campaign for Hunting were vital, but it was another financial burden for the Hunts, diverting money that could have gone into the sport. From 1994 Belvoir subscribers were each charged £35 per nominated day's hunting as a contribution towards the Campaign, and in the 1998-99 season the Hunt was making a contribution of about £7,000.

On 17 November 2004 the House of Lords persisted in making massive changes to the Hunting Act brought in by Tony Blair's government. The Lords wished to restore licensed hunting, and inserted a three year implementation process instead of the 18 months proposed by government.

Next day there was a farcical shuttling between the two Houses. There was a deplorable display of conflict between the Commons and the Lords. At 9pm in the Commons the Speaker, amid cries of 'Shame' announced the Hunting Bill had met all the provisions of the Parliament Act and would become law. Labour had mis-used the Parliament Act to over-rule the House of Lords, and force through a Bill which was to prove farcical and unworkable.

All subscribers and supporters of the Belvoir received the following letter, dated 16 December 2004 from Mrs Owen, Hunt Chairman.

'On 18 February 2005, hunting with hounds will be outlawed by a prejudiced and discriminatory House of Commons. We hope that this is temporary. The Bill is being legally challenged in the European Court of Human Rights, and in the High Court, and during this period of uncertainty the Joint Masters and Hunt Committee are determined to carry on whatever legal activities they can.

'Your continued support is vital to the well-being of the hounds, and to preserve as much of what we have inherited as possible. The Duke and Duchess of Rutland have generously offered Belvoir Castle for a Hunt Ball on Saturday 12 March. The Point-to-point will take place at Garthorpe on Saturday, 2 April.

'The meet on Thursday 17 February will be at Belvoir Castle, and a legal protest meet will take place on Saturday 19 February (in Melton Mowbray). Thank you for your support at this difficult time. Everyone's contribution is enormously important and hugely appreciated. Naturally all Hunts have unpalatable decisions to make. As Christmas approaches I hope you will particularly remember our hard-working and dedicated staff.

'We shall continue to fight with every tactic we have.'

BEFORE THE ACT

In the 2004-5 season, the Belvoir hounds achieved notably high levels of sport before the Hunting Act was imposed in February. There was a break with tradition when the Duke and Duchess of Rutland welcomed a good field at a meet at Belvoir Castle on the second fixture of the season.

Usually of course the Castle is the venue for the final Vale meet of the season, and as recounted above this was to be the scene of another meet, on 17 February, the day before the Hunting Act became law.

After the earlier Belvoir Castle meet hounds produced good sport around Eastwell and Waltham, and in the afternoon from Saltby to Buckminster.

There were good days throughout November, with temperatures falling fast, and snow blanketing most parts of the Midlands on 19 November. Fortunately it was clear of snow that day in the Fens where hounds achieved a busy day after the meet at Rookfield House, with Mr and Mrs Nick Coy as hosts.

Below: The Belvoir hounds, mounted and foot followers in the protest parade against the Hunting Act, through the streets of Melton Mowbray on 19 February, 2005.

The Belvoir mounted field on the Leicestershire side, led by Mr Joey Newton.

Next day Mr and Mrs John Pick entertained the meet above Long Clawson where some snow was still lying. Sherbrookes held a brace, and the bitches hunted one over Hickling back lane into the Quorn country, circling by Hickling Manor to come back to Lawson; a highly enjoyable ride for the mounted field.

They found again on the banks of the Smite, and there was a sharp hunt across Canal Lane to Hose, and up to Long Clawson where this fox was given best in the dusk.

After their meet at Walcot, where Mr and Mrs James Knight were hospitable as ever, hounds produced an enjoyable day, finishing with a fine circular hunt of five miles without a check.

On 17 December Jean Parry greeted the Saturday field at Allington, and a remarkable day followed. After two morning hunts over Allington Park, hounds found an outlier on Mr Lee's farm at Granby. They ran for Whatton Manor, but swinging over the Whipling and the old railway, crossed the River Smite at the footbridge, pushed on for Tithby Grange in the South Notts country, and crossed the Fosse beyond Cropwell Bishop.

They pressed on with determination, but with Radcliffe-on-Trent immediately ahead, and headlights on the busy Nottingham road becoming ever brighter, they were stopped near the golf course, opposite the RSPCA shelter, with only the Hunt staff with them.

The Belvoir

As reported by 'Old Bill' (Michael Saunby), hounds had covered more than ten miles, with a six and a half mile point. During the hunt they had crossed parts of three counties: Lincolnshire, Leicestershire, and Nottinghamshire, ending a long day some 14 miles from their point of departure in the Belvoir country.

HISTORY-MAKING SHOW APPEARANCES

In its report of the 1995 Great Yorkshire Foxhound Show, Foxford reported: 'Foxhunting history was made with the appearance of the Duke of Rutland's hounds, the Belvoir. I am assured this is the first time hounds have been shown in a public event in the Hunt's 245 history.

'Belvoir blood dominated hound breeding in general, and the leading prize-winners at Peterborough, in the late 19th and early 20th centuries. Successive Dukes of Rutland have insisted that their hounds have continued to be bred at Belvoir Castle on traditional English lines, without the admixtures of Welsh and other blood which changed so much breeding in this century.

'Well shown by their huntsman Martin Thornton, the Belvoir hounds were as confident and happy in the ring, as if they had shown for years, and they could be well pleased with their four reserves and two third placings in a show of predominantly 'modern' bred hounds.'

Below: Parading at Garthorpe – Mr Rupert Inglesant and hounds.

Autumn hunting - Mr Rupert Inglesant with hounds – and, on the grey, Miss Nina Camm, keen puppy walker, and Hon. Secretary of Belvoir Hunt Supporters Club since 1996.

In 2005 Peterborough Royal Foxhound Show made a major change in policy, and included a separate section for Old English type Foxhounds. The Belvoir made further history by showing for the first time at Peterborough. Seven other packs competed: the Brocklesby, Hurworth, Co. Limerick, Percy, Warwickshire, Sir Watkin Williams-Wynn's, and York and Ainsty South. The Old English hounds in their traditional Belvoir Tan livery were much admired, and one senior MFH said admiringly: 'Now those doghounds really look like doghounds.'

There were cheers from local supporters for the Belvoir when they won the unentered bitch class with Rapid, by Belvoir Poacher 98, who proved one of the most successful Belvoir sires of modern times, his daughter Poplin winning the bitch championship at Peterborough for the Heythrop.

After the appallingly drafted Hunt Act was made law in February 2005, Martin Thornton gave notice of intended retirement, but was asked by his Masters and the Hunt committee to continue after the Act for at least a season so that further plans could be made, and it is to his credit that he agreed to do so.

In March 2006 there was a farewell meet in Lincolnshire for a huntsman who had

The Belvoir

earned the highest respect and affection from followers that side of the country. At the meet at Osbournby, Joint Master Bill Bishop, not a man given to extravagant statements, said in a speech of tribute, 'I've hunted for 60 years, and seen a lot of huntsmen, but I haven't seen one who can compare with Martin.'

Nina Camm, Hon. Secretary of the Hunt Supporters' Club, and one of the most devoted hound lovers, whose parents Mr and Mrs Lol Camm were hosts at the meet, said, 'We get tremendous pleasure watching Martin handle the hounds; he's so patient with them. We love the hound work in this Lincolnshire country.'

MASTERSHIPS UNDER PRESSURE

The Belvoir benefitted from enthusiastic, locally-based, hunting people in maintaining the Hunt during the difficult years at the end of the 20th century and past the millennium.

Major John Parry CBE of Allington, a brewing executive and distinguished in other spheres, rendered great services as the Hunt's Hon. Treasurer for 16 years, from 1969-85, as Field Master for Lord Belper from 1976-77, and as Master from 1987-89, taking on this office when he was 66-years-old. In his first stint as Field Master, John gave a tremendous lead to hard-riding mounted fields on the Leicestershire side.

Miss Chloe Newton, daughter of Mr and Mrs Joey Newton, keen rider to hounds – and eventer.

Although at that time he wore a top-hat as Field Master there was no problem in observing who was leading the field. He was a consummate horseman, with an iron nerve. His wife Jean Parry, who he married in 1947, is known to generations of Belvoir followers as one of the last side-saddle riders following this pack, and their daughter Fiona, Mrs David Gibson, remains a popular member of the mounted field. Aged 91, Jean Parry was still attending Belvoir meets in the 2009-10 season.

When John Parry joined the Mastership from 1987 he proved he had lost none of his skills as Field Master, ensuring the obedience of the field with mild but firm commands, and giving an excellent lead.

Once he went to visit a smallholder to ask about the Hunt crossing his land. There appeared to be no-one about in the farmyard. John Parry, hearing a noise coming from a stable went to investigate. He peered over a door to find himself gazing into the yellow eyes of a full-grown, black-maned lion. He beat a hasty retreat.

There was much sadness at Major Parry's death, aged 81, in an accident while fishing in the River Spey in 2002.

James Knight, from one of the keenest sporting families in Lincolnshire, was Joint Master on that side of the country (1983-90). Marjorie Comerford, former international three-day-event rider, proved her durability as a rider after some horrendous injuries in falls. Equally durable is her constant support of the Belvoir, serving as Joint Master from 1988-92.

Continuity from within the Belvoir country was well-established when Joey Newton joined the Mastership in 1989, with John Parry, John Blakeway and James Knight.

Joey inherited a love of hunting and racing as the son of the late Hon. Mrs Ursula ('Urky') Newton, and her husband the late Lance Newton who founded the Melton Hunt Club. A grandson of Lord Rank, Joey farmed extensively in the Wednesday country at Saltby, and he was a top-class amateur 'chase rider, winning the Aintree Foxhunters' twice, and point-to-point racing for many years.

He is senior steward at Liverpool, and stewards at Newmarket and other leading racecourses. He receives considerable backing and support from his wife, Emma, a keen rider to hounds and a descendant of the Forester family so much associated with Leicestershire hunting.

After John Blakeway's retirement from the Mastership in 1992, Joey ably carried the Field Master's role on the Leicestershire side. From 1990 he had formed a new Mastership including Mrs Tor Owen, whose husband, the late Barry Owen, made considerable services to the Hunt as Hon. Treasurer. Tor Owen, with John Martin looked after the Lincolnshire side.

With the pressures of modern life, the increasing complexities of running a Hunt, and the burdens of financing the operation, the Belvoir shared the increasing trend throughout the sport for more Masters serving shorter terms. Joey Newton's brother-in-law, Steve Taylor, former National Hunt jockey, husband of Joey's sister, Carol, joined the Mastership for five seasons (1993-98) and added further strength to the lead the mounted field enjoyed from the 'front end', since Steve proved an excellent Field Master across any country.

Joining the Belvoir Mastership just before and after the millennium, were Sten Bertelsen and Richard Morley, both in 1998;

The Belvoir

James Henderson and Bill Bishop in 2000; and David Bellamy in 2001.

Joey Newton resigned as Joint Master in 2000, and in 2003 the Mastership was augmented by the Hon. Vicky Westropp, daughter of the late Lord Manton who was a brilliant man across country with the Quorn for many years. With her husband Harry Westropp, a keen hunting man, Vicky made a wonderful restoration of their home Goadby Hall, inherited from her late godmother Monica Sherriffe. It is a beautiful lake-side setting for Belvoir meets hosted by Harry and Vicky Westropp, keen members of the Belvoir mounted field. Harry, an experienced businessman, serves on the Belvoir's Finance Committee.

Mr Martin Brown became a Master from 2003-4, and rejoined the Mastership for the 2010-11 season; his father, Charles Brown, transport businessman and farmer on the Melton Mowbray border, is a veteran Belvoir member, and one of the keenest riders to hounds. Martin Brown served as a Field Master in the Leicestershire country.

After Tor Owen's retirement from the Mastership in 1999 she took on the role of Chairman of the Hunt, on the retirement of Lord King, and Mrs Owen had to bear the heavy burdens on all Hunt executives when the Hunting Bill arrived in 2005.

Richard Morley, James Henderson, Bill Bishop and Vicky Westropp were the Joint Masters when the Hunting Bill was enacted, following all the politics and campaigning described above.

Just a few of those who turned out for the sombre Belvoir Castle meet on 17 February, 2005.

AFTER THE HUNTING ACT

On Saturday 19 February 2005, the Belvoir played its full part in the impressive mounted protest parade through the streets of Melton Mowbray. They were part of a parade of over 600 riders with fellow supporters of the Quorn, Cottesmore and Oakley Foot Beagles. Pavements along the route were packed with about 4,000 well-wishers as Martin Thornton and the other huntsmen, whippers-in and hounds led their mounted followers in full Hunt dress through the streets of Melton, historic 'capital' of Shires foxhunting, since the Belvoir, Quorn and Cottesmore all have borders on the town's perimeter.

The parade ended at the Cattle Market where the Rutland and Melton Conservative MP Alan Duncan addressed the crowd, and pledged his support for a parliamentary battle to repeal the unjust Act which he thoroughly condemned as an unwarranted attack on the countryside.

The protest parade was organised by hunting farmer Mr Geoff Brooks and a regional Countryside Alliance team. At the Cattle Market meeting CA Regional Chairman, Michael Clayton, urged hunting people to keep their Hunts intact until a new government could repeal the Bill, and announced the Alliance's plan to petition the House of Lords against the government's use of the Parliament Act to ram through the anti-hunting Bill despite the refusal of the Lords to give it approval.

Richard Morley, retiring after eight years as a Joint Master, and appreciated as Leicestershire Field Master, wrote in *Belvoir Tan*: 'In the last eight seasons the Belvoir and its supporters have been at the forefront of the campaign to keep hunting. We have attended every major rally and march, and organised numerous events ourselves – remember the ride through Melton.

'These events have been very costly, and taken a lot of time, which could have been spent working in the Hunt country.

'Therefore, we should now be looking to open up more country, making jumping places, putting in culverts, cutting back rides and laying hedges. To do this takes time and money. Hunting nowadays has to compete with many other forms of equestrian activity to attract followers and thus bring in funds. Farming has had to diversify to survive – perhaps the Hunts need to do likewise. We certainly need to look for ways of encouraging more support in order to continue the way of hunting that we all enjoy.'

Working with the Chairman and the Hunt Committee, the Masters came to a decision to work through the 2005-6 season with the same team to see how the restrictions of the Bill could be operated in practice. Martin Thornton was considering retirement, but made a great contribution to the future of the Hunt by agreeing to continue for one more season, while the Masters and Committee could decide on their future course of action to keep the Hunt in being.

All Hunts were being urged to take this line by the Masters of Foxhounds Association and the Countryside Alliance. In all hunting countries the enactment of the Bill on 18 February, before the normal end of the 2004-5 season, caused immense stress and strain on everyone connected with the sport throughout England and Wales. Understandably, many thought the end of traditional hunting as intended by its opponents who supported the Act, would be the end of the sport. A BBC East Midlands TV crew attended the Belvoir's meet at Belvoir Castle on 17 February 2005.

At many meets throughout the country, foxhunters were feeling devastated by the prospect of losing a sport which they and their forebears had treasured as an integral part of country life for generations beyond count – and for which men and women had given their lives in two world wars in the expectation of preserving their way of life in the countryside.

There were some tearful sound-bites from foxhunters in the BBC's TV coverage from Belvoir, but the Duchess of Rutland gave a heartening response to a TV reporter, as she led one of her children on a pony from the meet. Asked if she expected this to be the end of hunting, she said: 'It's not over yet.'

The Belvoir, like all other Hunts, faced the 2005-6 season with trepidation, but with detailed advice from the MFHA and the Alliance, on what could be achieved within the new Act. Mounted and foot supporters turned out in similar numbers to the previous season.

The most important factor, which anti-hunting MPs in Parliament had not expected, was the tremendous support for the Hunts from farmers and landowners after the ban. The hated Hunting Act aimed to prevent them from making Hunts welcome on their land, by including clauses which made them liable if they were knowingly a party to infringements of the Act – but it failed.

The Act has numerous inconsistencies which says that a dog may hunt and kill a rat or a rabbit, but not a fox, hare, or deer. It allows a fox to be flushed by hounds from a covert to be killed with a gun, provided this is to protect game (amazingly, it does not say to protect farm stock). Basically, the Act seeks to eliminate the chase, and to prevent a fox being caught and killed by hounds, although accidents in which hounds may encounter a fox are exempt.

Hunts throughout Britain, with the guidance of their ruling bodies and the Countryside Alliance, have relied on hunting artificial trails, and on flushing the quarry when and where appropriate, including flushing to a bird of prey in the sport of falconry, which is an exemption under the Act.

VITAL SUPPORT FROM THE FARMERS

No hunting country's farmers and landowners were more staunch in their response to the Hunting Act than the Belvoir's. Everyone who hunts owes the farmers and landowners an immeasurable debt. They continued to welcome the Belvoir hounds in all parts of the country, just as before.

A system of assurances that Hunts were not seeking to break the law were made available to farmers and landowners throughout all hunting countries. But the rural community in general was disgusted with the Blair government's action in giving way to extremists on the hunting issue, and was perfectly prepared to cooperate with the Hunts to the hilt.

The Countryside Alliance since 2005 has been running a continuous campaign for repeal of the Hunting Act. The overturning of prosecutions against a minority of huntsmen for allegedly infringing the Act, has been a great encouragement. Most prosecutions were made privately by anti-hunting

The Fateful Nineties

organisations, and Magistrates and higher courts made it plain that the complexities of the badly drawn Act made prosecutions impossible, despite allegations made by camera toting 'hunt monitors' working for the anti-hunting lobby.

In May 2006, Tor Owen as Hunt Chairman wrote to all members and supporters of the Hunt:

'A big black cloud hovered over the Belvoir Hunt a year ago, and yet, a year on, it is seen to have a silver lining, or almost.

'Somehow the gloom and despondency have been dispersed, and the past season has been immensely enjoyable, for riders and car followers alike.

'Firstly, the landowners and farmers deserve our gratitude, in allowing us continued access to their land.

'Without this welcome, hunting would not

End of day – Martin Thornton with hounds boxing up.

145

have gone very far, as I am sure everyone appreciates. Perhaps that was the government's most serious miscalculation in their Bill to ban hunting. Secondly, there were the Belvoir hounds expecting to go hunting, and loyal hunt staff working extremely hard to maintain standards. From a careful and rather cautious beginning, every day was an unexpected bonus, and with the birds of prey giving necessary exemption, hounds were able to start hunting.

'Personally, I have enjoyed every one of my 39 days, and I am so grateful to the Joint Masters for their dedication in organising them. Martin and his staff have provided sport, and have always been very aware of the limitations of the law, and the extra care and control required.'

'Robert Morley reported the end of the 2005-6 season as 'the end of an era'. He paid tribute to Martin Thornton as 'a master of his profession, and my abiding memory of my time at the Belvoir will be the sight of Martin and the wonderful Old English hounds streaming across the Vale. The major problem for the rest of us was to keep up with them. Special mention of Sally Thornton who has so ably supported Martin both in the hunting field, the kennels and the home.'

Richard, always a fighter, declared presciently that they should look forward to a campaign to repeal the Hunting Act over the next few years, although it would take time, money, and political support. By the beginning of 2010, Richard's words were beginning to ring true, with the hunting world working for the return of a Conservative government which its leader, David Cameron, had pledged would bring in a Bill in government time to repeal the hated Hunting Act, although MPs would have a free vote on the issue.

The Belvoir Hunt Committee made a major decision well before the start of the 2006-7 season which enabled the Hunt to go forward with increased confidence. For the first time in its history, the Committee appointed a Master who would be sole huntsman of the hounds throughout the country. As this history has recounted, just after the first world war Major Tommy Bouch had hunted hounds, but only on the Lincolnshire side, and this applied to one or two other Masters who hunted hounds for short periods later.

The appointment of Rupert Inglesant as sole Master and amateur huntsman was warmly welcomed. Rupert is a Meltonian born and bred, the son of Jonathan Inglesant, known throughout the foxhunting world as the Quorn's highly effective Hon. Secretary for 18 years until 1976, and thereafter a devoted foot follower of the Quorn and Cottesmore. Jonathan became an especially keen foot follower of the Belvoir pack hunted by his son.

Rupert Inglesant was born in 1964 and lived in the Quorn country while his father was Hunt Secretary. After school at Millfield, and officer training at Sandhurst, Rupert joined the Royal Artillery, and his eight years' service included active duty in The Gulf and Northern Ireland. He managed to fit in 366 days' hunting during his Army service, although he was not able to fulfil his ambition to hunt the Royal Artillery hounds.

He became Master and huntsman of the Tedworth in Wiltshire from 1993-6, and soon earned a reputation for producing sport which led to a move to the Ludlow as Joint Master and huntsman from 1996-2006. He gained valuable experience, and was popular with Ludlow supporters, by producing sport and giving leadership.

All Rupert's early experience of hunting was in Leicestershire, and he was keen to take on the challenge of hunting a leading Shires pack.

Living at the Hunt kennels, and supported by his wife Caroline, who took charge of the Hunt stables, Rupert tackled the challenge of hunting Old English hounds with great zest, and became an enthusiast of their traditional breeding.

With George Grant serving as kennelman, and Tim Coulson from the Hursley Hambledon as whipper-in, Rupert set about producing enjoyable sport in the Leicestershire and Lincolnshire countries, and his military service and previous hunting experience enabled him to tackle the running of the Kennels and the country with effective organisation. Wayne Keble from the Heythrop was second whipper-in for the 2006-7 season, going on to the Warwickshire, and succeeded by Ben Higgins from the Barlow for 2007-8. For the 2009-10 season Rupert Inglesant's first whipper-in was Chris Edwards, son of Mr Foster Edwards, chairman of the Supporters' Club.

Joey Newton operating as Field Master on the Leicestershire side was much welcomed by mounted fields during Rupert Inglesant's Mastership, and on the Lincolnshire side Field Mastership was well carried out by former Joint Master David Bellamy, and by Michael Bell, an enthusiastic rider to hounds for many years with the Belvoir and Quorn.

The 2009 puppy show at the Hunt Kennels was a success, well attended, and with a good show of young hounds warmly praised by the judges, Jonathan Seed MFH (Avon Vale) and Richard Tyacke MFH (Sir Watkin Williams-Wynn's).

However, in January 2010 there was disappointment throughout the Hunt when Rupert Inglesant decided with regret to hand in his resignation as Master from the end of the season, having been in office four years, and carrying alone the tasks of running the country as well as hunting hounds.

'It has been a tremendous privilege to be Master of the Belvoir and to hunt these marvellous hounds,' he said. 'The problem is not the Hunt, but my life has reached a point where I must take a breather, and change direction.'

The Hunt Chairman, John Martin, and committee, were faced with the prospect of finding new arrangements for Masters, a huntsman and staff, for the 2010-11 season. The news of Rupert's retirement came in January, and since Hunt staff contracts traditionally start from 1 February, time was short.

Mr Martin was able to announce before the end of the month that John Holliday, former Belvoir whipper-in, and huntsman of the Ledbury since 1995, would be returning as Belvoir huntsman for 2010-11. Lady Sarah McCorquodale, of Stoke Rochford, one of the keenest Belvoir subscribers, and with much experience on the Hunt Committee, would form a new Joint Mastership, with former Joint Masters Martin Brown and David Bellamy, long-time subscriber and Field Master Michael Bell, and Mrs Emma Taylor, daughter of Mr Jim Bealby, former Joint Master of the Quorn, and his wife Susan.

An exceptionally hard winter, with snow and ice cloaking the land from mid-December to mid-January, and an attack of coughing in the Belvoir kennel, impeded hunting frequently throughout the British

The Belvoir

Isles during the 2009-10 season, but Hunts have long survived the worst that winter can bring. Everyone was looking forward to the 2010-11 season with keen anticipation.

The possibility of a new government in the 2010 General Election brought some hope of repeal of the Hunting Act, and a return to traditional hunting practice.

With a proud history approaching 300 years, meeting many challenges on the way, the Belvoir Hunt could look forward with confidence to the future.

Below: Starting his season as huntsman with the Belvoir, after moving from the Ledbury where he hunted hounds since 1995, John Holliday exercises hounds in the park with Belvoir Castle in the background. He served previously with the Belvoir as a whipper-in from 1989–92.

CHAPTER 12

The Belvoir Hounds

by Rupert Inglesant

(Master and Huntsman of the Belvoir 2006-10)

'Hunting the Belvoir hounds is a massive honour and the greatest privilege.'

To gain some understanding of the evolution of the Belvoir pack and the development of the 'old English Foxhound' one can study portraits of three Belvoir Hounds between 1853 and 1910:

Rallywood 1853, *painted by John Fernley.*
Gambler 1884, *by Basil Nightingale.*
Daystar 1903, *by Cuthbert Bradley.*

A striking and beautifully-balanced hound with pure-white neck, legs and muzzle, tan quarters and head, and a black body, Rallywood displays an intelligent and well-set head and neck; a flexible but not too long top-line, proportionate depth and shape to the rib-cage, a sloping shoulder, a straight fore-leg, powerful rounded quarters rather like a harrier, and good hocks.

One might pass adverse comment about the length of his toenails but the pads of his feet appear to rest squarely and evenly upon the ground. His proud stern is a disappointment, as it does not form a natural extension to the spine. Despite this latter point, all in all, he would appear to have been a really handsome Foxhound who would not be out of place in a 'modern English' kennel, nor indeed, apart from his feet, would he particularly stand out in an obvious manner amongst a pack of Fell Hounds.

Within 31 years the 'type' has altered markedly. The renowned Gambler is certainly a very imposing fellow, featuring the dominant black and tan colour generally associated with the 'old English', with less pure white than one sees on 'Rallywood'.

It is interesting to note: Gambler, bred by Belvoir huntsman Frank Gillard, was a son of Weathergauge 1876, one of Gillard's most prized stallion hounds, siring 54 litters and that Gambler himself sired 33 litters. Also, Brocklesby Rallywood 1843 (the sire of the aforementioned Belvoir Rallywood 1853) features some 14 times in Gambler's pedigree.

However, the colour pattern is not the only thing to have altered. Gambler is a completely different specimen of Foxhound, and his measurements, which are written against his portrait, became a bench mark for the 'Belvoir type': 23" high (the same height as 'Rallywood'); a girth of 31"; 27" from point of the shoulder to limit of the quarter; 8½" around the arms, 5¼" (of 'solid bone') below the knee, 10" extended neck; 12" from elbow

The Belvoir

to the ground and weighing 80lbs.

Nineteen years later, and Daystar portrays all the conformation faults that were apparent in Gambler, and many of these faults are now seen at their most extreme: generally unbalanced, he displays a heavy head, set upon a swan-like neck; a flat top-line; straight shoulders; he is over at the knee; has cat-like feet which are almost certainly turned-in; and a lack of proportion between height and length of body. It is easy to see how those Masters and huntsmen who disliked the Belvoir type gave them the derisory nickname of Shorthorns, after the bulky cattle of the same name.

Rallywood 1853, painted by John Ferneley – '…a striking and beautifully balanced hound…'

Fashion and trend meant that the 'Belvoir type' was propagated through an overwhelming number of English Kennels. Today, looking back from our 'enlightened' times, it is not possible to identify exactly why the process of change and subsequent deterioration in hound conformation, described above, was set in motion. However, one must always bear in mind that history is written by the victor; beauty is in the eye of the beholder; and people will so often simply follow those who hold power and influence, purely because it is the safest and easiest route to adopt.

The widespread pursuit of a breeding policy for Foxhounds of the 'Belvoir type' ultimately divided the hunting community to the extent that Masters with opposing views would cross the road in order to avoid each other. Even in modern times, the deep strength of feeling for, but particularly against, the 'Belvoir type' remains. Although we cannot answer why the 'Belvoir type' was sought so vigorously in a breeding policy, we *can* identify how this came about, and the main characters who set the whole process in motion: the Masters of the Belvoir Hunt, and their huntsmen, during the second part of the 19th century.

The 6th & 7th Dukes of Rutland dominated this period as Masters (1858-

Gambler 1884 – 'a completely different specimen of Foxhound...'

Belvoir Daystar 1903, illustrated by Cuthbert Bradley – 'portrays all the conformation faults that were apparent in Gambler...'

Modern hound exercise at Belvoir — with kennel-huntsman George Grant, during Rupert Inglesant's Mastership.

1888 and 1888-1896 respectively), and the huntsmen were James (Jem) Cooper (1859-1870) and Frank Gillard (1870-1896). Based purely upon the 30 years' Mastership of the 6th Duke, and the long tenure in post as huntsman of Gillard, some 26 years, one can assume these two provided a dominant influence and momentum in developing the 'Belvoir type'.

In addition, it is very likely that close links through society and the hunting field between the families of the Dukes of Rutland and Earls of Yarborough gave substantial strength and broad influence to promulgate the qualities of the 'Belvoir type'.

Friends, acquaintances and supporters from other Hunts would have supported their ideas on hound breeding policy. This is exemplified when one recalls that the Dukes of Rutland never sent hounds to Peterborough Royal Foxhound Show, first held in 1878, but for many years the winners were drawn from hounds with Belvoir pedigrees and conformation of the 'Belvoir type'.

Foxhunting was at its zenith during this period; it was the first of the three great eras for foxhunting in the Shires. *('The Shires' referring to those packs hunting in Leicestershire.)* For reasons beyond the remit of this chapter, Melton Mowbray had become a Mecca for foxhunters, and celebrities of the time flocked to visit or stay in the district. As a result the

The Belvoir Hounds

A veteran Belvoir doghound of 1930.

coverage of 'Shires hunting' dominated the sporting and social press. Numerous writers and artists recorded the times and exploits of the hounds and personalities in Melton's hunting community.

The Belvoir Hunt, as the only ducal and family-owned pack in the Shires, would have deservedly benefited from this coverage. The Hunt's great reputation spread to every corner of the kingdom, and it is easy to recognise how and why other Hunts would wish to be associated with this great establishment.

It is not beyond possibility, therefore, to consider that sycophantic attitudes on the part of some Masters and huntsmen across England may have played a part in their support of Belvoir breeding. A huntsman would receive a gratuity from Masters who sent their bitches to be covered by that huntsman's stallion hounds. One can see that Cooper and Gillard would have benefited in no small measure from these gratuities.

From the English hunting fraternity the praise given to the 'Belvoir type' went virtually unquestioned, at least in public, until the early part of the 20th century. Subsequently one can now recognise how the momentum gathered which allowed the 'Belvoir type' dominance over the hound breeding policies of so many Hunts. And one might also tentatively suggest that this is a lesson with which today's, and future breeders of the 'modern English' Foxhound should acquaint themselves.

The links between the Belvoir and Brocklesby Hunts are the source for what became the 'old English' foxhound. A stallion hound from the Brocklesby, Dashwood, was first used at Belvoir in 1799.

However, the beginning of the 'old English' perhaps finds its identifiable source during the tenure of Will Goodall, the Belvoir's renowned huntsman from 1842 to 1859. It was he who obtained the notable stallion hound Brocklesby Rallywood 1843 from the Earl of Yarborough's kennel. Undoubtedly, it was the extensive use of Rallywood, and his immediate progeny, that

Belvoir Weaver, 1906 – type hunted by Ben Capell.

153

'Hound Exercise' by Sir Alfred Munnings, early 20th century.

laid the foundation for the development of the 'Belvoir type', and the creation of the 'old English' Foxhound. As such, Rallywood can virtually be described not only as the father of the 'old English' Foxhound, but also of the 'modern English' Foxhound, as both only exist because of the development of the 'Belvoir type'.

An exchange deal between huntsmen was arranged. The Brocklesby's Will Smith wanted to import the Belvoir Grappler 1843, and Will Goodall selected Rallywood in exchange, in spite of his having had a broken thigh. The exchange was never made, due to Will Smith's untimely death, and Grappler never left Belvoir. However, Will Smith junior succeeded at the Brocklesby, and renewed the negotiations, sending Rallywood to Belvoir in his ninth season, having already sired about a dozen litters.

In return, the Belvoir sent to the Brocklesby their Trouncer 1845, and later Raglan 1845, neither of which Smith particularly liked. These hounds appear to have been drafted from their home kennel relatively late in their lives. One can assume they were no longer capable of hunting with the pack, but were kept for stallion hound duties.

Brocklesby Rallywood 1843 was a grandson of Sir Richard Sutton's Ringwood, and they were said to be very similar to Brocklesby Ringwood, painted by Stubbs in 1792. Rallywood's pedigree also included Mr Osbaldeston's Furrier, a famous hound of Belvoir stock. Will Goodall was delighted with Rallywood as a stallion hound, and used him extensively.

Between 1847 and 1854 Rallywood sired 15 litters upon Belvoir bitches, a total of 35 entered Hounds. James Cooper succeeded Goodall as huntsman in 1859, having previously been Goodall's first whipper-in. During his 11 years as huntsman, Cooper pursued this line with great, one might suggest excessive, enthusiasm; by 1864 Rallywood was grand-sire to 43 litters, a total of 96 hounds being entered to the Belvoir pack from these litters. Up to the same year Rallywood's offspring also extended another two generations consisting of a further 136 Hounds entered from 60 litters.

Included in these figures are the offspring of Rallywood's most famous son, the aforementioned Belvoir Rallywood 1853, who himself sired 17 litters at Belvoir. This Rallywood was the pride and joy of Goodall's pack. The huntsman praised his hound's intelligence, character, conformation, and working abilities, especially his durability in being able to hunt a fox late in the afternoon with just as much vigour as earlier in the day. Goodall claims he passed all these attributes on to his progeny, although one must bear in mind that Goodall actually only bred and hunted three of the 17 litters sired by this Rallywood.

When Cooper was huntsman among the 30 litters entered to the Belvoir pack in 1863 and 1864 that contained the Brocklesby Rallywood's pedigree, both the sire and dam were related to him in 11 instances. In 1863 the Belvoir entry of 17 couple consisted of 16½ couple of 'Rallywood's' descendants. The following year 14½ couple from another entry of 17 couple were again descendants of Rallywood.

Rallywood was held in such high esteem that upon his demise in 1853 he was buried in the garden in front of the huntsman's house at the Belvoir Kennels. For many years a redcurrant tree blossomed over his remains that are now marked by a stone.

The extensive policy of inbreeding at this time is probably the reason why the overall conformation of the Belvoir pack began to alter. The large proportion of hounds within the pack related to Rallywood will have compounded the matter. It appears that Rallywood's pedigree was held sacrosanct above all others. Could it be that sheer blind enthusiasm for this one blood-line created a mistake from which there was no turning back? Whatever the reason, whether knowingly or unwittingly, the foundations for the 'Belvoir type' and the 'old English' Foxhound, and the subsequent development of the 'modern English', had been well and truly laid down.

By the time Frank Gillard took over from Cooper as huntsman in 1870, with the 6th Duke continuing as Master, the change in hound conformation must have been well underway. For reasons that are very difficult to discover or understand, both the 6th Duke and Gillard appear to have been determined upon breeding hounds of great substance.

The aforementioned Belvoir Gambler 1884 should serve as proof of their on-going policy. Gambler was born mid-way through Gillard's time as huntsman. Gambler's sire, Belvoir Weathergauge 1876 was bred six seasons after Gillard became huntsman, and he considered this hound to be one of his prized stallion hounds. One must assume that by this time the 6th Duke and Gillard would have determined upon the qualities they wished to see enhanced within the pack.

As remarked above, history is written by the victors, and Belvoir history during Gillard's time was written by the huntsman himself. No matter how late he returned to kennels, Gillard wrote the reports of his pack's achievements in the hunting field, and passed them to the 6th Duke. Nor was Gillard afraid to offer his opinions regarding the quality of his hounds when asked by correspondents and authors. Cuthbert Bradley's book, *Hunting Reminiscences of Frank Gillard* is a wonderful read, and no doubt it is testimony that the hunting community held Gillard in extremely high regard.

The importance of good, athletic conformation cannot be overstated, however one thing is certain: the handling of a pack by a huntsman is the key factor in making them perform well in the hunting field. Hounds will come to reflect their huntsman's character, and if the huntsman is skilled enough, the most extraordinarily mixed pack will achieve good sport for the followers to enjoy.

It is worth remembering that the pressures upon huntsmen in the Shires to 'get forward', and 'be quick', are generally considerably greater than other hunting countries. Under such pressure it is easy for a huntsman to forget that a confident pack of hounds with drive and determination to be about their business, will always be quicker than a man on a horse. Unless, of course, the huntsman is a genius, and there are precious few that achieve such acclaim.

During Gillard's final years as Belvoir huntsman, and for the next couple of decades into the 20th century, the Belvoir Hounds were increasingly criticised on their durability, and this coincided with a backlash against the 'Belvoir type', and an increasing pressure to seek improvements in the conformation of the Hounds.

The most famous advocate of using Welsh crosses in English hounds was the American Master, Mr Ikey Bell. Mr Bell introduced blood into his Kilkenny pack from the white hounds of the Curre pack, bred by Sir Edward Curre at Itton, Montgomeryshire from 1896-1930. These hounds were lighter framed, and more athletic than the Belvoir type, and won praise for their 'fox sense', their ability to use their own intelligence in finding a fox, and their concentration in sticking to his line, with less reliance on direction from the huntsman.

As the years progressed more packs sought out-crosses to improve the conformation of their hounds. This ensured that the Foxhound breeding pendulum began to swing away from the 'Belvoir type' which we can now refer to as the 'old English' Foxhounds.

Unfortunately, some of the advocates of the new breeding policies were particularly scathing, and publicly so, in their criticism of the 'old English'. In return the traditionalists blamed the modernists for 'ruining the English Foxhound'!

Despite this, other packs continued to draw upon the Belvoir pedigrees and the Belvoir's Puppy Show continued to be well supported by Masters and Huntsmen. One must, therefore, ask: *why?*

As indicated earlier, Masters and huntsmen were drawn to the 'Belvoir type' when this was fashionable. However, it should be emphasised that the 'old English' Hounds, and the Belvoir pack particularly, possess historic qualities that every pack should seek to maintain: they are tough and hardy; they possess drive as a pack and can maintain an exhausting momentum; they think and operate as a team; they are persistent and determined in their work; they display a particular talent for sticking to a fox to the exclusion of all others, whilst not permitting any obstacle to stand between them and their quarry; and they rarely leave much evidence of their fox after they have caught him.

Visiting judges, Mr Jonathon Seed MFH Avon Vale, and Mr Richard Tyacke MFH, Sir Watkin Williams-Wynns with hounds shown by George Grant.

At Belvoir the policy through the 20th century was consistently aimed at maintaining the 'old English'. This did not mean there was no opportunity to redress some of the conformation issues that befell the 'Belvoir type'. On the contrary, there was plenty of opportunity to breed a lighter type of hound by careful selection from within the restricted gene pool. Beginning with Major Tommy Bouch, who was Master from 1912-24, this has been achieved by various Masters and huntsmen, although Bouch was firmly forbidden to engage in outcrosses. Major Bouch hunted non-Belvoir type hounds on the Lincolnshire side, but these were his own small pack that he brought into the kennel for this purpose.

Despite all the controversy, Foxhounds are bred for work, and the truth is that Belvoir blood is in the breeding of a great many of the kennels throughout the British Isles, and the working qualities of the Belvoir hounds have played a great part in ensuring sport in all sorts of conditions in widely varied hunting countries.

When Lord (Toby) Daresbury, Master of the Belvoir from 1934-1947, took Belvoir-bred hounds to form a new pack in County Limerick immediately after the second world war, these hounds were faced with hunting the fox over a big bank and ditch country. It was an extremely different environment to the Leicestershire and Nottinghamshire terrain of the Vale of Belvoir, the Wolds surrounding Melton Mowbray and Grantham, and sloping down to the fenland deeper into Lincolnshire. The Co. Limerick

The whole pack shown to spectators after the 1992 Puppy Show.

pack, bred entirely on Belvoir lines, excelled in their new surroundings, and have produced tremendous sport for generations of followers ever since.

The enthusiasm demonstrated by Lord Daresbury, and subsequently the Earl of Harrington as Master, and the huntsman Hugh Robards at the Co. Limerick, for the 'old English' Foxhounds contributed to a much higher proportion of Irish Hunts maintaining this type of hound than in the United Kingdom. Of the 38 registered Foxhound packs in Ireland, six maintain either exclusively or in part the 'old English'. Whereas, of the 196 registered packs in England, Wales and Scotland only seven have remained faithful to the 'old English'. Without the ongoing enthusiasm among the latter packs, the gene pool for the 'old English' would be dangerously small. Foremost amongst the current Irish supporters is Graham Bustin; his reputation as a huntsman was made hunting the 'old English' at the Waterford, and he was to become huntsman to the Co. Limerick on 1 May 2010.

In recent times the Belvoir was fortunate to secure the services of Martin Thornton as huntsman. A strong Mastership initially consisting of Messrs. Joey Newton, Steve Taylor, John Martin, and Mrs Tor Owen, ran an efficient and highly-professional establishment. Although Thornton was already an experienced huntsman, having previously hunted three packs of 'modern English' Hounds, he still had a hard act to follow: Robin Jackson had shown great sport for nine seasons up to 1992. Thornton retired in 2006, and many will recognise that he firmly established his reputation as one of the foremost and naturally gifted huntsmen of the modern era. What many will not appreciate is that, with the guidance and support of Mrs Owen, Thornton achieved more for the reputation of the Belvoir Hounds than probably any other huntsman in the previous 100 years. Mrs Owen and Thornton achieved a number of things that many people would probably have thought impossible.

The 'old English' Hounds have always held a reputation for being somewhat tough to handle in the field and in the kennel. It is especially important in this day and age that all hounds are 'people friendly', that they are relaxed and can be relied upon not to misbe-

Mr Robert Henson MFH, Prince Charles and Lord (Toby) Daresbury at the Kennels, when they judged the 1980 young entry.

Martin Thornton showing hounds at The Great Yorkshire Show, 1995. It was the first time the Belvoir showed at a Hound Show.

The Belvoir

have either in the kennels or especially when in the public domain. During his 14 seasons at Belvoir, Thornton can rightly claim to have bred the most biddable and professional pack that can be recalled in living memory whilst enhancing their ability to hunt and catch foxes in style.

Both Mrs Owen and Thornton, with the enthusiastic support of the other Masters, and later Bill Bishop when he became Joint Master, recognised the ongoing need to try to improve the overall conformation of the pack. With a limited gene pool to choose from, and the need to protect the traditional Kennel lines, this was never going to be an easy task. However, they quickly appreciated that, other than the bloodlines common between the Belvoir and Co. Limerick, there was a relative abundance of untapped 'old English' bloodlines in Ireland. Lines of communication were soon opened with the Masters and Huntsmen of these Irish packs.

Without neglecting the established links from Belvoir with the Co. Limerick, Brocklesby and Wynnstay, in 1994 Belvoir Tackle 1991 was covered by Waterford Primate 1988. Subsequently, Belvoir bitches were covered by doghounds from the Waterford, Muskerry, Louth and Duhallow.

As a consequence of diligently selecting the bitches and doghounds from which to breed, there was an almost immediate improvement to the pack's general conformation. By 2006 Thornton handed on to his successor, who can recall the Belvoir Hounds from 30 years previously, an 'Old English'

Mr Rupert Inglesant MFH enjoying his hounds – in the snow.

Martin Thornton shows young hounds at 1992 Puppy Show.

pack that in general terms and without losing its distinctive type, was considerably more athletic than he could ever have anticipated; much lighter of bone, displaying improved sloping shoulders, and less crooked in the leg.

These rapid and positive developments were recognised not only by the Masters and huntsmen of the 'old English' packs, but also by a small number of very discerning breeders of the 'modern English' hound.

The great reputation of the late Capt. Ronnie Wallace as a hound breeder is fully recognised by the hunting world. What is less well known, is that Wallace, whose reputation is synonymous with great post-1945 improvements of the 'modern English', recognised the importance in breeding, of the need occasionally and diligently to cast back. It is likely this lesson was not lost upon one of his successors as Master of the Heythrop, Mr Richard Sumner, when he approached the Belvoir to use Poacher 1998.

Poacher was drafted to Belvoir as an unentered hound, and as a result of Mrs Owen and Thornton's liaison with the 'old English' packs in Ireland. Poacher was a particularly well-made hound, by Muskerry Cricketer 1994, and out of Duhallow Pastime 1992.

One of the two resulting litters included the remarkably attractive Heythrop Poplin 2001 and she was selected Bitch Champion at Peterborough Royal Foxhound Show in 2003. This was a great triumph, not only for the Heythrop, but for the 'old English' Foxhound and its loyal supporters. The triumph was capped by both litters proving themselves on the hunting field, and three subsequent litters being entered with the Heythrop.

It will be interesting to see if any other reputable 'modern English' breeders will be brave enough to heed Capt Wallace's advice and follow Richard Sumner's example.

Perhaps the most difficult challenge Mrs Owen and Thornton had to face was the threat and impact of the Hunting Act

The Belvoir

2004. Motivated by social politics, this Act of Parliament posed a massive threat to hunting in all its forms. Consequently and specifically it posed a dreadful threat to the very existence of the Foxhound as a breed.

Hunting has managed to continue, albeit with a dark cloud hanging over the sport. However, it is difficult for hunt supporters to fully appreciate the degree of stress and worry that every huntsman was put through in 2004 and 2005. Thankfully, the worst case scenario has not yet materialised, and with luck the Hunting Act may yet be consigned to the waste paper bin.

The priority for Mrs Owen and Thornton was to protect the precious Belvoir lines. In order to achieve this, their only option was to draft hounds abroad and many went to Ireland. This may seem a harmless process, but they were effectively dismantling 250 years of living history. To hunt any pack of hounds is to be part of a team, the majority of whom cannot talk, but they always communicate.

Hounds consistently and regularly demonstrate a degree of loyalty to and hard work for their Huntsman that is incomparable with any situation in the modern world. It is a relationship that is beyond explanation in words. For Thornton it must have been an extremely emotional and distressing task to plan and carry out.

Thankfully, the pack and its heritage did not need to be completely dismantled. Although Thornton handed over to his successor a reduced pack, it retained bitches from two vitally important tail-female lines. Both lines can be traced back from dam to dam in unbroken succession as part of the Belvoir pack for in excess of 200 years.

The first and most important of these two tail-female lines began with Fanny 1793, by Mr Musters' Freeman, and out of Tresspass. Unfortunately, the Hound breeding records detailing the period 1781-1791 were lost, and it is impossible to ascertain a year of entry and to confirm that Tresspass was bred at Belvoir. If this were the case, it is likely that this line extends back even further to when the Dukes of Rutland first maintained a pack at Belvoir in order to hunt foxes. The second line began with Trinket 1801, by Lord Fitzwilliam's Traitor and out of his Destiny.

In conclusion, I should try to answer a question put to me by quite a number of people: What is it like to be huntsman of a pack of 'Old English' Foxhounds?

Well, to begin with I'm not the huntsman of a pack of *'Old English'* Foxhounds, I am the huntsman of the Duke of Rutland's Hounds; at least that is what the hounds told me, repeatedly, over the course of my first few weeks at Belvoir.

Beyond this, it is awesome; nerve-wracking; thrilling; scary; a pleasure; a nightmare; a freedom; a burden; contentment; frustrating; breath-taking; heart-rending; but above all, a massive honour and the greatest privilege.

CHAPTER 13

Supporters All

They set about organising events…

Fund-raising and fun: on both counts the Belvoir Hunt Supporters' Club has been a success since it was formed in the summer of July 1967.

In 2010, under its energetic chairman for the past decade, Mr Foster Edwards, the Club continued to play a vital role in enabling many people to become involved in the Hunt, strengthening the hunting community throughout the Belvoir country.

The 1967-68 season was to be spoilt by a severe outbreak of foot and mouth disease, causing a drop in Hunt incomes. It could not have been a better time to start a Supporters' Club, and a number of Belvoir followers thought it was worth trying.

The Belvoir Hunt Supporters' Club was launched in July 1967 with what amounted to the first ever Kennels Open Day, brought about by the Hunt Secretary, Brig. Tubby Cooper who was keen to see the Club succeed. The Open Day proved a great success, and some 175 members were enrolled.

There was also a horse show in the summer of 1967 at Easton Park, thanks to Sir Monty and Lady Cholmeley, followed by a supper dance at Marco's night club in Grantham, which was equally successful.

An inaugural BHSC meeting was held on 3 August at the George Hotel, Grantham, with former Joint Master Col. James Hanbury in the chair. Approval for starting the club came from the Master, John King, later Lord King, who consented to be the first President.

Brig. Cooper said the Hunt Committee would give a £50 loan to launch the new Club. This proved the best investment the Committee ever made, financially and in maintaining enthusiastic support throughout the country.

The £50 was repaid well before the first Annual General Meeting of the Club a year later, in July 1968, and ever since BHSC has made increasing donations to the Hunt. This was welcome from the start, but nowadays an annual contribution from a supporters' club is vital to the existence of virtually every British pack.

At the end of the first year the membership had soared to 540, and the bank balance was £82.63 shillings. BHSC was founded with a 'subscription for life' of only £2. Thirty years later subscriptions had only risen to £5 per person annually, with a £45 Life Membership, and by 2010 the sub was £10 a year, or £20 for family membership (two adults and children under

BHSC Chairman 1969-83, the Rev. John Ashley, Rector of Woolsthorpe-by-Belvoir, a true sporting parson who adored his hunting.

16), still a bargain for an annual programme of events providing entertainment for people throughout the hunting country, and raising funds for the Hunt.

The Club's first chairman was Mr Frank Kirk; vice-chairman, Mr John Grubb; Hon. Secretary, Mrs Wildman, the first Hon. Treasurer was Mr John Baggaley, but succeeded in a year by Mr John Moore; Mr J.E.P. Knight was elected as Liaison Officer.

The first committee represented four areas of the hunting country: Tuesday country – Mr J. Rowe, Mr G. Wilde, Mr G. Baines; Wednesday – Mrs J. Webster, Mr S. Manchester, Mr W. Skelton, Mr E. Stannage; Friday – Miss J. Gathercole, Mrs E. Sly, Mrs A. Musson; Saturday – Mr P. Hornbuckle, Mr J. Clayton, Mr S. Spence.

They set about organising events throughout the hunting year which became the foundation of today's Supporters' Club: whist drives, cricket matches, Belton Show, dinners and dances, and much was made of the Vale tradition of a skittles week at Croxton Kerrial during November.

Apologies to the many who contributed so much to the success of the Club who cannot be mentioned in these pages through lack of space, but officials of the Supporters' Club are listed in Appendix III.

At a meeting in October 1968 the committee discussed whether marshals should be on duty on Wednesdays and Saturdays to help organise the many car followers who were welcome, but could block country lanes for other road users, and perhaps head foxes on roads. It was decided tactfully that

Supporters All

John Moore, who gave tremendous services to the Club for about 25 years. At the Long Clawson meet in 1970 John Moore handed over the keys of the Land Rover to John King watched by a large crowd of BHSC members. Mr Moore said that in three years the Club had collected over £1,200.

At the 1971 annual meeting, John King said their accounts, showing a surplus of £718.82 on the year, were 'a credit to the Belvoir Hunt and the whole community. It has been a tremendous help, and a fine example of what a Supporters' Club should be.'

Major Peter Postlethwaite, Hon. Sec. 1983–88

each committee member should help in a rota to 'give advice and help' to car followers to get the best fun from the day's sport.

On 31 October 1970 the Supporters' Club presented their first major gift to the Hunt – a new Land Rover. The Hon. Treasurer and vice-chairman since 1968 was Mr

Mr Foster Edwards, BHSC Chairman since 2000.

The Belvoir

The Supporters' Club was fortunate when the Belvoir's highly popular hunting parson, the Rev. John Ashley, Rector of Woolsthorpe, took over as chairman in 1969. At the '71 annual meeting he called for fresh ideas for fund-raising, but he told members that promoting goodwill was just as important as raising money. At that meeting Mr Baines was elected vice-chairman and Mr Moore re-appointed as treasurer.

At the Club's annual meeting two years later, in 1973, the Rev. Mr Ashley warned of 'a threat hanging over our sport' from future governments. He urged an increase in membership, and called for car followers of the Belvoir to be 'a little less enthusiastic'.

He declared, 'The support of the Belvoir hounds is very good, but it is sometimes spoiled by the over-enthusiasm of car followers. If you could help other people to restrain their enthusiasm, the Master would be very pleased because it makes for sport for all. We are depending on you to discipline the Hunt followers.'

At the '82 meeting BHSC members heard with regret of the resignation of their President for the past ten years, Mrs Ann Reid Scott. She offered to the Club a trophy for annual competition in whatever manner they chose.

Unanimously elected as the new President was Joint Master Mr Nicholas Playne. A hunter trial was started at Mr Playne's home, Aswarby Park, run at first by Graham Daws and then handed over to Martin Hills. The event continued until 1987.

Hound sponsorship day in 2008.

BHSC Open Day at the Hunt Kennels 2009.

In 1983, the Rev. Mr Ashley announced his retirement as BHSC chairman, after 15 years in office, and was warmly praised by the President, Mr Playne, who said the hunting parson had worked very hard for the club in a quiet unassuming manner which everyone had appreciated. Rev. Ashley died in December 2010 aged 82.

He also thanked the vice-chairman, Mr Steven Manchester, who was also retiring. Lady Sally Cholmeley was elected the new Chairman, with Dr Graham Dawes as Vice-Chairman; John Moore continued as Treasurer, and Mrs Margaret Palmer as Secretary.

John Moore reported they had purchased land and equipment worth £15,000, part of a total of £24,000 raised in the Club's 16 years. They had recently bought a winch for the Hunt's flesh cart.

The Hunt continued to make useful contributions during the 1980s. At the 1986 annual meeting the Club reported a profit of £3,970.

In 1987 a major new annual attraction was the first Belvoir Team Event, which was to become one of the premier team 'chases in Britain. This was organised under a separate fund-raising effort, called the Enterprise Committee, run by the Hunt Hon. Treasurer John Richardson. It was set up at the instigation of Lord King to raise money, but not to clash with the activities of the Supporters' Club.

It was a daunting prospect to build two separate courses on Richard Chandler's Canal

The Belvoir

Farm at Long Clawson, but it turned out to be more of a pleasure than a big challenge due to Richard's enthusiasm, expertise and support. The initial courses were built by Richard, Geoff Perfect, Graham Daws and Keith Adlam all to eventing standards of safety.

The original committee was chaired by Tony Fenwick who was succeeded by Michael Bell, Robert Henson, Simon Brodie and David Selby. Graham Daws took on the organiser's role after Guy Wathen moved away to Norfolk and he was succeeded by Debbie Nicholls and then Simon Brodie before David Selby took control in 2007. David was still the chairman and organiser in 2010.

After the 2003 event Richard reluctantly decided that a change of farming policy was needed and so the event moved to Garthorpe after 15 years. Richard gave plenty of notice of this and consequently three separate course were built from scratch at Garthorpe by David Selby, Graham Daws, Richard Chandler and Martyn Carter, all of whom are still involved with course upgrading at the site.

Another successful riding venture associated with the Hunt has been Buckminster Park Horse Trials, initiated by Miles

Open Day 2004 with Martin Thornton and hound admirers.

Team Chase at Garthorpe.

Mr John Martin, Hunt Chairman since 2005.

Howard in 1989 as an affiliated event to the British Horse Society, now British Eventing. From 1991 the event was run to raise funds for the Belvoir Hunt Supporters' Club, with Jane Clarke (nee Tucker) as organiser. Graham Daws succeeded as organiser from 1995 to 2000 when the event moved away from BHSC control, although Graham continued as cross-country controller.

In 1988 Lady Cholmeley said at the annual meeting the BHSC had provided money for planting a four acre covert at Waltham, since known as 'Greenall's', in memory of former Master, the late Lord (Toby) Daresbury, on land owned by his daughter-in-law, the Hon. Mrs Greenall. Other projects included extra stabling at the Hunt Kennels, to be used as isolation boxes, and re-concreting of the hound yards.

Tom Hudson succeeded as BHSC chairman in 1989 from Lady Cholmeley who had served six years. Formerly the Hunt Secretary (1970-81) Tom was increasingly busy as a commentator at county shows

The Belvoir

Mrs Tor Owen, Joint Master 1990–99 and Chairman 2000–5.

The first issue gives a fascinating 'snapshot' of the Hunt at that time. Charles, the 10th Duke of Rutland wrote the Foreword in which he stated:

'I am immensely proud of my hounds. They are as much a part of Belvoir and Belvoir tradition as the castle itself. That is why I am so anxious to ensure that the breeding policy should follow our traditional lines of distinctive colour and conformation. These undoubtedly have evolved over the 200 years the pack has been in existence. Soon after the first war one of the Hunt Masters tried to introduce an element of white Welsh hound breeding into the breeding. This caused great offence to the Duke and was immediately changed.

My family has always taken pleasure in collecting works of art, including many sporting pictures. We are fortunate at Belvoir to have many pictures of the hounds, huntsmen and horses painted by famous artists, such as Ferneley, who as a young man used to paint the farm carts on the estate.

These pictures hang in the Castle, and are a frequent reminder of the Belvoir Hunt, and are part of our heritage. Also we have a remarkable collection of hunt diaries covering a period of over 100 years, up to the start of the last war.

These describe every day's hunting, written by the huntsmen at the end of each day. They show only too clearly that the tradition and sport is still, today, very much the same, hunting the same country with many familiar names of meets and coverts. Foxhunting today is a popular sport giving great pleasure to people from all walks of

and national and international horse shows, including London's annual Christmas show at Olympia. One of the initiatives during Tom Hudson's chairmanship was the launch of the Hunt magazine *Belvoir Tan*, first published in the 1990-91 season, with Debbie Nicholls as Editor.

Mr Tom Hudson, BHSC Chairman, 1984–99

life, as well as farmers and those who live in the country.

I am pleased that my hounds have such a high reputation, for speed and sport, and that our Hunt staff and Masters have an equally high reputation. Field sports and foxhunting are part of our British way of life, and I truly believe have had some influence in the formation of our character.'

We learn in the first issue that the Belvoir team won the Lincolnshire Show Inter-Hunt relay challenge trophy for the second year running, the team comprising whipper-in John Holliday on his wife's horse, Sarah Lanni on her brother Matthew's horse, and Tim Brown who 'borrowed' a likely prospect from his own yard.

The first issue of *Belvoir Tan* reported a record 89 teams having taken part in the 1990 Belvoir Hunt Team Chase, with the Odds and Sods team emerging as victors. Richard Chandler, the host, rode with the Boring Gorings to come fifth.

Richard is also reported in this issue as having made a three day trek to Czechoslovakia to take part in the awesome Velka Pardubicka steeplechase. He drove for three days to Pardubice in his horse box, carrying his mount Red Cheval. In the race he managed to clear the infamous Taxis fence, but his horse refused three fences later, and he had to pull up. He was planning to have a second crack at the race on a different horse, Clonroche Stream.

The fine sport the Belvoir was enjoying at that time is well represented in *Belvoir Tan*, including Foxford's report from *Horse and Hound* on the 18 miles marathon run achieved by the hounds, hunted by Robin Jackson, after their meet at Plungar on 2 December.

Lord King, Hunt Chairman, made a presentation to James Knight who had retired after seven seasons in charge of the Friday country in Lincolnshire where he had been universally popular.

Chairman Tom Hudson made presentations at the 1993 annual meeting to John Moore who was retiring as treasurer after tremendous service virtually since the Club was formed, and to Arthur Birch, the Belvoir's fence repair man, 'a fantastic diplomat' who was also retiring. Andrew Gibson was elected the new treasurer, with Richard Snodin as vice-chairman, and Margaret Palmer, secretary.

Later reports of the Supporters' Club in the 1990s include praise from Tom Hudson for the work of Graham Daws and his sub-committee in running Buckminster Horse Trials, which was an excellent money-

The Belvoir

Mr David Faulkner, Hon. Sec. 1981–83

raiser. The Country Fair, which took over from the 'Open Day' proved to be successful. From 1998 *Belvoir Tan* was under the editorship of Foster Edwards, who with his wife Jackie, had run Easton Park Show with much success. Foster, then manager of Belvoir Fruit Farm, is a lifelong hunting enthusiast, and in 1999 succeeded Tom Hudson as Supporters' Club chairman.

By 2002 the Club was contributing £10,000 to the Hunt, and continued making increased contributions. The Belvoir Hunt Supporters' Club, like all others, is an integral part of the Hunt's budget, and its social calendar. Under Foster Edwards, the Supporters' Club was contributing some £20,000 per year to the Hunt when it was so much needed, before and after the 2005 Hunting Act. Foster formed a strong team, with Nina Camm as Secretary.

The outbreak of the dreaded Foot and Mouth disease in 2001, and the Hunting Ban in 2005, were times of crisis for the Hunt. On both occasions, members of the Hunt rallied to help by their generous support of two auctions which raised very considerable amounts of money for Hunt funds.

The annual BHSC Open Day at the kennels has been organised in recent years by Nina Camm and Judy Glossop. They have revamped the event which now attracts up to

Mr Tim Hall-Wilson, Hon. Secretary of the Belvoir 1988–96.

Mrs 'Bambi' Hornbuckle, Hon. Sec. since 1996.

The Belvoir

A presentation in 2000 to the retiring Chairman, Lord King (centre), by the Duke of Rutland, with new chairman, Mrs Owen.

2,000 visitors, including dignitaries from the local councils. As well as being a significant fund-raising event, the Open Day promotes the image of the Belvoir Hunt in the area and beyond.

BELVOIR HEDGE-LAYING

Foxhunting in Leicestershire has for over 300 years been a major influence on the county's beautiful terrain of sweeping pastures broken by cut and laid hedges, and dotted with fox coverts. The Hunts have encouraged the planting of coverts where foxes live, and laying hedges by hand, all of which gave the landscape its special character – and of course the hedges have long been cherished by foxhunters as exciting obstacles to jump during a hunt.

Another special Shires feature is 'ridge and furrow', a rolling expanse of undulations in a pasture. It derives from ancient forms of village agriculture where drainage was created by permanent furrows between lines of hand-sown crops. It is still to be found in some parts of the Belvoir country, usually near villages.

The Belvoir encourages the traditional rural craft of hedge-laying through

Millennium 2000 line-up of Belvoir Masters, huntsmen and staff past and present :
Front – l. to r. Mr Charles Harrison, Mr John Parry, Mrs Ann Reid Scott, Maj.Gen. Sir Brian Wyldebore-Smith, Lord King, Duke of Rutland, Mr John Blakeway, Mr Robert Henson, Mrs Marjorie Comerford.
Centre – l. to r. Mr James Knight, Mr Bill Bishop, Mr Keith Hollingworth, Mr Steve Taylor, Mr Richard Morley, Mr Nick Turner, Jim Webster, Mr Nicholas Playne, Bill Lander, Mrs Barry Owen, Mr John Martin, Mr Joey Newton and Mr James Henderson.
Top – l. to r. Michael Little, Keith Challenge, Richard Markham, Martin Thornton, George Grant and Julian Brewitt

The Belvoir

annual competitions. Tom Kingston of Long Clawson took over as organiser in 2005 from Stuart Buntine, with help from Roger Chatterton, Conrad Underwood, Paul Palmer and Andrew Miller.

The Belvoir runs a one-day contest in November where competitors each lay a ten yard section of the same hedge over about four hours.

In March they judge an on-farm competition in which farmers and landowners are invited to enter a hedge laid in the last season. Both are sponsored by local businesses and individuals.

The 2009 open hedge-laying competition was won by Rob Thompston for the second year running, out of a strong field of ten competitors producing a high standard of work on a fair hedge. The best Belvoir competitor was Chris Smith who came third. The novice class was won by Paul Crothers on a challenging hedge.

Cut and laid hedges, and strategically planted coverts, are an example of practical conservation. They offer habitat for all sorts of mammal as well as foxes, and they are a haven for valuable insect life.

It is one of the key examples of hunting's contribution to the quality of life in our countryside.

Brig. T.G.G. (Tubby) Coooper, Hon Sec. 1957–70.

Belvoir Pony Club member Jessica Newton tackles a strong fence with style in the hunting field.

CHAPTER 14

Point-to-Point

A great tradition of colourful racing...

How many people attending the Belvoir's annual point-to-point are aware of the Hunt's long and colourful role in helping to create the sport of steeplechasing, long before it became established at Garthorpe?

During the early 19th century the Belvoir country saw some of the earliest organised 'chase meetings'.

In 1811, the 5th Duke of Rutland approved an annual race meeting on the Belvoir estate at Croxton Park where the family had a hunting lodge, built early in the previous century by the third Duke.

Croxton Park Races remained a permanent fixture for flat and jumping races in the local sporting calendar until the outbreak of the Great War in 1914, but it was not revived after the war.

Quite separately from Croxton, other races were taking place in the country on the Lincolnshire side. A race was run over natural country, parallel with the old North Road, at the foot of Gonerby Hill, back in the 1860s. The course ran about four miles, starting below Foston, with riders making their own way up to Gonerby.

According to the *Random Recollections*, 'the course was flagged, a real stiff one, with rough wild fences and two natural brooks, and demanded bold and big jumpers.' The winner was the owner-rider Tom Walker on his grey gelding Peter Simple, bred in Lincolnshire by Arbutus.

The Belvoir country's reputation for hard-riding was just as evident in its thrilling cross-country races as in the hunting field.

A subsequent race recalled in the *Random Recollections* started below Barrowby Toll-bar, running on the right of the Nottingham turnpike nearly to Sedgebrook, where the riders bore left to cross the road, and returned in a four mile line to finish within a couple of fields of Barrowby Church.

In the 1870s a more formal race meeting was held for several years from Harrowby, on a course just east of Grantham, all now enveloped by the town. Mr W.R. Brockton was successful on this course with a difficult horse called Berserker who went on to win about 20 races.

Through lack of support these races were abandoned, but in 1884 they were revived as the Belvoir Hunt Steeplechases, held between Lenton and Ingoldsby, and instigated by a keen hunting man, Mr Burdett Coutts. This was the birth of the annual meeting which became the Belvoir Point-to-point of today.

The Rev. Thomas Heathcote, vicar at Lenton Parish Church was a hard-riding

The Belvoir

This picture in the Duke's Room at the Hunt Kennels shows 'Miss Mutter, daughter of Mr 'Berty' Mutter, the Agent at Aswarby, in a ladies' race at the Belvoir Point-to-point held at Lenton Pastures, at about 1921.'
Miss Mutter is presumed to be in front.

Belvoir follower. In 1875 he was seeking to restore the spire of this Church, and asked the Duke of Rutland for a subscription.

'Why should I subscribe to a church that is not on my property?' asked the 6th Duke.

'Because it is such a good landmark when your hounds run,' replied the foxhunting parson. The Duke promptly sent £5 towards the restoration of the spire.

The Belvoir steeplechase meeting was established over the stretch of grass country below Lenton Vicarage, just a year after Mr Heathcote's death, flourishing for the next 20 years, and owing much of its management to the Vicar's eldest surviving son, Mr Thomas A.R. Heathcote. The race card for the 1888 meeting at Ingoldsby was reproduced in the Belvoir point-to-point race card one hundred years later.

The Belvoir Hunt Steeplechases card for Thursday 16 March 1899 says they were run 'under National Hunt Rules'. Mr Thomas Heathcote was named as Hon. Secretary, Clerk of the Course and Stakeholder at meetings in the 1880s.

In 1908 the Belvoir Steeplechases moved back to Harrowby after a gap of 34 years, remaining there until the outbreak of the Great War in 1914.

After the war, the annual Hunt races resumed at a new course at Barrowby, west of Grantham, and became a highly popular sporting event during the inter-wars years.

The most famous record of racing at Barrowby is Sir Alfred Munnings' painting which he achieved during a stay with the Belvoir's Master, Major Tommy Bouch, during the 1919-20 season. Edward Prince of Wales was a keen amateur race rider, and the Belvoir meeting was among those where he competed.

In 1925 the Prince of Wales presented to the Belvoir meeting a silver cup to the winner of what was probably the equivalent of the modern Gentleman's Open Race. Nowadays it is presented to the leading rider at each meeting.

Mrs Ann Reid Scott recalls that among Belvoir owner-riders between the wars were Brig. General George Paynter of Eaton, Lt.Col. Peter Payne Gallwey of Knipton, Capt. W.F. (Tim) Player, and Lt.Col. J.D. (Donnie) Player, the Hon. Mrs Edward (Joyce) Greenall, Mr Tom Clamp of Stathern, and Miss Meriel Atkinson, daughter of a hunting doctor of Long Clawson.

Point-to-point secretary for much of the inter-war period was Col. R.C. (Bobby)

Swan of Barrowby Grange.

The Barrowby course offered good viewing, but it had a disadvantage in that it ran over the road which nowadays has become upgraded to the A52, the main road to Nottingham from Grantham. They closed the road for each race throughout the years at Barrowby, but by 1933 this was no longer acceptable to the authorities, and the meeting had to move yet again.

This time it was placed in the cream of the Leicestershire country, at Long Clawson, taking place above the village, on the fields between Waltham Lane and Pasture Lane, below Brock Hill; a permanent reminder is Mr Andrew Parker's 'Racecourse Farm'. The helpers who prepared the course were able to take local trains from Grantham to Long Clawson for a fare of 4s.6d. return. The 1939 point-to-point took place, but the war halted further meetings.

Hon. Secretary of the Long Clawson meetings was Lt.Col. R.W. Newton of Barrowby Old Hall, first cousin of Lance Newton who was to play a major role in point-to-pointing after the war.

The point-to-point made yet another move when it was resumed on 3 May 1947, having been postponed due to late snowfalls that winter.

The fixture had returned from 1947 to Lincolnshire, at Manthorpe, by the Lincoln road, just north of Grantham, with Col. Newton in charge, assisted by Mr Moore and Mr Newcome. The meeting benefited from easy access to the growing town, and surrounding villages.

At the 1948 meeting at Manthorpe, on 10 April, the paddock posts cost one shilling each, paint for the stand cost 6s.6d. white and 3s.8d black; Bill Benson provided the weighing scales.

Racing continued at Manthorpe until 1950, but local developments forced another move. The former racecourse is now partly covered by the golf course belonging to Belton Woods Hotel.

At the final Manthorpe meeting, in

Another stunning picture of ladies' side-saddle point-to-pointing in the Belvoir meeting at Lenton circa 1921.

Above: Spectators on wagon at 1926 Belvoir Point-to-Point. Bespectacled in foreground left is Joint Master Charles Tonge.

'Belvoir Point-to-Point at Barrowby Hill', 1924 by Sir Alfred Munnings. The scene to the left of the present A52 road, looking towards Sedgebrook and Bottesford.

Edward, Prince of Wales, at the 1926 Belvoir Point-to-Point at Barrowby, riding Park Courtier.

Point—to—Point

Prince of Wales upsides Mr E. Stokes in the Nomination Race, Belvoir Point-to-Point 1926.

Mr E. Stokes on Kind Knight winning the Nomination Race, with the Prince of Wales a distance behind.

1954, the winner of the last on the card, the Royal Horse Artillery race, was Lt.Col. Frank Weldon, later director of Badminton Horse Trials. He won the race on his highly versatile mount Kilbarry who became a top-class event horse.

The Belvoir Point-to-point Committee, with Lt.Col. F.E Bowlby as Chairman, and Lance Newton as Hon. Secretary, negotiated with the Buckminster Estate to move the fixture to Garthorpe, near Melton Mowbray, where it proved successful from the first. Clerk of the Course was Mr J.H. Moore, and members of the Point-to-Point committee were: Lt.Col. James Hanbury MFH, Mr R.L. Black, Lt.Col. W.E.H. Garner, Major F.H. Horton, Capt. H. Garner Bellamy, and Mr Wilson Newcome.

Lance Newton had begun farming the land at Garthorpe, which is part of the Buckminster Estate, and he and the farmer and race rider Dick Black decided it would make a marvellous course.

Libby Gilman, writing a history of Garthorpe for the Point-to-point Festival there, in 1994, looked back to the Belvoir's first meeting when 'tents were used for changing rooms, the first aid room and weighing room. There were no running rails, judges' or commentary box. John Berry, later Clerk of the Course, and Bill Pell, later the Timekeeper, were in charge of a primitive number board consisting of a blackboard, easel and chalk. The scales, in use for many years, came from Birmingham racecourse.

'The basic layout of the course has changed little since its creation, although the open ditch has had three moves.'

Libby recalled that in those early days, problems included 'car park dodgers at the Belvoir meeting, which necessitated 'No Car

The Belvoir

Scots Guards and Irish Guards Challenge Cup Race, Belvoir Point-to-Point, Barrowby, 1926.

Parking' signs being put up off the course; there were never enough ladies' loos, horses were always late into the paddock, and Claude Manchester and Jimmy Elwell had problems exterminating the moles.'

Some of the same names appearing at the 1955 meetings were still to be found on officials' lists in the 1990s and into the 21st century: Gibsons as attending veterinary surgeons, George Slack as Assistant Starter, and Claude Manchester as Clerk of the Scales – a task his son, Ian Manchester took over in the 1970s and continued until the 2010 meeting. Ken Botterill, another stalwart hunting farmer from Waltham, took over as judge. It was not always an easy task, and there was one incident where some excited punters besieged the judge in his box, but he came through unscathed.

Car parking at Garthorpe in 1955 cost £1 or ten shillings, and the commentators came free.

Dennis Applewhite, aged 86, looks back on winning the first race, the Members' at the first meeting at Garthorpe, in 1955.

'I rode Painter's Reward; it was owned by Major Freddie Horton, father of Mrs Ann Reid Scott,' he recalled.

'The new course rode very well, and I wasn't surprised when it became a permanent fixture for point-to-points.'

In 1955, the same year the Belvoir arrived at Garthorpe, Lance Newton founded the Melton Hunt Club as Hon. Secretary, with Col. Hanbury, then Master of the Belvoir, as Chairman. Original Committee members, from the Belvoir country, were: Dick Black, Jack Drake, Jimmy Elwell, Tim Molony, Claude Manchester and Tom Connors.

Mr Lance Newton and his daughter Mrs Pat Hinch.

The Cottesmore and Quorn Hunts joined the MHC in 1956, and Garthorpe became the venue also for their point-to-points, together with the MHC's own meeting. Urky Newton joined the MHC Committee in 1959, and took over as Hon. Secretary on Lance Newton's death in 1969, assisted until 1985 by Didi Powles, and then by Sally Hudson who became Secretary until 2008.

Dick Black, David Gibson, and Rupert Watson figured in Belvoir Members' race victories in the remainder of the 1950s. Jim Emerson's Syrup won in '57, and Treacle Tart again in 1960. In the 1960s Belvoir Members' race-winning riders included David Applewhite. Other amateur riders who made their mark at Garthorpe were Guy Cunard, Robin Collie, Tommy Philby, David Turner, Peter Greenall (who succeeded as Lord Daresbury), his brother Johnny Greenall, John Sharpe, and Joey Newton. Among leading lady riders at the meeting were Ancilla Cummin, Sybil Jessop, and Rosemary Cadell (nowadays Lady Samworth, wife of Sir David Samworth).

From the 1959-60 meeting, Lance Newton became Belvoir Point-to-point Chairman, with Col. Newton as Hon. Secre-

Lord (Rupert) Manton on Mr Speaker, owned by Hon. Mrs 'Urky' Newton, winner at Belvoir Point-to-Point at Manthorpe 1953.

The Belvoir

tary, and Mr Jack Drake continued as Clerk of the Course.

Col. Newton was succeeded as Hon. Secretary by John Berry from 1970, and he rendered great services to the Point-to-point until 1986, when he was succeeded by Rob Gardiner who remained in post for the next ten years.

At its meeting on 16 April 1988 the Belvoir Point-to-point race card celebrated 100 years of the meeting, although in fact it had started in '84, as recounted above.

Steve Taylor, Urky Newton's son-in-law, and former Belvoir Joint Master, took over as Clerk of the Course in 1990s, to be succeed by Brian Crawford.

From '96 the Hon. Secretary was Mike Chatterton, no-one keener as a Belvoir hunting man, point-to-point rider, and owner of horses ridden by his son Mark. Mike shared the role with his wife Anne, and they continued in office until 2009 when they handed over to Claire Chandler and Jan Lloyd.

As well as veterinary surgeons, the attendance of hunting doctors at point-to-points is a great boon. The Belvoir has been fortunate in generations of these valuable riders to hounds. Dr Tom Connors, the famous doctor and horse dealer, lived in Long Clawson and practiced there for many years. His wife Jill is the daughter of former Belvoir chairman, Lt.Col. W.E.H. Garner. Dr Michael Fitzpatrick was a partner of Dr Connors, and another keen hunting man. Dr Atkinson of Long Clawson was the previous hunting doctor in the Vale.

A list of Belvoir Point-to-Point Members' Race winners since 1955 is in Appendix IV. Thanks to continuing cooperation from Sir Lionel Tollemache and the Buckminster estate, owners of the course, a great tradition of amateur race riding is as strong as ever at well-attended meetings at Garthorpe. The Belvoir fixture, inheritor of a great tradition of colourful racing, is still an essential part of the sporting calendar in the East Midlands.

Dick Black on Misty Nook, owned by Hon. Mrs 'Urky' Newton, winner Belvoir Members' Race 1956.

CHAPTER 15

The Pony Club – our future!

by Sally Skelton

'...the big thing was the cross-country...'

It was on 1 November 1929 the Institute of the Horse, forerunner of the British Horse Society, started the Junior Branch of their organisation known as The Pony Club. Under the scheme the country was divided into Districts, which were the same as the Hunt countries throughout the country, and bore their names. The Belvoir Hunt Branch formed a committee by the end of 1929. A District Commissioner was appointed in early 1930, and by May of that year the Belvoir Hunt Branch was officially in existence.

One of the reasons for setting up The Pony Club was to help farmers' children in particular to improve their riding, and to help teach them how to look after their horses and ponies. Members joined with an entrance fee of two shillings and sixpence (12.5p.), unchanged until 1976, and an annual subscription of five shillings (25p.) Farmers' children paid a reduced subscription until the late 1940s.

The first District Commissioner was Sir Arthur Curtis, followed by Miss Baldwin, and in the late 1930s the post was filled by Miss Daphne Marsh, later Daphne Toulson, wife of the leading show rider Vin Toulson. Daphne was District Commissioner at the outbreak of war in 1939, and Miss L. Watson was Secretary. The branch had 40 members in August 1940, and struggled on until September 1943, when it was officially closed down and the branch funds sent to The Pony Club Headquarters. The branch restarted in 1946 at the express wish of the Hunt Chairman, Sir Hugh Cholmeley, who had written to The Pony Club. Miss L. Watson, the former Branch Secretary, formed a committee, but she did not wish to become District Commissioner. The committee elected Mrs Stella Sutcliffe to be District Commissioner, followed by Miss Ann Horton, later Mrs Ann Reid Scott.

The following have served as District Commissioners since then:

The Hon. Miss Ursula (Urky) Rank (later Mrs Lance Newton), Mrs Sally Hanbury, Hon. Mrs Brace, Mrs Barbara Davies, Mr Fran Jenkinson, Mr John Berry, Mr Peter Jenkinson, Mr Jim Bealby, Mr Peter Jenkinson, Mrs Sally Skelton, Mrs Jane Chatterton, Mrs Pauline Goodson, Mrs Diana Thompson, Mrs Jenny Leslie, and Mrs Alex Askew.

In 1930, the year Belvoir branch of The Pony Club was formed, a children's meet being addressed by Joint Master Charles Tonge, accompanied by Joint Master Gordon Colman, left.

In the 1950s The Pony Club was divided into Areas, and the Belvoir became part of Area 6 (East Midlands). The District Commissioners in each Area elected an Area Representative, who sat on The Pony Club Council which was the ruling body of the organisation. Each Area Representative organised Area competitions which were qualifiers for the Pony Club Championships; they were also responsible for representing the views of their branches on the Council.

In the 1960s Brigadier T.G.G. (Tubby) Cooper, the Belvoir's Hunt Secretary, became the Area Representative for Area 6, and went on to become national Chairman of The Pony Club in 1971 until 1975.

The Belvoir has provided the Area Representative ever since, with Hon. Mrs Urky Newton succeeding Tubby Cooper for 17 years, followed by Mrs Sally Skelton for another 17 years, and now Mrs Christina Thompson holds the position.

Urky Newton was well-known for her love of cross country riding, and in her memory The Pony Club has awarded 'The Urky Newton Bursary' since 1996. It is awarded to the member considered to have ridden the most competent cross country round in the Open Eventing at The Pony Club Championships, and the recipient has received a week of instruction with a top trainer.

One of the highlights of the Pony Club year has always been the summer camp. Before the war there was a camp at Harlaxton where all the members slept in tents. After the war the first camp was at Hungerton Hall, followed by others at Alma Park, Barkestone Heath Aerodrome, Aswarby Park, Waltham House, and Stoke Rochford Hall, where members slept in the newly-built Teacher Training Halls of Residence.

The Camp went back to Aswarby Park, then Rauceby Hall, before moving to the old Hunt Stables at Woolsthorpe in the late 1950s. The stables were still in use by the Hunt at the time, and one of the biggest chores for members was keeping the stable yard swept and clear of any pieces of straw. It was considered more educational for members because a lot more of the horses could be stabled, except for the smaller ponies which were housed in the indoor school. The members, however, remembered it for the fun fair that was in the village, because camp was held at the same time as Feast Week in Woolsthorpe.

In 1963 camp moved to Garthorpe Racecourse, and was to remain there for 33 years. At first most of the horses and ponies were turned out together with their hind shoes removed, and only a few from the top two rides stabled in the farmyard at Garthorpe.

The big attraction was the cross-country course, and other local branches were quite envious of the Belvoir. In the early days members slept in the hut, and the old school, since knocked down. The Tote hut added a bit more sleeping accommodation and the Hunt Supporters' tent was used over the years for sleeping, and for housing members' tack.

In the evenings after a lecture or demonstration there were many hours of fun in water fights, both organised and spontaneous. These fights often ended up in the stream where they descended to mud baths. A story grew about the 'Ghost of Garthorpe', but it was probably only a ploy by older members to frighten younger members back to the hut, so that the older members could

The Pony Club's junior show at Eaton Grange, 2005.

Above: Belvoir Pony Club Eventing Team on a trip to Spain (left to right): Angus Montieth, Nicky Newton, Alvaro Domecq, Fiona Montieth and Ashley Bealby (nowadays a Quorn Field Master)

enjoy midnight feasts out on the racecourse.

It was not unusual to have 130 children or more at one camp in the 1970s, but as the years went on, the annual camp was split into Mini Camp, Junior Camp and Senior Camp. All started out at Garthorpe but gradually moved to other venues. Mini camp has been at Croxton Park, Culverthorpe Park, Belvoir Castle, Buckminster Park and the Hendersons' at Eaton. The cost of temporary stabling

Belvoir Pony Club junior camp at Buckminster. (left to right): Lucy Doone-Guinness, Kitty Taylor, Lottie Jones, Marina Stephens, Susannah Fleming, Alexandra Van Doorn, Jessica Newton, Charlotte Leversha, and Sophie Blanchard.

became prohibitive at Garthorpe as more and more members wanted their mounts stabled, and so the other camps moved on to Elms Farm, Caythorpe, and now Arena UK at Allington.

Throughout the years the branch has organised working rallies for the children, which originally were only in the school holidays, but gradually over the years took place during term time, and now the activities are arranged throughout the year.

During the 1950s and early 1960s there was a Pony Club Ball, held at the George Hotel in Grantham, and one of the highlights of the night would be the horn blowing competition for members and the adults. The competition would be judged by the Huntsman, first George Tongue and then Jim Webster, who supplied the horn to be blown. The Ball went out of fashion and was replaced by a Christmas Party which has been held on and off since.

In 1964 The Pony Club introduced the Hunting and Country Lore Tests, and the Belvoir was one of the few branches to embrace them enthusiastically, especially at camp, but these tests no longer exist.

The Belvoir Pony Club has always

Award winners at senior camp: (left to right) Rebecca Hempstead, Rebecca Pell, Dominic Hurrell, John Willis and Alec Askew, with instructor Mathew Firth.

been very competitive, and over the years it has been most unusual if one of the discipline teams has not qualified for The Pony Club Championships. These teams have often been placed, and have won the Eventing Championship twice, and the Show Jumping once.

They first won the Team Eventing Championships in 1977 and included in the team were: Fiona Monteith, Nicky Newton, Ashley Bealby and Angus Monteith. The prize for this team was a trip to Spain to the home of Domecq, who were the sponsors of the competition. They all had a wonderful time with Urky Newton as their chaperone. Nicky Newton went on to win The Senior Individual Eventing Championship in 1978. The branch did not win the championship until 2008 when the team was: Laura Rowbotham, Annabel Henderson, Georgie Buntine, and Rebecca Crosbie-Starling.

The Show Jumping teams have won at Hickstead once, and the competition at Burghley Horse Trials on more than one occasion. In 1999 the Belvoir won the Show Jumping Championships of The Pony Club. The team was: Richard Robinson, Nikki Pyrah, Chloe Newton and Vickie Hayes.

Harriett Thompson won the Individual Members Tetrathlon Championships in 1997, and the following members have gone on to represent their country in Eventing: Chris Bealby, Nicky Newton, Camilla Cholmeley.,Chloe Newton and Willa Newton. Tim Grubb has ridden for his country in Show Jumping.

Many ex-members have ridden in point-to-points, and under Rules with great success, and probably the most famous of these is the current professional jockey Robert ('Choc') Thornton.

Belvoir members have sold race cards at the Belvoir Hunt Point-to-Point since the late 1940s, and possibly before. Members have helped the Hunt whenever requested, and the connection between the Hunt and The Belvoir Hunt Branch of The Pony Club has always been very close. Nearly all the District Commissioners were active hunting members of the Hunt, and many committee members have hunted. The link always was, and is, very strong.

Belvoir Pony Club member Laura Buntine, riding Ryan in the hunting field.

CHAPTER 16

Memories, Memories...

'We've had a helluva day... all but drowned two of the Hunt staff...
crippled the horses... and hounds have caught two brace of foxes...'

Celia Adcock (nee Berry), of Ingoldsby, remembers starting hunting with the Belvoir as a small child on a leading rein, and being blooded by George Tongue at Normanton Thorns, when she was eight. She is the third generation of her family hunting with the Belvoir.

'My grandfather, Hoyland Berry, died in 1936 after a hunting accident on the Lincolnshire side, riding a horse belonging to Herbert Jones,' says Celia.

Celia was a member of the Belvoir Pony Club, and so were her children and grandchildren; she walked puppies; and for 20 years handled the declarations at the Belvoir Point-to-Point. Celia is still hunting in the mounted field.

She recalls Jim Webster as a good friend of her parents – 'we loved him'. She recalls Robin Jackson as a huntsman 'who gave us lots of fun'; she thought Martin Thornton 'was a brilliant huntsman'; and she asserts 'Rupert Inglesant is doing a good job in difficult times...'

'We have had enormous fun in the past in Lincolnshire, including long hunts round our home which is not good country – no jumps! – but was well foxed.'

'I am enormously proud of our hounds; they are beautiful, and especially the doghounds which are my favourites, they have good voice. It was especially interesting watching Martin Thornton getting used to them.'

The Rev. John Ashley, retired Anglican priest, aged 81, Chairman of the Belvoir Hunt Supporters' Club 1969-83, started hunting with the Belvoir in 1966, and continued following on foot from about 1978. People still remember his wine and cheese parties held at the Woolsthorpe-by-Belvoir Rectory on the Thursday before the Grand National, when the draw took place.

As he had no horse transport the Rector was limited mainly to meets within hacking distance of the Rectory. He recalls especially a hunt on 12 January 1977 from Goadby Hall when the actor Gerald Harper came up for the day before speaking at a BHSC dinner.

'I was anxious to be out, so I had 'borrowed' horse transport. I had a funeral to take in Grantham, so my wife took my horse (Alconbury, a gift from Lord King on his retirement) on to the meet, dropping Gerald off at Wycombe to meet his horse, provided by Tom Hudson.

'I pulled in at the lay-by at the top of Lings Hill, to swop my cassock for my black coat, put on my spurs; my boots and stock were already on! We were delighted to discover that Prince Charles was having his first day with the Belvoir, which was why, in spite of frost, we had been assured the meet would take place.

'A good day followed. I left at second horses, but Gerald stayed all day, fell off twice, and could scarcely get off his horse at the end of the day, but recovered to dance after dinner at the Red House, Knipton.

'In spite of changing farming policies and other factors, it was still possible in the 1970s to have good runs with plenty of jumping.'

John Baggaley, aged 75, hunting farmer, of Normanton, blooded by George Tongue in 'Tot' Lees' stack paddock at Granby, when aged nine in 1943; hunt button presented by the 10th Duke; founder member as Hon. Treasurer of the Belvoir Hunt Supporters' Club.

'I hunted in the mounted field throughout Jim Webster's time, and one season with Robin Jackson... I especially remember a day in deep snow at Don Mitchell's at Aswarby. Jim took every hound in the Kennels... Robert Henson and Tom Hudson, and myself were all mounted... hounds hunted with the most outstanding music I ever heard, with the sun shining on the snow... I saw my first muntjac deer, and later a large red deer stag passed me in a ride. When I reported it to Jim Webster, he said 'Never mind. It must have been a Jersey cow.'

When it passed us again, I called out to Jim, 'Have you got your milking bucket?'

Of course, afterwards we went back to Don's for refreshment...

'I have seen many changes in my own patch... loss of Halfcrown Covert, Normanton Little Covert, and the hedge-cutting by machine... you could not see far across the country... it taught you to listen for hounds, and to look for a set of rails in the overgrown hedges... and put your arm up to protect your eyes in the real bull-finches...

'The Belvoir Hounds? They're the finest in the world...'

Mrs Margaret Musson, Field Secretary Lincolnshire since 1992.

Memories, Memories

Rick Beauchamp, Hunt Treasurer for three years during Tor Owen's chairmanship, started hunting with the Belvoir from 1988. He recalls Robin Jackson's testimonial day with special pleasure, and looks back on many happy days in the Waltham area on his favourite horse, Lively, a bright bay Warmblood 'who took me over country I could only dream about doing on other horses'.

Rick says, 'John Blakeway always sticks in my mind as a great Master, jolly, fearless across country and a nice chap to deal with; Joey Newton was, and still is, great across country... the Belvoir hounds should be exported to every pack in the country. They are the best!'

David Bellamy, aged 46, farmer, of South Rauceby, Lincs., Joint Master 2001-2, Field Master four seasons up to 2010, served on Hunt Committee five years, re-joined Mastership for 2010-11 season. Learned to ride aged 27 with sole purpose of hunting, and has only missed one season since.

'I've had too many good days to pick out one, but the best eye-opener was maybe my first Saturday after learning to ride late in

The Rev. and Mrs John Ashley.

Mrs Jean Parry.

life...it was from Farriers Forge, Hose...things just went up a couple of gears... John Martin helped me, and I helped him by building Hunt fences around the Tuesday country.

'The country in general has got noticeably smaller over my 19 years with the Belvoir, but I guess people have been saying that for the past 100 years...and we still have country to suit all tastes...The old English hounds are a breed of their own, and I am proud to be part of it, as there are so few of these packs around...I know they are not every huntsman's cup of tea, but they are a challenge.'

Marjorie Bird (formerly Marjorie Comerford) International Event Rider, Joint Master of the Belvoir (1987-91), of Stapleford, Melton Mowbray, hunted with the Belvoir for 36 seasons, four-days-a-week most seasons.

'Marje', as she is known to many in the hunting and equestrian world, says she looks back on a 'kaleidoscope of incidents' during her long hunting experience. She thought Jim Webster, Robin Jackson and Martin Thornton were 'all great hound men', and looks back on 'the sheer cussed independence of the doghounds, and the laughing, chattering enthusiasm of the bitches...'

Marje says she especially enjoyed hunting when John Blakeway was Field Master; 'he was brave beyond the call of duty.'

She recalls during her Mastership 'one of my responsibilities was the Hunt Stables. I bought grey horses which came to be a Belvoir tradition, although I did not buy this colour purposely at the beginning. At one time we had up to nine greys in the stables. One picture has the three Hunt servants changing from three dirty grey horses on to three spotlessly clean grey horses!'

John Blakeway, of Birdlip, Gloucestershire, retired fruit merchant, aged 84, Joint Master and Saturday Field Master (1983-92), among so many happy memories of hunting with the Belvoir, especially recalled the Langar Run, 18 miles as hounds ran and a seven mile point [reported Chapter 9]. Among John's memories: huntsman Robin Jackson: 'I got on very well with him, and he showed such a lot of sport.' John Blakeway's Joint Master Robert Henson: 'He was a good horseman, brave across country, loved hunting, and very agreeable to hunt with...the Saturday country

Frances Elson of Holwell, side-saddle rider of elegance and dash.

when I was Field Master was challenging and exciting to ride across...you needed a very good, quality horse to cross it...I was very proud of the Belvoir pack for their sharpness and speed.'

Rosie Capriles, of Hose, retired schoolteacher, aged 88 in March 2010, hunted in the mounted field with the Belvoir since 1955 until the 1980s, and continued following in the car ever since.

'I had such fun hunting my good grey, Berry. What lovely days, and I can honestly say all the huntsmen, and the Masters, were very kind to me, and that includes the Hunt Secretaries, because I hunted on a shoestring, and enjoyed every moment – it kept me sane in my teaching days.

'A few falls out hunting will always be remembered...Berry lost me a few times, never his fault of course, always rider errors. I was knocked off in mid-air when someone out of control cut straight into him. That time he was brought back by Sally Hudson, who remarked that he'd jumped the next two fences better without his rider.

'Once we jumped quite a nasty place below Clawson Thorns, and I didn't kick on enough, so he dropped a hind leg as he landed, lurched and again I fell off. This time Emma Newton saw him keeping up on his own, and kindly brought him back to me.

'I don't really recommend old age, but I have kept going in the car despite arthritis.

The Belvoir

I admire very much everyone who runs the Hunt since the Hunting Act; it must be a tough job, and they do very well.'

Richard Casswell, of Priory Farm, Horbling, says he is probably typical of some 'born-again' hunting people; his grandfather used to hunt with the Belvoir in the 1920s, although his parents never rode. Richard recalls attending a shooting dinner in 1998, when someone suggested the group should start hunting to support the sport in the face of the Michael Foster Bill.

'The host's dear wife quite sensibly pointed out that (a) none of us had ever ridden a horse, and (b) we were all in our 50th year,' says Richard. 'When we sobered up, only two of us were daft enough to have a go.'

His friend broke bones learning to ride, and gave up, but Richard persisted with lessons 'one hour a week on a hairy pony', and I only meant to have a few quiet days hunting, 'but it's quite addictive, isn't it?'

He has thoroughly enjoyed his hunting, mainly on the Lincolnshire side,

Below: Rupert Inglesant, Master and huntsman 2006-10, at the Hunt Kennels with his team of staff and Countrymen volunteers (left to right): Tom Grant, Martin Greet, George Grant (Kennel Huntsman and Countryman); David (Danny) Grange; Rupert Inglesant; Foster Edwards (Hunt Supporters' Club Chairman); Tim Coulson (1st Whipper-in, and following season Master and huntsman to the Lauderdale); Chris Edwards (following season 1st Whipper-in); Stuart Whatton, Ian Whatton, and Nick Edwards.

Lord (Peter) Daresbury, Jim Webster in retirement, the Hon. Migs Greenall, and Robin Abel-Smith.

and has served as a committee member and on the Hunt board. He especially recalls a day after a meet at Rookfield House, home of his neighours, Nick and Liz Coy, on 3 November 2000, with Martin Thornton hunting hounds.

'The point is that it was a completely un-classic hunt on the extreme east of our country – all arable farmland, no fences after we left the first field, but ditches and drains everywhere. The hounds hunted fantastically – the old pocket-handkerchief-would cover-all-of-them cliché – and very fast. Even Martin Thornton and Richard Markham failed to keep up with them.'

It was a highly eventful day, with some riders floundering in dykes, and hounds running parallel with the famous Forty Foot drain, leaving the field far behind. At Pointon Fen the huntsman and whipper-in 'came to grief when the horses got into a muddy drain and didn't have the strength to scramble out…they slid backwards into three feet of muddy water. Martin kept his feet, but Richard, went right under.' Joint Master Tor Owen was riding on the A52, and jumped a gate off the road onto the bank of the Forty Foot – and then went over the Billingborough Lode, 'quite a serious drain, but crossable, whereas you can only cross the Forty foot on a bridge.'

Tor Owen and Bill Bishop rescued the Hunt horses when they could not get out of their drain.

Martin and Richard continued on foot, and after running three fields they met hounds returning 'looking pleased with themselves'.

In the afternoon hounds caught another brace of foxes on the railway line, and finished with another fine run from Folkingham Big Gorse to Sempringham Osiers where they were successful again.

The Belvoir

Mrs Richard Casswell at her Meet for the Belvoir at Horbling in November 2010.

Richard Casswell summed it up: 'We've had a helluva day. By the end of the afternoon we'd all but drowned the Hunt staff, crippled the horses, and killed two brace of foxes. Nick had to send out for more port. The Hunt lorry drove round recovering exhausted nags from half the stables in the county, and we were all on the 'phone to the farrier to get things put right in the hoof and shoe department before next week.'

Richard's view of the Mastership: 'Tor Owen was particularly friendly and welcoming when I started, but they're all good in their own ways, and I'm grateful to anyone who'll do the job. Our country is wonderfully varied – a bit of everything except moorland; arable, complete with horse-friendly ELS headlands, grass, limestone heath, woodland, ditches, rivers, rails, fallen trees, dry stone walls, hedges.'

Mike and Ann Chatterton, of Merrivale Farm, Plungar, are life-long Belvoir hunting people, and served as Belvoir Point-to-Point Joint Secretaries for ten years. Mike's parents, George and Joan Chatterton, lived at Shelford Manor and bought a farm at Holwell in the 1960s to enable them to hunt as farmers with the Belvoir, with their five children. Roger, Mike, Judy, Ruth and Angela started hunting with the Belvoir in the late 1950s. Mike and Anne bought the farm at Plungar in 1965, and hunted with their three boys. Mike Chatterton was still hunting in 2010, with his son Mark, and two grandsons, George and Billy.

Mike recalls the Canal Dinners run by Tom Hudson to entertain farmers over whose land they hunted.

'They were memorable, great fun evenings at the Peacock pub in Redmile, with some farmers walking home dangerously along the canal bank, and others getting a lift home with the milkman.'

There are also memories of wonderful days from Melton Spinney, with fun in the Scalford pub with some colourful visitiors: the racing stars Willie Carson, Barry Hills, Walter Swinburn and others. Another popular post-hunting venue was the Red House at Knipton, with Jim Webster regaling the company on the day's sport.

The Chattertons recall giving the meet on 1 March Hunt Ball day in 1975, when hounds first scored a four-mile-point in a good hunt from Granby Gap to the gardens at Belvoir Castle.

From the Chatterton's kale there was an excellent hound hunt of 80 minutes on a long circle, a strong fox running by Jericho, past Elton, on to Whatton Hall, over the Grimmer, and to ground short of Jericho.

Mike Chatterton recalls Robert Henson's Mastership of 1978-87 with special pleasure: 'Robert headed the hard-riding Belvoir field with great courage. During his Mastership the Belvoir had some excellent

Four generations with the Belvoir: (right) Chairman 1954–9 Lt.Col. W.E.H. (Ted) Garner; (centre) his son-in-law and daughter, Dr and Mrs Tom Connors; (left) Mr John Chatfeild Roberts, his wife Doone (daughter of Dr and Mrs Connors) and sons Harry, 14, and Tom, 16.

seasons, with John Blakeway as Joint Master, and Tom and Sally Hudson backing them up as Joint Secretaries.'

Fiona Gibson (nee Parry), regular member of the Belvoir mounted field since childhood, of Barleythorpe, Rutland; daughter of Major John Parry, former Joint Master, and Mrs Jean Parry, long-time subscriber.

'I started hunting with the Belvoir aged 10 in 1964, with my late brother, Michael, and my mother, now aged 91, and my father.

'An abiding memory was when I was 12, and I was sitting at the top end of Holwell Mouth on a 13.2 hands pony, having never seen anything other than a Suffolk ditch before when out hunting. Spread below were endless green fields, but worryingly they were enclosed by vast hedges with ditches before or away – the most terrifying sight!'

Michael, Frances and **Benjamin Elson**, of Holwell (respectively self-employed, a cook on a yacht in Monaco, and a stockbroker), started hunting with the Belvoir in 1993 after previously with the S. Notts. Served as committee member for Hunt and Supporters, Point-to-Point and Pony Club, puppy-walker, earth-stopper, Frances [see page 195] rides side-saddle (an intrepid team 'chaser, she was first woman rider home in the Melton Hunt Club Ride side-saddle).

'Outstanding day in mid-January two seasons ago…lashing down with rain…we jumped a style near the Smite. One Alan Kasket took it well but could not pull up. His horse jumped into the brook with Alan. It was like Irish hunting. Benjamin jumped off his horse and followed Alan into the stream as his horse was stuck under a fallen tree. The two were swimming in full hunting kit, with Alan's top hat floating in the water. We finally got him and his horse out, and we all carried on 'til end of day.

'Any day is outstanding, especially as we can hack to most High Leicestershire meets from our farm. We think the Belvoir hounds are fast, pure-bred and wonderful to behold.'

Richard Grieve, started hunting with the Belvoir in 1999: 'There is no doubt the Belvoir has a wonderful and varied country, which I have come to love the more I have hunted in it.'

Richard points out that in the decade he has hunted with the Belvoir, 'the Hunt has had to change in difficult times, brought about by the threat of a hunting ban, loss of country, the strain on the farming community and other factors...the Belvoir was a four-day-a-week pack; it now does only two or three days and sometimes four.'

He says the decrease in visitors since the turn of the century has hit the Hunt's finances, but he feels 'the Belvoir seems to have grown into a more friendly Hunt than it was in 1999; less strangers about, plus the shared experience of sticking together through the bad times of the threat of the ban, has made the Hunt into a 'happy band of brothers and sisters' today.'

'It is only in the last two years that I have hunted in the Vale of Belvoir, and this is a wonderful piece of country with lots of jumping, and where, up to the present day, the followers continue to find great enjoyment in following the Belvoir hounds.'

Marian Bamber Hornbuckle (since the age of two known as Bambi) of Granby, 63-years-old-dairy farmer, Belvoir Hunt Secretary since 2000:

'I started hunting with the Belvoir at the age of 33, having learned to ride at the age of 32, so now I have hunted with the Belvoir for nearly 30 years. My family had no association with foxhunting whatsoever.

'I was a Pony Club secretary for seven years, and on the BHSC committee for a number of years. I served on the Hunt committee, and I was a puppy walker for 13 years.

'I have hunted with Jim Webster, Robin Jackson, Martin Thornton and Rupert Inglesant. Jim Webster and Martin Thornton were the best huntsmen and hound men you could wish for, but Robin Jackson was best for entertaining the subscribers. Rupert Inglesant was excellent as a Master organising the hunting and communicating with the farmers. John Blakeway was the Field Master I most enjoyed following. He always had a cheery word and gave the followers the best ride, and lead over the obstacles.

'The land in all areas in the Belvoir country hunts differently. I enjoy every day whether a jumping day or a 'flat' day. Seeing the hounds work, and people enjoying themselves, is the best feeling in the world. Even on a slow day there is no such thing as a bad day's hunting!

'The pure-bred English hounds are like the difference between a Thoroughbred horse and a cob. Both have their place, but the Belvoir hounds are the best. Yes, I am very proud of our hounds and I hope they will continue to be pure for many years to come.

'I am very proud to be part of the Belvoir Hunt.'

John Pick, farmer, Long Clawson in the Vale of Belvoir: 'I have followed the Belvoir hounds for many years in various ways: on foot, cycle, motorbike, and latterly in various cars, mostly one's able to go from nought to 60 in a quarter of an hour.

'I was lucky to be born in Long Clawson, the capital of foxhunting, where

New Mastership for the 2010–11 season at Belvoir Castle (left to right): Mr David Bellamy, Mt Martin Brown, Lady Sarah McCorquodale, Mrs Emma Taylor and Mr Michael Bell.

there is a fox covert at each corner of the village – Holwell Mouth, Sherbrooke's, Hazeltongue (Top Covert), Hose Thorns – and also from Long Clawson parish can be seen four if not five hunt countries, and 25 fox coverts. I started taking an interest in hunting when I was about five-years-old, as my father worked for Captain Heyman at the Manor as groom and gardener or vice-versa... In about 1937 my father had started farming on some of the land where the cross-country course was held much later. When hunting more or less stopped at the start of the war, Lord Greenwood gave father his hunter to work on the farm; in those far-off days hunters were not of the quality they are today.

'We had a house behind where Birleys Garage is now, which at that time was Dick Hart's, the Saddlers... Next door lived Foreman Miller, well known as Hunt Valet, often doing the Prince of Wales's hunting gear – I suppose he was the forerunner of Sketchleys.

'Around 1940, my family moved up the hill, which was a big step, as we had no electricity or mains water, and only horse power…After the war hunting struck up again. With the River Smite running through the middle of Holwell Mouth we used to get the Quorn on a Monday under George Barker… The fencing was done by

New Hunt staff team 2010–11 season: George Pierce, 2nd Whipper-in; Huntsman John Holliday and 1st Whipper-in Chris Edwards.

Deaf Alf, who was the landlord of the Black Horse at Grimston, coming round in a horse and cart.

'At this time, in 1950, I started earth stopping, taking over from Henry Freckingham, as it was getting a bit much for him...I have had one or two hair-raising moments when out stopping. One night on a farm in the pitch dark I thought: 'This ground's a bit boggy'. When I put my light on, I was walking on a 12 foot deep slurry lagoon. I still have nightmares about that one.

'Once in Holwell Mouth I saw this blue light like I had not seen before. I decided not to go near, as I felt scared. I thought it could be something from outer space. I went back to look next day – someone had set a moth trap.

'Another night in a barn at Little Belvoir, around the time people were claiming to be seeing a puma, suddenly there was a clatter. I thought 'it's got me' – turned out it was pigeons making their getaway.

'In the olden days the Earth Stoppers' Lunch was held at the Chequers Inn at Woolsthorpe from noon till around six o'clock. They were wonderful occasions. If you could attend, earth stoppers and keepers would receive a card in Jim's best handwriting, stating the number of finds, and telling you a bus would leave Grantham bus station for Woolsthorpe, returning afterwards... When Tom Hudson came as Secretary, it changed to an evening do, to allow people to attend without having a day off work.

'At one evening do, long before drink driving, I had too much to drink. Ken Skinner told me to follow him home. However someone got between my car and his. I followed it and realised I was wrong after going over the hump-back bridge at Redmile! I got home, woke up in the car frozen, thinking 'It's moonlight tonight', not realising it was seven o' clock in the morning!'

Giles Pitman, of Ware, Herts., 'outside' subscriber to the Belvoir since 1985, receiving his Hunt button in his second season. Among many happy memories he cherishes one of a great hunt – 'best morning of the season' – on Christmas Eve 1993 from Mount Pleasant, Hose. He especially enjoyed hunting with John Blakeway – 'always such fun for the field' – and says the Belvoir country was 'almost perfect in the top Saturday country around Long Clawson, and the best of the Wednesday country.

'The Belvoir hounds are brilliant to hunt so well, followed by so many of the field, like me, who mainly 'hunt to ride'.' Giles says it was 'a very great honour to be asked to serve on the Finance committee, to represent 'non-pats', i.e. outsiders.'

James Knight, of a well-known Lincolnshire farming family at Walcot, Joint Master 1983-1991, and current chairman of the Point-to-point committee, started hunting in 1955 aged five – and in 2010 was still hunting. His parents Peter and Joan Knight hunted all their lives; his mother walked 26 couple of puppies.

When she was a girl George Tongue was cross with her for teaching one puppy to beg, and this hound would always come to his mother at the meet to beg, and would usually be given a biscuit. James's grandmother Mrs S.K.(Sue)Watts was an extremely keen hunting lady, and he has a painting by Cuthbert Bradley of his grandmother jumping a gate.

Huntsman Martin Thornton and his wife Sally, at the last meet before the Hunting Act in February 2005.

In March 1950 James was christened at 10am and the Belvoir hounds met at his parents' house at noon. Col James Hanbury, George Tongue and many local hunting characters were present.

On James's 21st birthday the Belvoir hounds met at his parents' house and Col Hanbury came again, although now in failing health.

As a life-long admirer of the Belvoir hounds, James says, 'On a good scenting day the music, and their concentration on hunting as a pack is unique.'

Chris Markham was brought up on the Chatsworth Estate, in Derbyshire, and his earliest hunting was with the Barlow and the High Peak, later hunting with the Meynell, the DNS Beagles and the Quorn.

'However I had always wanted to hunt with the Belvoir,' he says.

Chris started in the early 'seventies, and has hunted regularly on Saturdays since. He recalls his first Belvoir day from Eaton Grange, when he was impressed by the country from the start.

'Put the Belvoir hounds running hard across their country under a huge wintry sky, and I am in heaven! Jim Webster gave us a great day, and the memory of those beautiful tan hounds running hard and leaving many empty saddles in their wake has never left me. I was hooked.

'As a pack they have always impressed me with their ability to draw well, pushing into the thickest cover, and once away they are rarely strung out, running with great drive and cry, swinging to cast and put themselves right when need be, and turning with great accuracy to stick to the line. When the horn is touched they respond quickly and are soon away again!

'Loving my sport as I do, on the last day of legal hunting in February 2005 I stood at the bottom of Pasture Lane as Martin boxed up, and I shed more than a few tears. However, on the following Saturday in Melton when the Belvoir Hounds proudly led over 600 riders through the streets of the town I knew then we had only lost a battle, and not the war!

'It's no use anyone moaning about things not being the same. Of course they aren't, but hounds are still running across the Vale and over the plough, albeit with changes to which we must adapt. There is certainly no place for 'armchair huntsmen' any more. What we have we must put up with, for the time being, and maximize the exemptions which the law allows whilst making certain that no-one is compromised during the day's activities.

'Two memories stick in my mind from the past season. The first was that late evening trail from the back of Clawson village across to Hose Thorns, over the lane to the old Harby cheese factory. I could just make out the shadowy figure of hounds in the dusk, but oh the cry! Wonderful! And the second memory was that trail from the old piggery at Wycomb round Mrs Greenall's land through Chadwell at top pace, and as I went under the old bridge at Scalford, hounds came down the big grass field, and you could have put a sheet over them as they drove at such pace.

'Most of them cleared the five-bar gate onto the lane, and then cleared the next off it. They flew to cross above Scalford village, and to the OFB kennels where the trail petered out. The Belvoir is a top class pack of hounds, steeped in tradition, able to work in some of the most beautiful countryside in Britain, and with a bright future in safe and capable hands of a team we should all be proud to support. That's why I follow the Belvoir hounds!'

Joey Newton, landowner and farmer of Stonesby, son of the late Lance and the Hon. Ursula Newton, has hunted with the Belvoir for 46 years, having served as a Joint Master (1989-2000), Field Master, and committee member. In the 2009-10 season he was still Field Master on the Leicestershire side, with Rupert Inglesant hunting hounds.

Joey recalls a wonderful hunt with Jim Webster hunting hounds, when the pack ran from Garthorpe eastwards to the A1.

'Jim Webster was a wonderful communicator, and a great ambassador for the Belvoir,' says Joey.

'Robin Jackson was well organised, and very helpful to new Masters. He always made sure the Masters understood what was expected of them. Martin Thornton was a brilliant huntsman, very easy to mount, and undemanding on his horses. I was very lucky to have so many happy years hunting with him.'

Joey says the Belvoir country from a Master's point of view is 'very spoiling due to the generosity of the farmers. Pockets of the hunting country are still the very best from a riding point of view. The majority is still unspoilt, and very good hunting.'

Joey's view of the Belvoir hounds: 'The old English, being different, are always difficult to compare with other types of hound. The breeding limitations of keeping the breed pure makes life easier because it removes the possibility of trying fashionable outcrosses, which have not always been that successful elsewhere. We are all very lucky still to be hunting with a pure traditional pack'.

Victoria (Tor) Owen started hunting with the Belvoir in 1970 when she married Barry Owen, who had been hunting with the Belvoir since 1955.

'I was then 25, I am still hunting, so I am coming up to 40 years with the Belvoir.'

Tor served on the Hunt Committee from 1988 until becoming a Joint-Master in 1990-91, with responsibility for the Friday country. She retired as Master on 30 April 1999, 'but one of the last things the 10th Duke of Rutland did before he died was to write to ask me to take over as Chairman from Lord King. So, I became Vice-Chairman in 2000, and then Chairman from 1 May 2001 until 30 April 2006.'

Tor started hunting on the Leicestershire side... 'Barry felt Lincs. was somewhere quite impossible, but I began to venture across from about 1975. Once I had the horses at home I was a free agent to zip off whenever I could!'

She especially remembers 8 January 1970, from Hose with a hunt from Sherbrookes in the afternoon, and 9 January 1975 from Goadby Marwood, with a hunt from Goadby Gorse after second horses. 'In both hunts I rode the same horse all day; an ex-Harvey Smith showjumper, he taught me to jump gates, but stop on a sixpence – while I carried on.

'They were two memorable days early on in my hunting career, but later hunts in the 'nineties were also terrific. My abiding memory is really the privilege of being able to go out on hound exercise in July and August before autumn hunting, riding through the Castle gates behind the Belvoir hounds on the same roads and tracks used for generations.

And of course, I shall never forget the kindness and generosity shown to me by the farmers and landowners while I was Master.'

Major Peter Postlethwaite, of Claypole, Newark, Hon. Secretary 1983-89, committee member 1993-98. Especially remembers the hunt on Christmas Eve 1983, after a hospitable meet at Wartnaby... 'they found straight away in Holwell Mouth, ran for Sherbrookes, into the Quorn country, and hunted for next three and a half hours over great swathes of their Monday country before returning to Harby Hills where home was blown.

'Because of strong Masterships, mounted fields of up to 200 on good Saturdays, full subscriptions and waiting lists, the 1980s and '90s were something of a mini golden era – excellent sport provided, and the Hunt's popularity widespread. I had excellent help as secretary from Mrs Blanche Wildman and her daughter Ann Creed. Lord King's strong leadership helped to maintain the Hunt's reputation during his Chairmanship.'

John Richardson, of Manor House, Bitchfield, Hon. Treasurer from 1985-92, hunted on the Leicestershire side with the Belvoir from 1955-92. He especially enjoyed hunting with Lord (Ronnie) Belper: 'His knowledge of hunting was excellent'. And retains many happy memories of Vale days, especially from Long Clawson and Holwell Mouth: 'The Vale was the best, and our hounds hunted brilliantly. What magical fun it all was.'

Stuart Spence, Farrier RSS, AFCL. 'On leaving the family forge at Knossington, in the Cottesmore country, my father Walter Spence moved to the forge in Hose in the Vale of Belvoir, the business then being called W. Spence. On building up the business up in the Vale and around, my father began shoeing for the Belvoir Hunt in 1948. I remember going to the kennels at the age of ten to help my father when at that time the huntsman was George Tongue and the Master was Major Hanbury.

Mr Stuart Spence of Hose, farrier who supports the Belvoir.

'I became a partner in the business with father in 1965, and the business was then called W Spence and Son. Sadly my father died in 1967, and I and my wife, June, took over the family business.

'In 1982 the business was changed to W Spence and Son (Blacksmiths) Ltd Farriers. My son Richard Spence DWCF AWCF joined the business in 1989. Throughout the years there have been over 30 apprentices trained with us.

'To this present day we are still farriers for the Belvoir Hunt, and offer support and sponsorship at the Belvoir Point-to-point, the Kennels Open Day, the Team 'Chase, the Supporters Club, and any other event organised by the Hunt.

'The Spence family has always supported and followed the Belvoir Hunt throughout the years, with my daughter, Sally Lee, and daughter-in-law, Rebecca Spence, hunting on horse back and others on foot in Leicestershire and Lincolnshire.

Rodney Vigne, chartered surveyor, of Freeby, Member of Hunt Supporters Committee for 15 years, and Hon. Treasurer for 12 years, member Point-to-point Committee, and Assistant Clerk of Course at Garthorpe. Followed Belvoir on foot since 1970, formerly keen on beagling and coursing. 'I never learned to ride properly... had a morning's cubhunting from the Kennels until I was bucked off! I remounted despite mild concussion and badly bruised ribs, and can remember little of the rest of the morning, but I achieved an ambition rather late in life.

'In my opinion Jim Webster was the greatest Belvoir huntsman I saw, a true Hunt servant.

'The country is not what it used to be 40 years ago. The plough has changed most of it almost beyond recognition – but there is nothing like seeing pure bred English hounds hunting over it, and I am proud of their uniqueness.'

Next page: Huntsman John Holliday in his first season with the Belvoir, 2010–11, with hounds moving off from a Meet at Belvoir Castle.

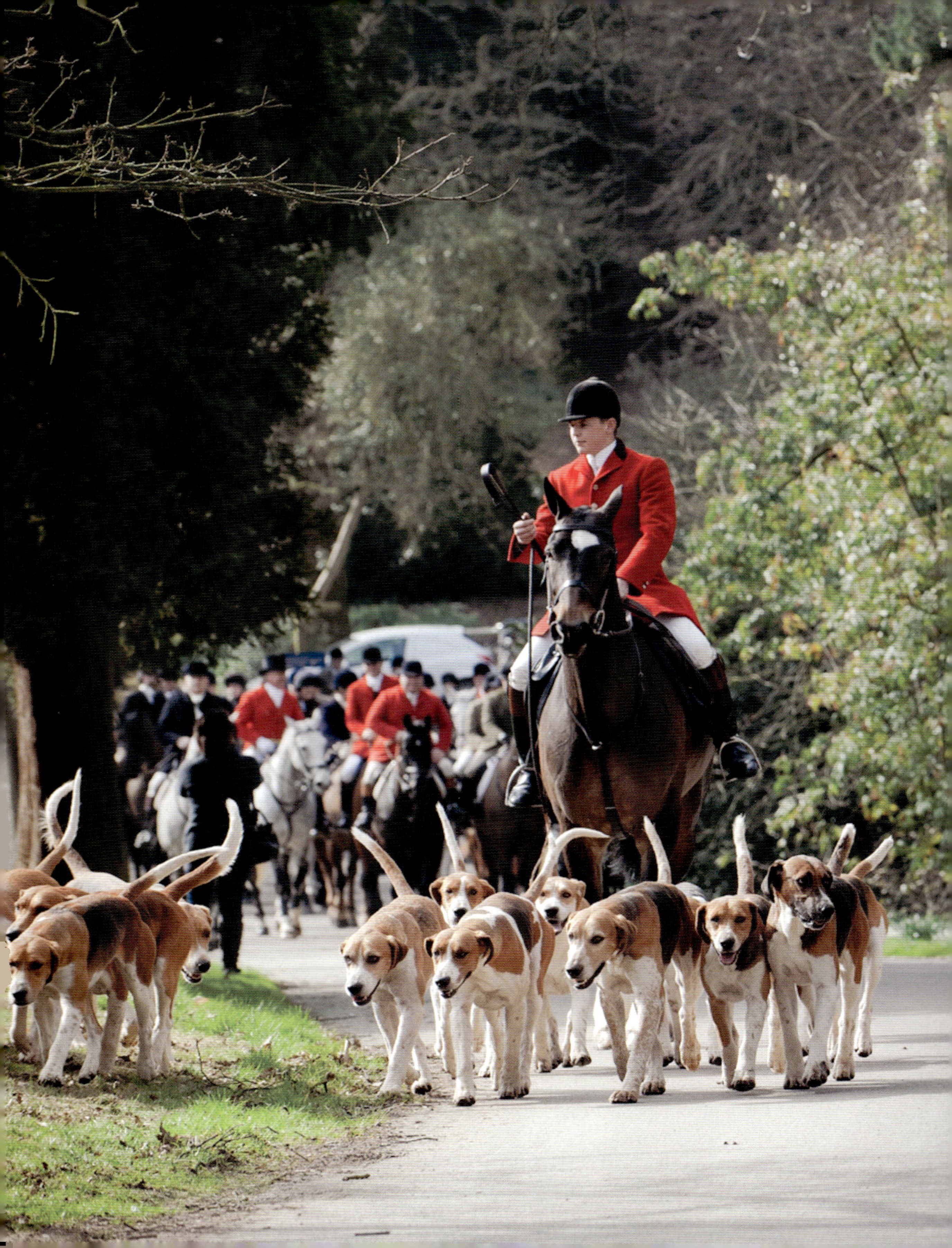

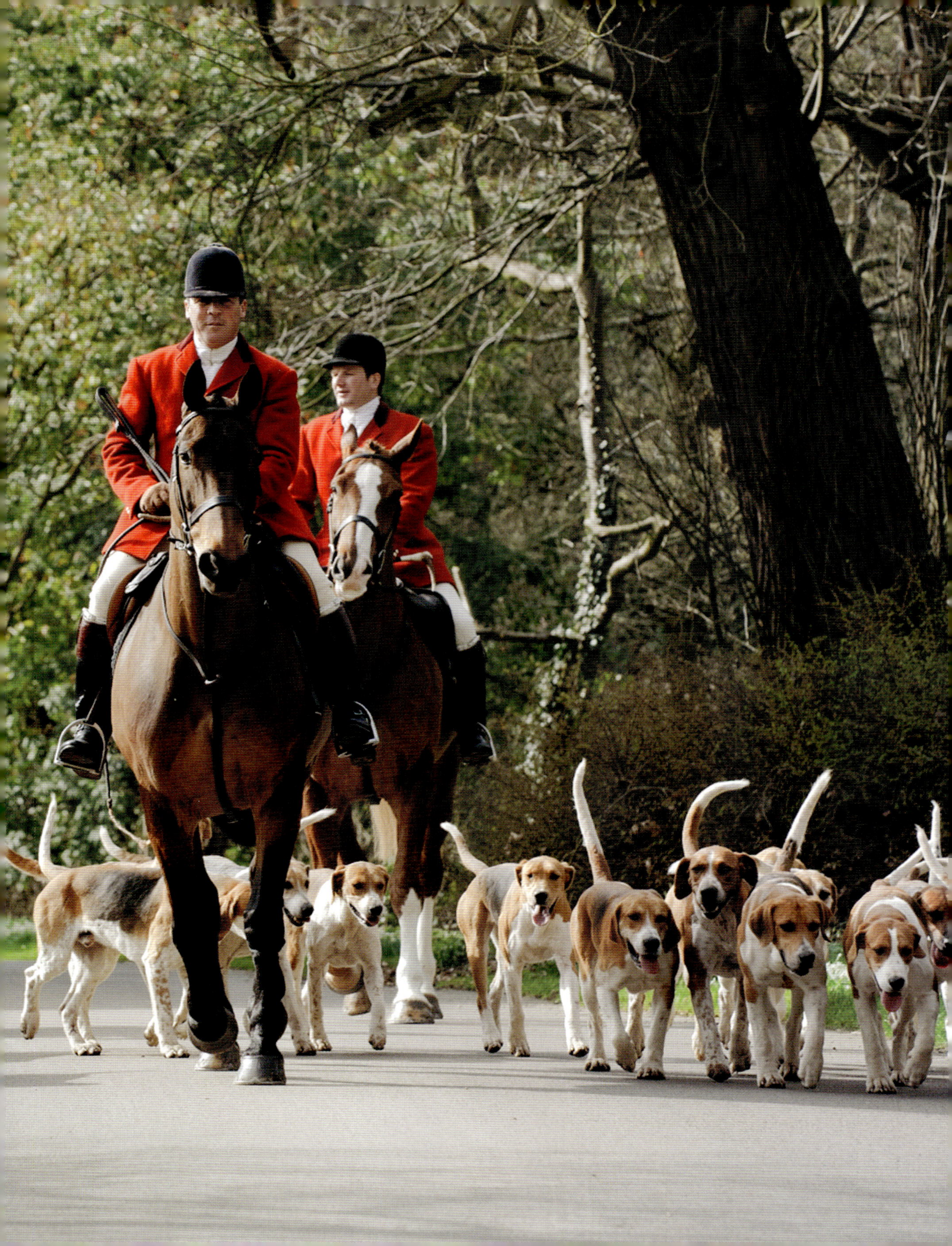

APPENDIX I

Masters and Huntsmen of the Belvoir

SEASONS	MASTERS	HUNTSMEN
1730-79	3rd Duke of Rutland	
1742-70	John Marquis of Granby	
1779-87	4th Duke of Rutland	John Smith
1784-91	(Lord George Cavendish & Sir Carnaby Haggerston, managers)	
1791-99	Mr Perceval	Newman
1799-1830	5th Duke of Rutland	'Gentleman' Shaw (1804-16)
		Thomas Goosey (1816-42)
1830-58	Lord Forester	Will Goodall (1842-59)
1859-88	6th Duke of Rutland	James Cooper (1859-70)
1888-96	7th Duke of Rutland	Frank Gillard (1887-96)
1896-1912	Sir Gilbert Greenall	Ben Capell (1896-1912)
		Jack Hewitt (1912-13)
1912-24	Major Tommy Bouch	Dick Woodward (1913-19)
		Major Bouch (1919-24)
1912-14	Lord Robert Manners	
1924-28	Capt. M.O. Roberts	Nimrod Capell (1924-28)
1928-31	Mr Charles Tonge	George Tongue (1928-56)
1928-30	Mr P.S. Ackroyd	
1930-39	Col. F.G.D. Colman	
1934-40 & 1941-7	2nd Lord Daresbury	
1940-52	10th Duke of Rutland	
1947-64	Lt.Col. James Hanbury	Jim Webster (1956-83)
1952-54	Lt.Col. F. Bowlby	
1953-4 & 1955-6	Major George Pretyman	
1954-55	Lt.Col. James Seely	
1955-66	Lord Belper	
1956-64	Lt.Col. H.L.V. Beddington	
1958-72	Mr John King (later Lord King)	
1971-73	Major General F.B. Wyldebore-Smith	
1972-78	Mrs Ann Reid Scott	

The Belvoir

1972-74	Mr Nicholas Turner	
1974-76	Mr John Hine	
1976-78	Lord Belper	
1978-79	Mr Philip Watts	
1978-87	Mr Robert Henson	
1980-83	Mr Nicholas Playne & Mr Nicholas Turner	
1983-88	Mr Charles Harrison	Robin Jackson (1983-92)
1983-92	Mr John Blakeway	
1987-89	Mr John Parry	
1983-90	Mr James Knight	
1988-92	Mrs Marjorie Comerford	
1993-98	Mr Steven Taylor	
1989-2000	Mr Joey Newton	
1990-99	Mrs Barry Owen	
1991-2004	Mr John Martin	Martin Thornton (1992-2006)
1998-2003	Mr Sten Bertelsen	
1998-2006	Mr Richard Morley	
2000-06	Mr James Henderson	
2000-06	Mr Bill Bishop	
2001-02	Mr David Bellamy	
2003-06	Hon. Vicky Westropp	
2003-04	Mr Martin Brown	
2006-10	Mr Rupert Inglesant	Mr Inglesant (2006-10)
2010-	Lady Sarah McCorquodale	John Holliday (2010-)
2010-	Mrs Emma Bealby	
2010-	Mr David Bellamy	
2010-	Mr Martin Brown	
2010-	Mr Michael Bell	

APPENDIX II

Hunt Chairmen and Hon. Secretaries

BELVOIR HUNT CHAIRMEN

1896	Col. Mildmay Willson
1901	Major William Longstaffe
1905	Maj. General Sir Mildmay Willson
1912	Mr Pearson Gregory
1912	Mr Charles Welby
1925	Brig. Gen. Sir George Paynter
1939	Major Herbert Turner
1946	Capt. Sir Hugh Cholmeley
1954	Lt.Col. W.E.H. Garner
1959	Major William T. Pott
1963	Mr Thomas H. Beddington
1967	Lt.Col. James Hanbury
1969	Lord Belper
1976	Lord King
2000	Mrs D.B. Owen
2006	Mr John Martin

BELVOIR HUNT SECRETARIES

Pre 1892	Mr Frederick Sloane Stanley
	Mr James Hutchinson
1892	Mr C.J. Parker
1900	Mr W. Pinder (died in office)
1902	Mr W. Newton
1905	Mr J.F. Cartmell (Leicestershire side)
1905–1932	Mr W. Newton (Lincolnshire side, and both sides during First War)
1919	Major F.D. Alexander (Leicestershire)
1923	Lt.Col. H. Webber (Leicestershire)
1925	Lt.Col. G. Cantrell-Hubbersty (Leicestershire)
1928	Lt.Col. J. Lockett (Leicestershire)
1933	Mr H. Garner Bellamy (Lincolnshire)

The Belvoir

1946   Capt. Garner Bellamy (one secretary both sides from 1946)
1947   Major F.H. Horton
1951   Mr Wilson Newcome
1957   Brig. T.G.G. Cooper
1970   Mr Tom Hudson
1981   Mr David Faulkner
1983   Major Peter Postlethwaite
1988   Capt Tim Hall-Wilson
1992   Mrs M. Musson (Lincolnshire Field Secretary)
1996   Mrs P. Hornbuckle

APPENDIX III

Officers of the Belvoir Hunt Supporters' Club

PRESIDENT

1967–1971	John King
1972–1980	Mrs Ann Reid Scott
1981–	Nicholas Playne

CHAIRMAN

1967–1970	Frank Kirk
1971–1982	Rev. John Ashley
1983–1988	Lady Sally Cholmeley
1989–1999	Tom Hudson
2000–	Foster Edwards

SECRETARY

1967–1971	Mrs Cis Wildman
1972	Diane Webster
1973–1975	Mrs Helen Forster
1976–1994	Mrs Margaret Palmer
1995–1996	Mrs Sue Dawson
1997–2002	Nina Camm
2003–2004	Vacant
2005–	Nina Camm

TREASURER

1967	John Baggaley
1968–1993	John Moore
1994–1996	Andrew Gibson
1997–date	Rodney Vigne

PURCHASES MADE BY BELVOIR HUNT SUPPORTERS' CLUB

1970	Bought Land Rover
1972	Bought covert on Harby Hills
1975	Bought land at Stathern; bought Flesh cart
1976	Bought new Land Rover
1978	Bought Shipmans covert
1979	Bought tent
1980	Bought new silo crusher; installed heating for staff rooms
1982	Bought new winch
1984	Paid for new flesh house and new post and rails at Kennels
1985	Paid for repairs to whelping pens; bought tent
1986	Paid for planting of Harby Hills; new work in Duke's Room
1988	Paid for stable block
1989	Paid for planting of Lord Daresbury's covert; bought Land Rover; Yard at kennels concreted
1991	Bought Scalford Ashes
1992	Paid for planting of Folkingham Big Gorse
1994	Bought flesh wagon and tent
1995	Bought lorry
2000	Bought 2 hunt horses
2002	Bought computer and photocopier for Hunt office
2007	Bought new quad bike
2008	Bought trailer for Quad bike and hurdles
2009	Bought new Quad bike and pressure washer; new signs for kennels; Paid for repairs to whelping lodges

APPENDIX IV

Belvoir Point–to–Point

Winners of the Members' Race for the Duchess of Rutland's Challenge Cup – since 1955, the first year the fixture was run at Garthorpe.

1955	Major F. Horton's	Painter's Reward	Mr D. Applewhite
1956	Hon Mrs R.L. Newton's	Misty Nook	Mr R.L. Black
1957	Mr J.T. Emerson's	Syrup	Mr R.L. Black
1958	Mrs J.R. Hanbury's	Merrywell	Lord Patrick Beresford
1959	Mr R.L. Newton's	Misty Devil	Mr D. Gibson
1960	Mr J.T. Emerson's	Treacle Tart	Capt. R. Watson
1961	Hon Mrs R.L. Newton's	Turf Fire	Mr R. Abel-Smith
1962	Mr J.T. Emerson's	Syrup	Lord Patrick Beresford
1963	Mr J.L. King's	Tax Relief	Mr R. King
1964	Mr R.L. Newton's	Misty Wood	Mr T. Philby
1965	Mr J.L. King's	Half Asleep	Mr R. King
1966	Hon. Mrs E.G. Greenall's	Egg	Mr A.L. Smith
1967	Mr R.L. Newton's	King Fin	Mrs P. Hinch
1968	Mr D.C. Samworth's	Tadoro	owner
1969	Mr D.C. Samworth's	The Black Moth	owner
1970	Mr D. Gibson's	Master Cagire	owner
1971	Mr D. Gibson's	Master Cagire	owner
1972	Hon. Mrs Newton's	Santa Grand	Miss Carol Newton
1973	Mr J.T. Emerson's	Home Cured	Mr Andrew Berry
1974	Mrs J.R. Henson's	Poached Turf	Mr Andrew Graham
1975	Hon. Mrs R.L. Newton's	Urlanmore	Mr Joey Newton
1976	Mrs D. Hinckley's	Irish Flyer	owner
1977	Hon. Mrs R.L. Newton's	Urlanmore	Mr Joey Newton
1978	Miss S Berry's	Urlanmore	owner
1979	Hon. Mrs R.L. Newton's	Chief Witness	Mrs Emma Newton
1980	Hon. P. Greenall's	Harry Hills	owner
1981	Hon. Mrs R.L. Newton's	Donogue	Mr Joey Newton
1982	Hon. Mrs R.L. Newton's	Church Newton	Mr Joey Newton
1983	Mr Joey Newton's	Ryedale	owner
1984	Mr R.A.L. Roberts's	Double Earning	Miss Helen Roberts

The Belvoir

1985	Mr P.T.S. Bowlby	Scort	Mr Ashley Bealby
1986	Mr Joey Newton's	Periscope	owner
1987	Mr P.J. King's	Mirquest	Mr R. King
1988	Mr C. Vale's	Terry's Lad	owner
1989	Mr C. Vale's	Terry's Lad	owner
1990	Mr R. E. Gardiner's	Pendor	Mr C. Bealby
1991	Mr Joey Newton's	True Dowry	Mrs J. Willis
1992	Mr D. Applewhite's	Carats Major	owner
1993	Mr D. Applewhite's	Carats Major	owner
1994	Mr M.G. Chatterton's	Rain Mark	Mr Mark Chatterton
1995	Miss A. Hinch's	High Edge Grey	owner
1996	Mr W. Tellwright's	Monarrow	owner
1997	Mr M.G. Chatterton's	The Difference	Mr Mark Chatterton
1998	Mrs A. Bell's	Romany Ark	Mr N. Bell
1999	Mrs A. Bell's	Zam Bee	Mr N. Bell
2000	Mrs C. Price's	Square One	Mr J. Docker
2001	*No Meeting Due to Foot and Mouth Disease*		
2002	Mr M.G. Chatterton	Deel Quay	Mr Mark Chatterton
2003	Mr W.J. Moore's	Trouvaille	Mr M. Mackley
2004	Mrs J. Knight's	Bengal Boy	Mr N. Pearce
2005	Mr and Mrs B. Holt's	Hi Up Brenkley	Mr R. Armson
2006	Mr and Mrs B. Holt's	Hi Up Brenkley	Mr R. Armson
2007	Miss J. Henfrey's	Niembro	Mr M. Seston
2008	Mrs F. Macfarlane's	Just Jove	Mr A. Corbett
2009	Mrs C.H. Covell's	Picabo Kid	Mr M. Mackley
2010	Mr J.H. Henderson's	Aztec Warrior	Mr G. Henderson
2011	Mr J.H. Henderson's	Aztec Warrior	Mr G. Henderson

Index

ABEL-SMITH, Billy 58
ABEL-SMITH, Robin 58, 197
ACKROYD, Peter 58, 63, 68
ADCOCK, Celia 191
ADELAIDE, Queen 26, 27
ADLAM, Keith 168
ALBERT, Prince Consort 26
ALDIN, Cecil 14
ALVANLEY, Lord 23
AMBROSE CLARK, F. 70
ANCASTER, Lord 42
ANDREWS, Harvey 68
ANYAN, Frank 60, 68, 72
APPERLEY, Charles James (Nimrod) 20, 25
APPLEWHITE, Dennis 182, 183
APPLEYARD, Charles 90
ARGYLL, Duke 23
ASHLEY, Margaret 193
ASHLEY, Rev. John 164, 166, 167, 191, 193
ASKEW, Alec 189
ASKEW, Alex 185
ASTON, Richard 103
ATKINSON, Dr 184
ATKINSON, Meriel 77, 178
AUSTEN-MACKENZIE, Mr 33

BAGGALEY, John 118, 164, 192
BAILEY, James 64
BAILLIE, Arthur 55
BAINES, G. 164
BALDWIN, Miss 185
BARCLAY, Edward 50
BARKER, George 65, 202
BARKER, Capt. Fred 114, 115
BARNARD, Matt 9
BARRETT, Howard 9
BEALBY, Jim 147, 185
BEALBY, Ashley 188, 190
BEALBY, Susan 9
BEAUCHAMP, Rick 193
BEAUFORT, 4TH Duke 19, 20
BEAUFORT, 10th Duke 65, 66

BEDDINGTON, Hugh 97
BEDDINGTON, Thomas H. 97
BELL, Reg 75
BELL, Ikey 63, 65, 66
BELL, Michael 130, 134, 147, 168, 201
BELLAMY, David, 132, 134, 147, 193, 201
BELPER, Lord 82, 83, 96, 99, 121, 140
BENJAMIN 199
BERRY, Hoyland 191
BERRY, Godfrey (Goff) 90
BERRY, John 184, 185
BERTELSEN, Sten 127, 141
BEVAN, Jack 126
BIRCH, Arthur 171
BIRD, Marjorie (née Comerford) 105, 107, 141, 175, 194
BISHOP, Bill 128, 139, 142, 160, 175, 197
BISTON, William 68
BLACK, Dick 81, 182, 184
BLAKEWAY, John 105, 111, 118, 175, 194, 199, 200
BLANCHARD, Sophie 187
BOTTERILL, Ken 182
BOUCH, Major Tommy 45-52, 63, 146, 157
BOWSER, Mr F.G. 46
BOYLES, Dennis 90
BRACE, Hon. Mrs 185
BRADLEY, Cuthbert 29, 31, 41, 156
BREWITT, Julian 109, 112, 126, 175
BROCKLEHURST, Alfred 68
BROCKTON WADSLEY, Mrs 47
BRODIE, Simon 132, 168
BROOKS, Geoff 143
BROWN, Charles 142
BROWN, Martin 132, 1 42, 201
BROWN, Tim 171
BROWNING, Jim 81
BROWNLOW, Lord 32, 33

BRUMMELL, Beau 23
BRYANT, John 9
BUNTINE, Laura 190
BUNTINE, George 190
BURGESS, William 48

CAMM, Mr and Mrs Lol 140
CAMM, Nina 140
CAPELL, Ben 36-42
CAPELL, Nimrod 50, 53, 57, 59, 79
CAPRILES, Rosie 195
CARTER, Martyn 168
CASSWELL, Mrs Richard 198
CASSWELL, Richard 196, 198
CHALLENGE, Keith 175
CHANDLER, Claire 184
CHANDLER, Richard 94, 167, 168, 171
CHANDOS POLE, Mr 44
CHARLES, Prince of Wales 93, 95, 109, 110, 120
CHATFEILD ROBERTS, Harry 199
CHATFEILD ROBERTS, Doone (née Connors) 199
CHATFEILD ROBERTS, John 199
CHATFEILD ROBERTS, Tom 199
CHATTERTON, Jane 185
CHATTERTON, Joan 198
CHATTERTON, Mark 184
CHATTERTON, Ann 119, 184, 198
CHATTERTON, George 198
CHATTERTON, Michael 111, 117, 119, 184, 198
CHATTERTON, Roger 117, 119, 198
CHAWORTH MUSTERS, John 30
CHOLMELEY, Camilla 190
CHOLMELEY, Lady Sally 163, 167, 168
CHOLMELEY, Sir Hugh 74, 163
CLAMP, Tom 178

219

Index

CLARK, Ann 9
CLARKE, Jane 169
CLAYTON, John 164
COLEY, Stuart 90, 109
COLLIE, Robin 183
COLLINS, Suzanne (née Lumb) 103
COLMAN, Peggy (née Brocklehurst) 68, 69, 73
COLMAN, Col. Gordon 63, 65, 68, 73, 186
CONNORS, Dr Tom 97, 118, 182, 199
CONNORS, Mrs Jill (née Garner) 184, 199
CONYERS, Lord 65
COOPER, Brig. "Tubby" 163, 176, 186
COOPER, James, 27, 29, 30, 152, 154, 155
COULSON, Tim 130, 196
COUTTS, Burdett 177
COY, Nick 136
CRAWFORD, Brian 184
CROSBIE-STARLING, Rebecca 190
CUMMIN, Ancilla 183
CUNARD, Guy 183
CURTIS, Sir Arthur 185

DALE, T.F. 18, 19
DARESBURY, Lady (Frances) 33, 36, 38
DARESBURY, Lord (Hon. Toby Greenall) 36, 37, 38, 43, 57, 69, 70-77, 109, 120, 157, 158
DARESBURY, Lord (Sir Gilbert Greenall) 33-42, 51
DARESBURY, Lady (née Joyce Laycock) 71
DARESBURY, Lord (Hon. Peter Greenall) 9, 77, 183, 197
DAVIES, Barbara 185
DAWS, Graham 166, 168
DE TODENI, Robert, 15
DENT, Lizzie 28
DENT, Tom 28
DIANA, Princess of Wales 93-5
DOONE-GUINNESS, Lucy 187
DOUBLEDAY, John 94

DOUBLEDAY, Garth 116
DOWN, Tom 65
DRAKE, Jack 182
DUDLEY WAR, Winifred 70
DUNCAN MP, Alan 143

EDWARD, Prince of Wales (King Edward VIII) 53, 62, 69, 72, 181
EDWARD, Prince of Wales (King Edward VII) 29
EDWARDS, Lionel 9, 59
EDWARDS, Chris 147, 196, 202
EDWARDS, Foster 9, 147, 163, 165, 196
EDWARDS, Nick 196
EGGLESTONE, Ken 95
ELSON, Frances 195, 199
ELSON, Michael, Frances, Benjamin 199
ELWELL, Jimmy 182
EMPRESS OF AUSTRIA 31

FARRIN, Michael 110, 123
FENWICK, Tony 9, 31, 168
FERNELEY, John 23, 26
FIELD, Don 132
FILMER-SANKEY, Billy 71, 72
FIRR, Tom 40
FIRTH, Mathew 189
FITZPATRICK, Dr Michael 184
FLEMING, Susannah 187
FORESTER, Lord Cecil 23
FORESTER, Lord John 24, 25
FOSTER, Robin 90
FOUNTAIN, Sarah 55
FOUNTAIN, Johnny 9, 11, 55
FOX-PITT, Marietta 103
FOX-PITT, William 103
FREEMAN, Frank 37, 40

G00DALL, Frances 28
GAINSBOROUGH, Earl 18
GALE, George 75, 76
GARDINER, Rob 134
GARNER BELLAMY, H. 69
GARNER, W.E.H. 97, 184, 199
GATHERCOLE, Miss J. 164
GIBSON, David 183
GIBSON, Andrew 171

GIBSON, Fiona (née Parry) 9, 101, 199
GILLARD, Frank 30-32, 39, 152, 155, 156
GILLSON, Charles 48
GILLSON, Sam 39
GLOUCESTER, Duke of (Prince Henry) 53, 62, 65, 67, 70
GODDARD, James 68
GOODALL, Stephen 25
GOODALL, Will 25-28, 154, 155
GOODSON, Pauline 185
GOOSEY, Thomas 22-25
GOSDEN, Charlie 48
GRANBY, Marquis 19
GRANGE, David (Danny) 196
GRANT, George 172, 152, 175, 196
GRANT, Sir Francis 22, 24
GRANT, Tom 196
GREENALL, "Migs" 77, 80, 88, 197
GREENALL, Hon. Edward 71, 77, 80
GREENALL, Hon. Gilbert 71
GREENALL, Hon. Johnny 183
GREENALL, Cyril 47, 48
GREENALL, Mrs Edward 54, 178
GREET, Martin 196
GRIEVE, DUNCAN 76
GRIEVE, Richard 200
GRUBB, Tim 190
GRUBB, John 164
GUPWELL, Brian 79

HALLS, Tom 48
HALL-WILSON, Tim 9, 60, 63
HANBURY, Evan 78
HANBURY, Col. James 74, 78, 79, 81, 96, 182, 204
HANBURY, Joss 78
HARDING, Oliver 126
HARDY, Capt and Mrs 43
HARPER, Gerald 191
HARRINGTON, Earl 158
HARRINGTON, Countess 65
HARRISON, Charles 105, 175
HARRISON, Geoff 90, 123
HART, Roy 109
HARVEY, Ron 123

220

Index

HEATHCOTE, Rev. Thomas 177-8
HEATHCOTE, Thomas A.R. 178
HEMPSTEAD, Rebecca 189
HENDERSON, Annabel 190
HENDERSON, James 130, 142, 175
HENSON, Bill 106
HENSON, Gino 105
HENSON, Richard 89, 106
HENSON, Robert 9, 94, 95, 105, 106, 109, 113-122, 159, 160, 175, 192, 194, 198
HEWITT, Jack 33, 39, 45
HIDE, Tom 48
HIGGINS, Ben 147
HILL, Lord Francis 56
HILLS, Barry 92, 198
HILLS, Martin 166
HILTON GREEN, "Chatty" 65, 66, 77
HILTON-GREEN, Lady Helena ("Boodley") 77
HINCH, Pat 182
HINE, John 102, 104
HODGKINSON, Capt. 65
HOLLAND, Fred 65
HOLLAND, Henry 68
HOLLIDAY, John 109, 112, 147, 148, 171, 202
HOLLINGWORTH, Keith 175
HORNBUCKLE, "Bambi" 173, 200
HORNBUCKLE, P. 164
HORTON, Capt. Freddie 65, 101, 182
HOWARD, Miles 168
HOWELLS, Jack 107
HUDSON, Tom 100, 103, 115, 118, 169, 191, 192, 199
HUDSON, Sally 115, 118, 171, 195, 199
HUMFREY, Charlie 104
HURRELL, Dominic 189

INGLESANT, Rupert 9, 127, 138, 139, 146, 147, 149-162, 191, 196, 200
IRVING, Edward 126, 127

JACKSON, Dorothy 107, 111
JACKSON, Robin 95, 105, 107-12, 194, 200
JENKINSON, Fran 185
JENKINSON, Peter 185
JERSEY, Lord 23
JESSOP, Sybil 183
JONES, Ian 126
JONES, George 39
JONES, Herbert 46
JONES, Lottie 187
JOYNES, Gary 109
JUDD, Harry 85
KEBLE, Wayne 147
KENT, Duke of (Prince George) 62, 69
KING, Lady 98, 174
KING, Lord (John King) 87, 88, 93, 94, 96, 97-101, 142, 165, 175, 191
KIRKBY, Laurence 123
KNIGHT, Brian 67
KNIGHT, Doris (née Tongue) 67
KNIGHT, James 103, 105, 137, 141, 175, 203
KNOWLES, Mr R.M. 44

LANDER, Bill 89, 175
LANNI, Sarah 171
LAWRENCE, William 67
LAYCOCK, Sir Joseph 55, 58
LAYCOCK, Joyce 56
LAYCOCK, Peter 56
LAYCOCK, Rosemary 54-57
LEE, Sam 111
LEOPOLD, King of Belgians 27
LESLIE, Jenny 185
LEVERSHA, Charlotte 187
LITTLE, Michael 175
LLOYD, Jan 184
LOCKETT, Col. 65, 69
LORD, H. 65
LOVETT, Alice 67
LUCAS, Philip 109

MANCHESTER, Claude 182
MANCHESTER, Ian 9, 182
MANCHESTER, Steven 164, 167
MANKEE, Ralph 109
MANNERS, Lord Robert 37, 45, 46, 47
MANNERS, Betty 43, 54
MANNERS, Lady Isobel 67
MANNERS, Lady Katherine 24
MANNERS, Lady Mildred 45, 50
MANNERS, Lady Violet 62
MANNERS, Lord Robert 23, 43, 49
MANNERS, Lord Charles 23
MANNERS, Sir Thomas 15
MANTON, Lord Rupert 142, 183
MARKHAM, Chris 204
MARKHAM, Richard 126, 175, 197
MARSHALL ROBERTS, Mrs 54
MARSHALL ROBERTS, Capt. 53, 54, 59
MARTIN, John 112, 127, 130, 147, 158, 169, 175, 194
MAXWELL HYSLOP, Sandy 103
McCORQUODALE, Lady Sarah 134, 147, 201
McNEILL, Charlie 43, 44
MEADS, Jim 9
MEEKS, Trevor 9
MOLONY, Tim 182
MONTAGUE-DOUGLAS-SCOTT, Lady Alice 70
MONTEITH, Angus 188, 190
MONTEITH, Fiona 188, 190
MOORE, John 164, 165, 167
MOORE, William 9
MORGAN, Nico 9
MORLEY, Caroline 129
MORLEY, Richard 127, 141, 143, 146, 175
MORRIS, Harry 75
MORRIS, Wil 65
MOUNCER, Alan 103
MOUNTAIN, Mr J.C. 49
MUNNINGS, Sir Alfred 9, 180
MURRAY SMITH, Ulrica 78
MUSSON, Barbara 192
MUSSON, Mrs A. 164
MUTTER, Bertie 178
MUTTER, Miss 178
NEWMAN, Tom (Beaufort huntsman) 65

221

Index

NEWMAN, Tom 19
NEWTON, Joey 112, 125, 126, 127, 137, 141, 142, 147, 158, 175, 183, 193, 205
NEWTON, Nicky, 188, 190
NEWTON, Willa 190
NEWTON, William 69
NEWTON, Chloe 140, 190
NEWTON, Hon. Ursula ("Urky") 9, 89, 103, 114, 118, 184-186
NEWTON, Jessica 176
NEWTON, Lance 78, 181, 182-184
NEWTON, R.W. 181, 184
NICHOLLS, Debbie 168
NORMAN, Herbert 36, 39

ONIONS, Arthur 68
ORR, George 107
OWEN, Barry 141
OWEN, Tor 11, 99, 126, 133, 135, 141, 142, 145, 158, 159, 161, 162, 170, 174, 175, 197, 198, 205

PAGET, Guy 42
PALMER, Jack 94
PALMER, Mrs Margaret 167, 171
PARKER, Bernard 111
PARRY, Major John 9, 101, 105, 140, 141, 175, 199
PARRY, Jean 9, 101, 137, 141, 194, 199
PATEMAN, Bert 79
PAYNE GALLWEY, Miss 54
PAYNE GALLWEY, Peter 58, 178
PAYNTER, Alba 57
PAYNTER, Brig.Gen. George 178
PEACOCK, Charles 51
PEARSON, James 112, 126
PELL, Rebecca 189
PERCE, George 202
PERCEVAL, Edward 19, 20
PERCEVAL, Spencer 19
PERFECT, Geoff 168
PERKINS, Richard 68, 75, 79, 87
PHAYRE, Lt. Col. R.A 88
PHILBY, Tommy 183
PICK, John 137, 200-204
PINDER, William 69
PITMAN, Giles 203

PLAYER, J.D. (Donnie) 178
PLAYER, W.F. (Tim) 178
PLAYNE, Nick 105, 109, 166, 167, 175
POPE, Will 87
POSTLETHWAITE, Peter 165, 206
PRETYMAN, George 81
PRICE, Ron 90
PURSE, George 48
PYRAH, Nikki 190

REID SCOTT, Ann 63, 64, 87, 101, 102, 104, 121, 166, 175, 182, 185
RICHARDSON, John 98, 167, 206
ROBARDS, Hugh 158
ROBERTS, Graham 87, 90
ROBINSON, Richard 190
ROLLO, Lady Kathleen 56
ROLLO, Bill 56, 58
ROWBOTHAM, Laura 190
ROWE, J. 164
RUTLAND, Duke 1st 17
RUTLAND, Duke 3rd 18
RUTLAND, 5th Duke 20-27, 177, 178
RUTLAND, 6th Duke 27-31, 151
RUTLAND, 7th Duke 32, 151
RUTLAND, 8th Duke 62
RUTLAND, 10th Duke 73, 74, 77, 81, 98, 109, 170, 192
RUTLAND, 11th Duke 7, 9, 74, 131, 136
RUTLAND, Duchess 74, 125, 127, 131, 136, 144, 174, 175

SAMWORTH, Lady (née Rosemary Cadell) 183
SAUNBY, Michael 9, 11, 81, 101, 108, 124, 137
SEED, Jonathan 147, 157
SEELEY, W.E. 82
SEELY, James 82
SELBY, Graham 168
SHARPE, John 183
SHAW, "Gentleman" 20, 21
SHERRIFFE, Joan 71
SHERRIFFE, Monica 9, 60, 71, 142
SHIPMAN, Margaret 9, 29

SHIPMAN, Philip 28, 29
SIMESTER, Jack 89
SIMPSON, Mrs Wallis 69
SKELTON, Sally 9, 10, 185
SLACK, George 182
SLY, Mrs E. 164
SMITH, Will 154
SNODIN, Richard 171
SOMERSET, Lady Mary 19
SPENCE, S. 164
SPENCE, Stuart 206
STANNAGE, E. 164
STEPHENS, Marina 187
STOUPH, Ron 87, 90, 93
STUBBINGS, Philip 126
SUMNER, Richard 161
SUTCLIFFE, Stella 185
SWAN, Col. Robert Clayton 39, 49, 61, 63, 178
SWAN, Hester 54, 63

TAYLOR, Steve 112, 141, 158, 175, 184
TAYLOR, Carol 9, 141
TAYLOR, Emma (née Bealby) 147, 201
TAYLOR, Kitty 187
THATCHER, Arthur (Atherstone) 79
THATCHER, Arthur (Cottesmore) 78
THOMPSON, Diana 185
THOMPSON, Rob 176
THORNTON, Sally 123, 204
THORNTON, Martin 112, 123-126, 133, 138, 139, 145, 158, 159, 160, 161, 168, 175, 191, 194, 197, 200, 204
THORNTON, Robert ("Choc") 23, 190
TOLLEMACHE, Sir Lionel 184
TONGE, Charles 9, 58, 60, 61, 65, 66, 180, 186
TONGUE, George 57, 64, 67, 72, 75, 76, 79, 81, 83, 84, 89, 189, 192
TOULSON, Daphne (née Marsh) 185
TURNER, Nick 89, 96, 101, 102, 105, 109, 175

TURNER, David 183	WATTS, Philip 105	WILLIS, John 189
TURNER, Di 89	WEBSTER, Sheila 93, 108	WILSON, Roderick 126
TYACKE, Richard 147, 157	WEBSTER, Jim 68, 72, 81, 83, 84, 85-96, 99, 103, 104, 108, 114, 175, 189, 191, 192, 194, 198, 200	WILSON, W. 65
		WING, Malcolm 88
VAN DOORN, Alexandra 187		WOODHOUSE, Michael 126
VERE NICOLL, Graham 118	WEBSTER, Arthur 85	WOODWARD, Dick 48
VICTORIA, Queen 26, 27	WEBSTER, Clarence 86	WRIGHT, Fred 51
VIGNE, Rodney 207	WESTROPP, Harry 129, 142	WRIGHT, Kenwyn 114
	WESTROPP, Hon. Vicky 9, 128, 129, 142	WROUGHTON, William 50
WADSLEY, Mrs Brockton 47		WYLDBORE-SMITH, Sir Brian 101, 175
WALKER, Tom 17	WHATTON, Ian 196	
WALLACE, Capt Ronnie 90, 161	WHATTON, Stuart 196	WYNDHAM, Hon. W.R. 47
WARNER, William P. 39	WHICHCOTE, Sir George 48	WYNNE GRIFFITH, Edward 33
WATCHORN, Neville (Tom) 67	WHICHCOTE, Sir Thomas 28	
WATHEN, Guy 168	WILDE, G. 164	YORK, Duke of
WATSON, Miss L. 185	WILES, Brian 95	(King George VI) 23, 47, 48, 53, 70

Also published by Merlin Unwin Books

Hunting in the Lake District
Seán Frain £14.99

Willie Irving
Huntsman, Terrierman and Lakelander
Seán Frain £17.99

The Hare
Jill Mason £20

The Otter
James Willliams £20

How to Watch a Bullfight
Tristan Wood £20

The Racing Man's Bedside Book
Compiled by Julian Bedford £18.95

Apley Hall
The Golden Years of a Sporting Estate
Norman Sharpe £12

That Strange Alchemy
Pheasants, Trout and a Middle-aged Man
Laurence Catlow £17.99

The Shootingman's Bedside Book
Compiled by BB £18.95

Advice from a Gamekeeper
John Cowan £20

The Private Life of Adders
Rodger McPhail £14.99

Vintage Guns for the Modern Shot
Diggory Hadoke £30

...and many more

www.merlinunwin.co.uk